A Child's Parent Dies

A Child's Parent Dies

STUDIES IN CHILDHOOD BEREAVEMENT

Erna Furman

NEW HAVEN AND LONDON, YALE UNIVERSITY PRESS

Published with assistance from the foundation
established in memory of Amasa Stone Mather of the
class of 1907, Yale College.

Library of Congress catalog card number: 73–86894

ISBN 0–300–01719–7 (cloth)
ISBN 0–300–02645–5 (paper)

Designed by Sally Sullivan
and set in Times Roman type.
Printed in the United States of America by
Vail-Ballou Press, Inc., Binghamton, N.Y.

12   11   10   9   8   7   6   5   4   3

Contents

Foreword

A Child's Parent Dies is a remarkable publication which merits a prominent place among the psychoanalytic investigations of childhood and its problems. Despite the intentional narrowing down of the topic to parental loss by death, with loss through rejection, separation, and abandonment excluded, the scope, depth, and thoroughness of the study is impressive; so is the backing up of every piece of reasoning by the display of clinical material, taken from one source exclusively, namely from child-analytic treatments carried over a number of years.

It is much to the credit of the author and contributors that they reject all simple answers to the problem of bereavement in childhood. Although they emphasize the importance of chronological age and developmental stage when the loss occurs, they add to these determinants a whole host of other factors such as the actual details of the traumatic happening, the lost parent's role for the child's physical and emotional well-being, the availability of inner coping mechanisms and of environmental sources of comfort, explanation and help in affective abreaction. In short, they show convincingly that it is on the one hand the total character and personality of the child and on the other hand the totality of environmental circumstances which determine the outcome of the experience. Here, as in all other areas of the child's life, the interaction between internal and external forces decides between the possibility of normal developmental progress and the incidence of pathological developmental distortion or arrest.

In an extensive and painstaking discussion of the relevant literature, the author relates her own work to other studies of mourning. What she is too modest to envisage is the fact that in the future her and her collaborators' efforts may rank much higher and be considered as more comprehensive and helpful than any of the single explorations of the subject that have gone before.

London   ANNA FREUD

vii

Preface

This book is the outcome of many years of cooperative work of a group of child analysts in Cleveland. Each analyst contributed his clinical material and theoretical thinking. Each shared in our many discussions and helped to evolve our ideas in a concerted effort to learn and to understand. It would be impossible to single out those whose experiences were most instructive as source material or to attribute specific ideas and formulations to individual members. The theoretical sections represent the work of all. They bear my name because, as project director, I gathered together the strands of our thinking, gave it written form and, in some instances, extended it to implicit conclusions.

The members of the research group were Marion J. Barnes, Joanne Benkendorf, Elizabeth Daunton, Eleanor S. Fiedler, Elizabeth Fleming, Erna Furman, Robert A. Furman, M.D., Myron W. Goldman, Anny Katan, M.D., Maurits Katan, M.D., Marilyn R. Machlup, Marie E. McCann, Arthur L. Rosenbaum, M.D., and Edward J. Schiff, M.D.[1]

This entire group's deep gratitude and appreciation go to our patients and their families for sharing with us their feelings and thoughts and for enabling us to learn with them at a most trying period in their lives. Several of them, through their generous and kind permission, made it possible for the reader to share by way of the individual case reports included in this book. Many others may recognize themselves in excerpts or illustrative examples. In each instance we have attempted to prevent possible recognition by others without falsifying the internal truth of the material. Our aim throughout has been to share what might be helpful to those who work with bereaved children but to do so without exposing or hurting our patients or their families.

In the case of the children who attended the Hanna Perkins Nursery School and Kindergarten we owe special thanks to Lois D. Archer,

1. David Crocker, M.D., joined us for a short period.

educational director, and to the head teachers, Sandra Redmond and Marilyn R. Machlup. Their observations, ideas, and daily educational care were invaluable to the individuals involved as well as to the analysts who worked with them.

Our work was made possible through the facilities of the Cleveland Center for Research in Child Development and the devoted assistance of its director, Robert A. Furman, who took responsibility for administration and finances. Some of our patients were treated in the Center's Child Analytic Clinic or by participants in the Center's Analytic Child Psychotherapy Training Program. The latter treatments were supervised by members of the training program faculty, Elizabeth Daunton, Erna Furman, and Alice Rolnick.

In the Child Analytic Clinic the patients' fees are assessed according to their financial means; some are able to contribute only the cost of transportation. Although all analysts work for the Center at reduced rates, the need for financial subsidy is very great. From its inception the Clinic has been most generously and consistently funded by the Cleveland Psychoanalytic Society Foundation; this support was augmented by that of the Cleveland Foundation and by the Ittleson Family Foundation. Without these grants a number of bereaved children and families could not have received help.

The treatments-via-the parent at the Hanna Perkins School are made possible by the cooperative work of the Division of Day Care and Child Development of the Center for Human Services. The New Land Foundation has for many years been a steady supporter of this work, joined in the last two years by the Ittleson Family Foundation.

The cost of the preliminary bereavement-group study was carried by the Cleveland Center for Research in Child Development, assisted initially by the Codrington Foundation. During a two-year period of intensive research-group study, we incurred considerable expense for secretarial work. This was generously compensated by the Association for Child Psychoanalysis from its special fund for study groups. As we engaged in the actual task of writing the manuscript, the project director, the analysts contributing case reports, and the group's editorial committee needed to devote a great deal of time to their tasks. The secretarial work took on a new dimension. The Ittleson Family Foundation came fully to our help at this time and, through its special grant, enabled us to reach our goal.

We are most grateful to all who supported our work. Without their assistance, this study, reaching back over so many years, would not have been possible.

Throughout these years Eleanor Whiston, executive secretary of the Cleveland Center for Research in Child Development, shouldered a particularly arduous task. It was shared by her assistants Lydia Furman, Elizabeth Fink, Gayle Perl, and Tanya Furman. They typed and distributed the notes of our meetings and, later on, prepared the manuscripts for the editorial committee and the publishers. We thank them most warmly.

Personally, I am especially grateful to the members of our research group's editorial committee, Elizabeth Daunton, Elizabeth Fleming, and Arthur L. Rosenbaum. Untiringly and thoughtfully they read all the first drafts and final manuscripts and made many important suggestions and corrections. Our meetings and discussions improved the presentation of the material and were most helpful and meaningful to me.

Last but not least, I thank my family—my husband, Robert A. Furman, for discussing with me all the theoretical and clinical facets of this difficult subject over many years, and my children for bearing with me patiently during the two long years of writing this book.

1. How This Study Came to Be

The Beginnings

During the past fifteen years, twenty-three children who had lost a parent through death were treated by child analysts associated with the Cleveland Center for Research in Child Development. This group of children included black and white, rich and poor, of various religious denominations and cultural backgrounds. The youngest child was only ten weeks old when her mother died, the oldest lost his father at age thirteen. Fourteen of the children received individual psychoanalytic treatment and were seen in five sessions weekly over periods of two to six years. The other nine were in treatment-via-the parent; that is, they were children under five years of age attending the Hanna Perkins Therapeutic Nursery School and Kindergarten, while a child analyst, in weekly sessions, assisted the surviving parent or parent substitute, to work with his child therapeutically.[1] This form of treatment continued with each patient over a period of one to three years and, in some instances, even preceded nursery school attendance.

Except for one child, none of these patients came for help because of the parent's death. With eight of them the parent died during the course of the child's treatment; the bereavement had not been anticipated at the start of the work. The others were referred for a variety of symptoms which seriously interfered with their age-adequate functioning, for example, amnesia, learning problems, difficulties in social relationships, self-hurting tendencies, inhibitions of speech and motility, sleep disturbances, disciplinary problems. In some of these cases the referring parent surmised that the death of the other parent was related to his child's difficulties. In many instances, however, the parent's death initially figured as one among many incidents in the patient's history. The treatment work only later uncovered the

1. This method was developed at the Hanna Perkins Nursery School especially for the treatment of certain forms of emotional disturbances of early childhood (E. Furman 1957, 1969).

1

significance of the parent's death and of its circumstances for the subsequent pathology.

It is noteworthy, too, that neither individual child analysts nor the agencies with which they were associated ever sought cases of bereaved children. Until quite recently the community was not aware of our growing interest in this subject. In fact, none of the investigators had a prior inclination or plan to study this topic. Like most people, we started out essentially reluctant to acknowledge the frequency of these tragic occurrences and unclear about their impact on the children's emotional life. How then did we come to focus our interest on this topic?

About twelve years ago two youngsters in our Hanna Perkins Nursery School lost their mothers through death within the short span of a few months. The mothers were young women, succumbing untimely to the rapid and intense grip of disease and leaving behind them sadly distraught husbands, children, parents, and friends. Their deaths also had a most distressing effect on the schoolmates of the bereaved children and, last but not least, on the professional staff of educators, child analysts, and therapists who had worked with these children and their families. The hard months and years that followed taught us a great deal about the children's reactions. The analysts most immediately concerned with the children's care published some of their experiences (R. A. Furman 1964, 1964a; Barnes 1964; McDonald 1963, 1964).

This, however, was only the beginning. These two tragic incidents alerted many of us to the fact that the death of a young parent is not as rare as we like to believe.[2] By that time several other children were already in treatment who had lost a parent earlier and, during the succeeding years, several more such patients started therapeutic work. Those of us who regularly consulted for local nursery schools, day care centers and community agencies were frequently called upon to help with the management of a tragic situation resulting from a parent's death. It is possible, perhaps even likely, that bereaved chil-

---

2. According to the 1971 Statistical Abstract of the United States published by the U.S. Department of Commerce, Bureau of the Census, which uses as its source the Department of Health, Education and Welfare, Social Security Administration, there were as of July 1970, among children under age 18, 3.4% paternal orphans, 1.3% maternal orphans, 0.1% full orphans. Thus 4.7% children under 18 years of age have lost either their father or mother through death. These percentages have varied but very slightly since 1955.

dren as a group show a higher incidence of emotional disturbances and therefore are referred for therapeutic help in relatively greater numbers. Our experience, however, appears to have been particularly unfortunate in that a parent died unexpectedly during the child's treatment in eight instances.

We realized also that, even barring loss of a parent, all children encountered death and bereavement in some form—death of a grandparent, family friend, pet. We learned that these experiences, though of incomparably lesser impact, often were difficult for parents and children to cope with. Increasingly we felt that it was important to understand better the effect of loss through death, and particularly a parent's death, on children in order to assist them better at a time of loss and, if possible, to outline some prophylactic educational measures that could pave the way for coping with such experiences. From our group, R. A. Furman (1967, 1968, 1970, 1973) published some of his thoughts on these lines.

In time, the child analysts' scientific interest, stimulated by the gradual unraveling of these patients' mental responses as well as the severe emotional stress of empathizing with their feelings, prompted a need to share what had been learned and to learn from one another. During our weekly meetings, headed by Dr. Anny Katan and attended by most local child analysts, ongoing analytic cases of bereaved children were studied and a special series was devoted to presentation and discussion of such cases. Another forum for pooling and deepening our knowledge was the weekly staff conferences at the Hanna Perkins Nursery School, also chaired by Dr. Katan and attended by the entire educational and therapeutic staff. At these meetings the educational and therapeutic material on bereaved children in treatment-via-the parent was regularly reviewed.

In 1966 the Cleveland Center for Research in Child Development sponsored a special bereavement research group to meet our increasing need for detailed and continuous study. Throughout the next three and a half years we devoted an evening once a month to discuss the ongoing treatment of a little girl whose mother had died when she was four. The members of this small group,[3] as well as I as research consultant, contributed their own experience with cases of parent

3. Marion J. Barnes, Robert A. Furman, M.D., Myron W. Goldman, Marie E. McCann, Edward J. Schiff, M.D., Erna Furman.

loss by way of comparison or contrast, thereby enlarging our understanding. This group formed the nucleus for our later research project.

At these different but interrelated meetings, significant contributions were made by child analysts who worked with children who had lost a parent not through death but through adoption, separation, or divorce. These helped us to understand the impact of different forms of parental loss. There was, unfortunately, also ample clinical experience from the analyses of children whose siblings had died, enabling us to compare the effects of these losses with those of the death of a parent. Further, those analysts who also worked with adults could shed light on the differences between bereavement in later and early life and, in some instances, trace the effects of a parent's death in their patient's youth, thus providing us with a long-term perspective.

Finally we felt the time had come for all of us who treated bereaved patients to get together, to collect our data and gather our thoughts, and to work toward setting them down explicitly while the material was still fresh in our minds. We knew that the value of our experience lay primarily in the nature of our clinical material, gained through the exacting long-term intensive use of the psychoanalytic method of investigation. The most important aim of our project was to understand what our patients had taught us.

Methods of Study

In the fall of 1969, when we decided to embark on our present project, the most important part of our work had already been accomplished; the treatments of our orphaned patients had either been concluded or were under way. The analysts who had worked with these children and their families had kept records of their work so that most of the data were collected and ready at hand. Through long years of close professional cooperation, most of us were familiar with almost all the cases. We had attended the case presentations in seminars and had participated in the discussions which always followed. The data thus had already become the main basis of our thinking.

In spite of our familiarity with the cases, when we began to enumerate them we were shocked at the length of our list and, indeed, we initially "forgot" some of them. At this point we began to realize how painful and distressing it was to address ourselves to this topic in a concentrated effort and how alert we needed to be to recognize and prevent untoward emotional influences.

The first step in organizing the project was to invite the participation of all analysts and child therapists who had worked, or were working, with bereaved children. Our colleagues' response was most enthusiastic. Fourteen analysts and child therapists agreed to work together and did so during the next three years. I participated throughout as project director.

We decided to meet twice monthly, devoting about two hours to the joint work, and continued the meetings for two academic years. One of my tasks was to keep detailed notes and type them up for distribution to all members well in advance of the next meeting so they could be studied at leisure. The meeting always started with a review of the minutes, noting corrections or omissions, adding further thoughts and comments. During the many months when the meetings centered primarily around the study of individual cases, I used my notes to write up a full report of the case that had been presented and discussed, and submitted it to the child's analyst for correction before distributing copies to all members. In some instances the analyst presented his case from his own written report which then, together with the discussion notes, became a part of our project records. The detailed records of the meetings eventually served as the basis for a brief published account of our project (E. Furman 1970). After about one and a half years of study, both theoretical and clinical excerpts and summaries were presented for discussion to the Cleveland child analytic group in three consecutive Monday evening seminars chaired by Dr. Anny Katan.

During our third year of cooperative research we utilized our records for the task of writing up our findings and preparing them for publication. During this year we met less frequently as a group. Our discussions centered on specific questions of format, sequence, and style of presentation. It was decided that I would use our detailed records to write the theoretical chapters and discussions of the cases and the literature. The clinical illustrations would be contributed by the child analysts or child therapists concerned with the individual cases. Much thought was given to the selection of the clinical material. We realized that it was impossible to include everything; the book would be too bulky, the reader overwhelmed. Further, a considerable portion of the cases, or parts of them, had to be excluded for reasons of confidentiality. This decision was made by each analyst for his own patients. We also had to decide in which sequence or grouping the case reports should be arranged. Several important criteria suggested themselves—whether father or mother had died; whether we had worked with the child at the actual time of the parent's death or later; whether the death occurred suddenly, followed a prolonged debilitating illness, or was a suicide; whether the form of treatment had been analysis or treatment-via-the parent. Although these and other factors were considered germane and necessary for the purpose of discussion, the factor of the child's developmental stage at the time of the parent's death was agreed to be of overriding significance in the context of our work. The case material was selected on this basis to represent as nearly as possible examples from the different developmental levels and arranged in chronological sequence.

An editorial committee was formed to review and correct the manuscripts. The members worked together during the third year of our project and until the final drafts were ready.

Clinical Data

From the start our difficulty lay in having to select from too much clinical material. We had, unfortunately, much experience in helping the bereaved, both in terms of the nature of the loss and form of treatment. The latter included psychotherapy and consultation work of varied duration and intensity in nursery schools, community agencies, and private practice.

We agreed readily that, for the purpose of this psychoanalytic project, we would include only cases which had been treated either in five-times-weekly individual psychoanalysis or in treatment-via-the parent while the child attended the Hanna Perkins Nursery School. Our professional training, as well as our varied clinical experience, convinced us that these two forms of treatment would furnish us with the most detailed, comprehensive, and reliable data. The unique research value of data gained through the use of the psychoanalytic method in individual treatment has long been accepted in our field.

The research value of data gained through treatment-via-the parent is, in many respects, different: our understanding in this work derives first from the long-term direct observation of the child by psychoanalysts and analytically trained teachers, and second from the regular work with the parent who, with the analyst's assistance, treats his child, helping him to resolve external and certain forms of internalized conflicts. Long-term observation and a direct opportunity to understand the parent–child relationship provide special data in treatment-via-the parent.

We had much more difficulty in deciding which forms of bereavement to include in the study. In addition to children whose parent had died, there were analyses of children whose sibling had died or who had lost a parent through separation. Cases of adults were available who had suffered bereavement in childhood or as adults. All offered important insights. We had to leave this question open at first. After some months of intensive study we were clear in our own minds that a child's loss of his parent through death is psychologically a unique and complex circumstance that needs to be considered separately. Other types of bereavement can at best serve to highlight the differences. An approach combining the study of several forms of object loss would confuse rather than clarify the issues. In research meetings we often availed ourselves of material and insight gained in work with children who had suffered other losses. We utilized them for purposes of comparison, and they contributed in this way toward our better understanding, but we did not attempt to study them for their own sake. It was not till the final stages of our work that we decided also to set aside cases of adults. We did so because they introduced a multitude of additional factors and because we had so much material from the analyses of children that we feared to overextend ourselves and overburden the reader. Ultimately we selected only cases of children who had been orphaned through the death of a parent and who had received five-times-weekly psychoanalysis and/or treatment-via-the parent while attending the Hanna Perkins Nursery School. There were twenty-three such cases. The clinical reports in this book are from this group.

Plan and Procedure

The main aim of the project was to study in detail all the available data. To facilitate our own grasp, however, we felt that we needed first to state clearly some basic definitions, especially those of grief, mourning, and depression. We hoped that the considerable literature on the subject would help us in our efforts. I was charged with an additional survey and report on articles dealing with childhood bereavement, while all members studied selected contributions. Our first two meetings were spent on a review and discussion of a portion of this scientific literature. We found to our dismay that different authors used the basic terms very differently, depending on their theoretical background as well as on the nature and utilization of their clinical data. We realized that, in order to assess the great variety of approaches, we would have to start by formulating our own concepts and defining them to the best of our ability.

The task of collecting and reviewing the wider literature on the topic was delegated to me as a separate undertaking. In addition, it became my responsibility to report to the group specific papers that might prove especially helpful and pertinent to any topic under discussion. In practice, many members shared this latter task by contributing from their knowledge of the literature. We began by concentrating efforts on the study of basic works and on our own resources to arrive at agreed definitions, to delineate areas of interest, and to state open questions. Throughout these discussions clinical material served as the basis for each theoretical step. Since our use of terms derived mainly from the works of Sigmund Freud, Anna Freud, and the publications by members of our group, we reviewed their pertinent papers to assist us in our discussions.

In our study of individual cases we usually devoted an entire meeting to the presentation and discussion of one case. We focused on understanding the material in its individual context and specific aspects as well as on comparing these with similarities and differences in other cases. In this way we gradually found some answers to our earlier questions but also became aware of new areas whose importance we had overlooked or simply not known and which, in turn, raised new questions. Occasional meetings, or series of meetings, would then be held to bring together our insights, understanding them metapsychologically, reformulating our previous ideas when indicated, or outlining new areas of inquiry.

The end of our work was not set by a predetermined date. We had never attempted to frame our project in a specific span of time. Rather, the end was felt spontaneously by all of us when we had reviewed our clinical material, had gained as much theoretical understanding as we could from it, and—perhaps—had expended as much emotional effort as we were capable of in dealing with parental death. In some areas we were satisfied with the validity of our conclusions, in some we were keenly aware of their tentative nature, while in others we had been able only to point to the need for further psychoanalytic investigation.

Now, after some years of concentrated cooperative study, the members of our group realize more than ever that bereavement in childhood is a vast, complicated, and extremely painful subject; that our experience and insight are limited and our conclusions tentative. In sharing our data and thinking with others, we do not aim at a comprehensive, exhaustive presentation but rather at a contribution to the understanding of the effects of a parent's death on his children.

Throughout the work, in our direct contacts with our patients and their families, in our private thinking and in our research discussions, we lived with the intense distress, pain, and anguish engendered by bereavement. We have come to understand that this emotional stress is an inevitable burden for all who work with bereaved children. It is essential in facilitating appropriate empathy and insight, and helpful in integrating an intellectual grasp of the psychic processes within the patients' personalities. Only those willing and able to bear the impact with feeling can hope to work with bereaved children fruitfully and to understand them scientifically.

We realize that we place some of this burden and expectation on the reader. To an extent he is spared in that he does not know the children personally, is not directly involved with them, and need not feel their pain daily for many years. His task is made more difficult, however, by being deprived of the opportunity of active participation in the clinical setting and in the theoretical discussions. In selecting and arranging our material we have tried to keep the reader in mind, hoping neither to overwhelm him nor to exclude him from our experience. We trust that the reader, for his part, will allow himself an empathetic approach.

Scientific understanding, however, is not achieved by empathy alone. The emotional strain of the work has to be matched by intensive intellectual effort in order to bring about an integrated comprehension. We hope the reader will also participate in this aspect of our endeavor and will, like ourselves, find that the theoretical thinking helps to contain and structure the clinical material.

The sequence of chapters in this book reflects the unfolding process by which our group discussions related theoretical thinking and clinical experience. In presenting this work in written form I could not fully preserve the close and constant interplay between theory and practice. Inevitably, some chapters concentrate more on theory, others deal primarily with case material, and still others attempt to apply what we learned to educational and prophylactic measures.

Since our own work with bereaved children was prompted by clinical considerations and geared to the task of assisting our patients and their families in their distress, we decided to start with some practical applications.

The definitions of mourning and its processes form the basis from which we explore the specific clinical ramifications—the many different aspects that affect the individual child's bereavement and his ability to master this stress, as well as some effects of the parent's death on personality development. We devoted special attention to crucial questions—criteria for mourning in childhood, the difference between the child's task of mourning a parent and adult bereavement, the incidence and nature of depression and apathy in bereaved children.

Our views differ considerably from those of others. It seemed essential therefore to explore other authors' viewpoints, concepts, and data and to relate our findings to them. This integration enabled us to state meaningful comparisons, and to delineate areas in which the study of bereavement still lacks sufficient data or needs theoretical clarification and refinement.

Ten clinical reports are included to highlight the many different ways in which children experience and react to the death of a parent. These reports are inserted in the text at points where they illustrate some aspects of the adjacent chapters and are also grouped to facilitate comparison between children of similar ages.

2. Helping Bereaved Children

Work with our patients made us painfully aware that we are all help-less in the face of the death of a loved person. The way each of us copes with this experience depends on many internal and external factors and can be influenced only to a certain extent. In the light of this it seems contradictory to speak of methods of handling a death or helping a bereaved child, for this implies that we are dealing with general rather than specific experiences, and that we can be active and effective. Perhaps the only general statement that can be made is that anyone concerned with bereavement needs to appreciate the limits of his helpfulness and the unique impact of each death. When we are aware of this we are not tempted to misuse activity and generalities to ward off the inevitable emotional burden of tolerating our own feelings and of empathizing with those we wish to help. Ul-timately, each step in assisting a bereaved person becomes valid only when it grows out of full acceptance of, and respect for, the feelings and facts that comprise the individual's personal situation. Without that the best measure may prove useless or even harmful because it would not be in tune with the individual's need at a given time.

We found that what we had learned from our analytic patients in the course of years of treatment stood us in good stead in other forms of therapy. These included assisting bereaved families psycho-therapeutically in private practice or in clinics and treatment centers, or in consulting for child care agencies. Our experience did not en-able us to spare ourselves or other professional workers, much less the bereaved themselves, from emotional hardship, rather, we learned that when a child's parent dies he faces an incomparable stress which threatens the further development of his personality. This danger can be averted if the child can be helped to mourn his parent as fully as possible, and children from toddler age on can be assisted in this dif-ficult task. The detailed clinical evidence and theoretical implications underlying these findings form the substance of this book, together with an exploration of the many grave difficulties to be faced both by the bereaved child and his surviving family. Our findings have proven useful in our own clinical work but they are too limited to make up a set of definitive conclusions; they serve as suggestions only as the reader may be willing and able to utilize them.

When his parent dies, a child finds himself in a unique situation because of the special nature of his ties to the deceased. An adult distributes his love among several meaningful relationships—his spouse, parents, children, friends, colleagues—as well as in his work and hobbies. The child, by contrast, invests almost all his feelings in his parents. Except in very unusual circumstances, this single relationship is therefore incomparably rich and intense, unlike any close adult relationship. Only in childhood can death deprive an individual of so much opportunity to love and be loved and face him with so difficult a task of adaptation. We cannot compare mourning in children and adults without taking this into account.

This understanding made us decide to devote our presentation solely to the death of a parent in childhood and to exclude reactions to other bereavements for the purposes of this study.

Although all aspects of a child's dealing with the death of a parent are closely interwoven, for the sake of clarity we group our ideas under three headings, which are discussed in the remainder of this chapter.

How can a child be helped to develop the personality attributes that will enable him to master the task of mourning?

This question sometimes arose in our own minds when we came to understand that some of our patients' difficulties in coping with their bereavement stemmed from personality problems which long preceded the death of the parent. Many times, concerned parents whose equanimity had been shaken by the recent death of a contemporary asked if they could do anything to ensure that their children would be safe emotionally should such a tragedy befall them.

Apparently the child's chance of coping with the death of a parent is better the older he is (the further advanced in the independence and structuralization of his personality) and the healthier he is emotionally (the more he has achieved integrated development in all areas of personality functioning). Also, the more mature and healthy the child, the less is the physical and emotional burden of those who care for him after his bereavement and assist him with his mourning. It would be a mistake to underestimate the essential role of each personality factor in the total effort of dealing with this major stress. There may be considerable merit in a comprehensive account of how each factor contributes to and affects the individual's manner of responding. This, however, is beyond our knowledge and immediate scope. Some aspects are discussed in subsequent chapters; some have been detailed in other publications (McDonald 1964; R. A. Furman 1968, 1970). Here we wish to focus only on several aspects which directly affect the child's capacity for handling parental death and are within the parent's control to a considerable extent.

We found repeatedly that a child's ability to understand the death of a parent was helped considerably if he already had a realistic concept of death in its concrete manifestations. All children encounter death in their daily lives in the form of dead insects, worms, small animals. Usually by the age of two they can begin to develop a concrete concept of death if adults help them to understand and integrate their observations. This understanding can then be extended to the children's occasional experiences with the deaths of animals and people they knew and liked but on whom they did not intimately depend (grandparents, neighbors, friends of the family, pets).

In our experience the introduction of religious and philosophical concepts of death confused and frightened young children because their capacity for abstract thinking was not yet developed. Children in latency and older could grasp abstract beliefs when they were helped to add them to their concrete understanding rather than to replace it. We enlarge on this important topic of the child's concept of death, and the adult's role in helping him to develop it, in several contexts.

The closer a child felt to a deceased loved person the more did he also need help in differentiating himself from that person's fate before he could appropriately apply his intellectual understanding. Every person needs to deal with his fear of death by distancing himself from the fate of the dead, yet feeling close enough to allow empathy and sympathy. When his parent dies, a child experiences special difficulty in this area; it is easier to help him with the death of a person less close. For example, a parent might explain, "Mr. X died because he was very old and had a sickness that only very old people get. This cannot happen to you or to mommy and daddy. We are much younger and expect to live for a long, long time." With such deaths it was also appropriate to support the child's remembering and longing, to share and talk over with him the parents' similar reactions and means of mastery.

The children we knew were considerably helped in developing a realistic concept of death when they could learn to distinguish real from imaginary causes. The prelatency child, particularly, was apt to feel that his angry thoughts, sometimes in the form of outright death wishes, could cause a person to die. Unwitting parents sometimes reinforced the child's confusion by reacting very harshly or anxiously to such verbalizations. Other parents, by contrast, could acknowledge, "I know you are very mad at me but that cannot make me die. People don't die because someone wishes it." Similarly, a parent was sometimes hesitant to assure the child when he worriedly asked, "Will you die, mommy?" because she did not wish to deceive him. Yet complicated explanations about each person's ultimate fate and its unpredictability actually tended to mislead the young child. It usually worked out best when the parent could explore the child's question calmly so that his answer met the real concern. Many times it arose not from intellectual curiosity but from the child's worry about the power of his infantile hostility to the people he loved most.

As adults we understand the concrete aspects of death but we vary greatly in our religious or philosophical beliefs and in our emotional attitude to death. Through the model of our own handling of the topic we can influence the child's chances of developing his understanding. A number of parents found that they could not begin to address themselves to the subject of death with their children until they had clarified their own ideas, knew where their own uncertainties lay, and sifted out the essential from the vague and peripheral. They could then help their children to understand the concrete realities of death and to distinguish between what we can objectively perceive from what we believe about death privately or according to our religion. In our society, and perhaps universally, this is a difficult task. We explore it repeatedly in this book.

A child's ability to tolerate and express longing, with its accompanying feelings of sadness and anger, bears directly on his potential for dealing with the loss of a parent. The role of longing in mourning and the development of the child's ability to bear these feelings are detailed later. At this point a brief summary serves to highlight some of the child's developmental steps. Longing occurs primarily when he has been separated from a loved person but is also experienced when he loses something else he loves, such as a pet or a home. This may even extend to a beloved old pair of shoes he has to discard or to a pleasure he wants to outgrow, such as being washed by or read to by mother. In the following chapters we stress the difference between a loss due to death and one due to separation, regardless of whether it is a temporary or permanent separation. We do not wish to confuse the two but rather to focus here on the one aspect in which they are similar, namely the experience of longing. Normally developed children are capable of longing after they have reached the beginning of object constancy, usually in the last part of their first year. At that time their emotional experience is intense and primitive, with little or no differentiation between the feelings, little tolerance for them, and with only bodily means of discharge. The child matures in these areas, so that in the latter half of his second year he can differentiate sad and angry feelings. He can endure and contain them better and, helped by adults, learns their names and begins to express them verbally (A. Katan 1961).

The extent to which a child can develop the ability to tolerate and express longing depends on many factors. There are no doubt considerable constitutional variations which make it easier for some than for others to tolerate painful inner tensions. To a large extent it depends on the child's maturational level: the older he gets the more capable he tends to become in this respect. A most important factor is the nature of his experience with stressful times of longing. It is helpful when the length of time for which he has to suffer his feelings is within the limits of his endurance and when he does not have to cope with other stresses at the same time which significantly augment his emotional burden. Other things being equal, we assume that an infant or toddler can long for a much shorter time than an older child. Whenever the length of the separation exceeds the child's capacity for tolerating painful feelings, he either becomes overwhelmed or has to resort to defensive measures which enable him to ward off feelings. In such a situation his developing capacity for recognizing, bearing, and expressing sadness and anger in interfered with temporarily or permanently. By the same token, if a child is never exposed to tolerable separations, his capacity for coping with longing may also be interfered with. He has no opportunity to "practice" the necessary mental skills.

Last, but not least, the child's capacity for bearing longing depends on the educational help he receives from his parents, both in terms of the example they set and in terms of their support of him. This includes helping him to recognize his feelings and encouraging him to tolerate them and to express them age-appropriately. The occurrence, length, and circumstances of separations are not always within the control of the parents. Insofar as they are, it is helpful to adapt them to the child's developmental needs at any given time. Educational help in recognizing, tolerating, and expressing feelings is much more within the realm of parental control. It is a common fallacy to think that a young child who "does not mind" when his parents leave him or when he leaves them has coped well with the separation. The child who really copes well allows himself to miss the absent loved one, to feel sad, lonely, and perhaps angry, and to express his feelings age-appropriately. The death of a parent engenders a longing of incomparable amount, intensity, and longevity. The child's previously acquired ability to deal with lesser distress cannot truly prepare him for such an event but stands him in good stead in his efforts to cope with it.

Sometimes we have been asked whether a child would not be spared the pain of longing for the parent if two or more people cared for him. Insofar as this question refers to upbringing in an "extended family," the answer lies outside the scope of this work. It would involve a detailed discussion of the complex ramifications of multiple parenting. Suffice it to say that its effects on a child's developing personality are so extensive that it would be misleading to single out the factors here under discussion, namely the effect of separation on longing and the tolerance of its pain. If, however, the question refers to the role of the parental substitutes, it may be pertinent to share some of our findings.

It is well known that having a consistently available and liked babysitter, from within or without the family, is very helpful to the child in easing the circumstantial stress during a separation from the parent. The sitter is a parent substitute, rather than an additional parent, and does not claim the child's equal affection. One of the important roles of such a short-term parent substitute is her ability to sympathize with the child's feelings of longing for the real parent, to assist him in tolerating and expressing his feelings, and to inform the parent on his return of the child's responses: "Johnny missed you especially when it was time to go to bed and I told him I would tell you that he was very lonely for you."

In chapter 5 we describe how much a child was helped both in mastering the immediate stress of parental death and in his mourning when he felt assured of consistent adequate care and feelingful empathy from a trusted person. Some of our case reports unfortunately illustrate the difficulties caused by a lack of such a relationship, for example Geraldine and Jim (pp. 69 and 88). In each instance the availability of the surviving parent proved particularly helpful and so did the familiar home surroundings and the presence of other family members. When the surviving parent was not able to assume all the care—for example, when a father was left with very young children—the additional presence of a loved parent substitute was necessary. In some cases, parents had kept these needs of their children in mind in their practical planning. Adequate insurance benefits made it possible for some fathers to employ a competent full-time housekeeper; some mothers could remain with their children in their own home instead of having to move or leave them to earn a living. It was especially fortunate when advance planning made it possible for a congenial member of the family, such as a grandparent, to be available. We want to stress that even in such relatively fortunate circumstances the surviving parent and parent substitute do not spare the child the pain and distress of mourning. Rather, it is their care and support that help the child to bear it.

How can a child be helped to integrate the realities and feelings that face him at the time of his parent's death?

It is the terrible nature of death that we cannot anticipate or control either its timing or its form. Each death is unique and is experienced differently by the survivors. Generalities do not apply and at best have to be adapted to the specific situation and need.

It is a paradox that the very person who is deeply afflicted himself, namely the surviving parent, is, from the child's point of view, best suited to help him grasp and handle the tragic event. When the surviving parent can sensitively fulfill this task during the difficult period of the other parent's terminal illness or at the time of his sudden death, his long-standing relationship with his child serves as a support and makes the realities more bearable for the child. Such parent–child communication during the immediate stress becomes a helpful basis for the long hard future when the child needs the parent's help with mourning.

This difficult and important role of the surviving parent presupposes the kind of personality that enables one to face the anxiety-arousing realities of the spouse's dying, to tolerate the intense feelings it engenders, and to mourn appropriately. No parent can go through such an experience without at times either becoming overwhelmed or resorting to defensive measures. Overall and long term, the surviving parent's response sets a helpful model for the child and forms the basis for his empathy with the child's feelings. The younger the child the more crucial is the surviving parent's influence in this respect.

A long or short illness preceding the parent's death poses the problem of helping the child to understand and integrate what is happening to his sick parent and how this affects the family and the child himself. Children are so observant of and sensitive to their parents' moods and nuances of behavior that, in our experience, it is impossible to spare them from knowing or to deceive them about the true nature of events. Several case histories in this book as well as many vignettes included in the text show the difficulties that arise when the truth is kept from the child. However, the reality has to be presented in such a manner that the child can integrate the pertinent facts and feelings over a period of time. A two-year-old can initially understand, "Mommy has an 'ouch' in her tummy. The doctor helps her get better." A school-age child can grasp that mother needs the doctor's help because something has grown in her stomach that does not belong there and is a sign of sickness. Both children will react with a variety of concerns and feelings to such an explanation and will need opportunity to ask questions in words or actions and to express their feelings. Their chances of coping depend on many factors, among them the extent to which they can feel assured that they themselves will still be cared for physically and emotionally. At a time of such stress even the healthy parent usually has to reduce the amount of time he can spend with his child. It is all the more important that he not withdraw in feeling too. Just as the healthy parent finds some comfort in actively caring for his sick spouse, the child can also be encouraged to do something kind or helpful for his needy parent. A small service, a visit, a gift of a crayoned picture or of a small bouquet of dandelions, all help to overcome helplessness and left-out feelings. They also reaffirm in the child's mind his love for his sick parent at a time when the frustration of the parent's unavailability arouses anger and guilt.

Often it is helpful both to the child and to the sick parent to maintain personal contact for as long as the parent has not drastically altered in appearance or in ability to communicate with feeling. Other things, too, need to be considered. It is impossible for young children to sit passively in the sickroom for long periods. Some children prefer to play with toys or to work on hobbies and school assignments during their visits, recreating the kind of togetherness typical of their usual home life. It is helpful when visits do not become an unbearable burden or force the child to discontinue all his other activities. The parent for his part needs privacy for his personal care or medical and nursing procedures. This interrupts or prevents the child's stay at times.

It is always especially difficult to know when to tell the child that his parent is going to die. One deciding factor is whether the dying parent himself is conscious of his fate. The children often sense the parent's concern and sometimes ask, "Is daddy going to die?" In order to protect the parent and his last interactions with his child it proves helpful at such times to acknowledge and sympathize with the child's concern and to share with him what the physician has told the dying parent. "I can well understand that you worry that dad will die. I have thought about it too. Right now the doctor tells daddy that there are still things to do and medicines to take that can make him feel better." When the parent is so close to death that the child can no longer visit or phone him it becomes possible to inform him that the doctors now have no further way of curing the sickness and they can only make sure that the parent will be comfortable until he dies. There will be hard and sad times ahead but they will be faced together and everyone's needs will be taken care of as well as possible. R. A. Furman (1964a) and Marion Barnes (1964) have movingly described two families coping with this distress.

It is most helpful when, by the time of such a conversation, it has been possible to arrange for the children's consistent daily care in the home, either by the surviving parent or by another family member or housekeeper. The latter arrangement usually becomes necessary when the mother is dying. It is then especially helpful when the person who takes on the mother's tasks has an opportunity to learn the routines from the mother herself. This not only makes it possible to reduce the number of changes and omissions but is also more easily accepted by the children because it carries mother's special stamp of approval.

The circumstances are different but no less painful in the case of a parent's sudden death. Whereas prolonged terminal illness sometimes presents the family with seemingly endless anxious anticipation, the agony of a sudden death lies in its abrupt shock. Its form is often violent and is witnessed by the child, who may sustain an injury himself. In these instances the child appears to be helped best when the surviving parent can, as soon as possible, acknowledge his child's observations and clarify his misperceptions or misinterpretations. If the family does not discuss the child's experience, in the hope that he has not been aware of what has gone on, or if they contradict his observations in the hope of presenting a more palatable reality, a barrier is created in the parent–child relationship. The child then has to struggle alone with his frightening experiences and confused conclusions.

With some sudden deaths the child has no direct involvement. He then seems to be helped most when the surviving parent can broach the news himself right away. A brief preliminary remark helps the child to brace himself a little. "I have something very sad to tell you." The extent to which specific facts can be helpfully shared depends on the child's ability to integrate them. Sometimes all the details are not even known at first. Children seem to feel better when the parent tells them that he does not know all the circumstances and will share them as he learns about them, than when he delays all information until he knows the full story. Since, with a sudden death, the surviving parent is as unprepared as the child, it is particularly difficult for him or her to deal with his own as well as with the child's reactions at the same time. Children cannot deal well with a flood of frightening details or speculations, nor with controlled silence, but they can take in stride a parent's overt upset and tears. A sudden death may also intensify the survivor's fear of the immediate future and leave him at a loss. However bleak the outlook may seem to the adult it is even more frightening for the child, who is helpless to take any active steps. The child, therefore, profits especially when the parent can reassure him that the family will remain together, that his needs will be taken care of as best possible, and that he will be told step by step as each arrangement is planned.

The immediate planning at the time of death concerns the funeral arrangements and the question of the child's participation in the rites. When a family feels comfortable with a particular set of customs— ethnic, religious, or personal—the bereaved adults are usually able to achieve a measure of equanimity during the days of preparation and at the time of the services. The implied certainty of, "This is the way things are done," often provides so much reassurance for the young child that he can take in stride some aspects that would otherwise upset him. Burlingham and A. Freud (1942) found that youngsters did not become unduly anxious during air raids as long as their mothers could contain their own anxiety. Similarly, we have learned that sometimes young children were not overwhelmed at open-casket funerals, apparently because the mothers held their hands throughout and remained in touch with the children's feelings in spite of their own stress. By contrast, children who did not get such support or could not utilize it sufficiently, were severely frightened and confused by the sight of the dead parent's body or by the demand that they touch or kiss it.

Some families sensitively modify their customs to ease the experience for the child and yet make it possible for him to participate with them; they shorten the service, do not insist on the child's bodily contact with the corpse, or arrange for a closed casket. Sometimes families wish to spare the child the anguish of the concrete aspects of the funeral and burial and to spare themselves the additional burden of caring for the child and dealing with his reactions at that time. In some cases this works out well, especially when the child is very young and can remain at home with a trusted adult who can help him with his questions and feelings. When this arrangement is made for older children, they tend to feel left out, deprived of the opportunity to share their feelings with the family and to understand what has happened to the body of the dead parent. Several of our accounts of individual children's treatments show how helpful this could be to the child in grappling with the concrete aspects of death and in affirming his relationship with the surviving parent—important steps toward facilitating the mourning proper.

Even when they have some previous concept of death, for many children the death of the parent is the first death of a loved person. They therefore need a great deal of help to understand at least intellectually what death means, how the family deals with its practical aspects, and why. Unfortunately, some adults are so busy with the arrangements that they cannot devote enough time and thought to the children; others take defensive refuge in being overly busy. Many parents nevertheless are able to help their children to a surprising extent at this time.

Some mastery of the experiences of the first stressful days is often important in its own right and also sets the stage for all aspects of the mourning—the understanding and acceptance of the concreteness of death, the attitude to stressful feelings, and the need for the surviving parent's physical presence and emotional closeness. As long as these goals are kept in mind, different families find their own ways of achieving them.

How can a child be helped to maintain his personality functioning and to mourn his parent in the period following his parent's death?

Once the funeral and ceremonies related to it are over, the hectic pace gives way to the loneliness which stretches into the unforeseeable future, filled only with the concerns of daily living and the weight of seemingly unbearable feelings. Whereas our work with our bereaved families focused on understanding and helping them with their internal stress, we were acutely aware of their external hardships and of the extent to which the latter affected the former. Mourning is a difficult task at best. When it has to be undertaken under anxiety-arousing external conditions it becomes almost impossible. In our later discussions we detail many of our findings in this respect, particularly from the point of view of the child. Our concern is also extended to the stress of the surviving parent, caused, for example, by uncertain sources of income or the burden of being both homemaker and breadwinner. In the context of this study, however, we kept our focus on the child and included the surviving parent's distress only so far as it affected his vital role with his child.

For the parent, one of the hardest things to effect is the kind of setting that is so important for the child's mourning. We found that the child, like the adult, could best undertake the task of mourning when he felt personally safe and could rely on his remaining object relationships. In the child's terms this meant that he could remain with all the surviving family in his own home, that his needs were fulfilled adequately and consistently by the surviving parent or by one continuously available familiar person. This also meant that there were minimal changes in the routines of his daily life and that he could count on the support of his loved ones in his struggle with the facts and feelings of his bereavement. To arrange for the continuity of the home and the consistency of care was often so difficult that the surviving parent was easily tempted to compromise unless he was very aware of their great importance for his child. A quick move sometimes saved money and effort or a day care placement was cheaper and more convenient. Sometimes changes were dictated by dire necessity but, with a number of our patients, practical choices were possible. The decision was influenced by personal factors.

To cope with the difficulties of providing adequate personal care and consistent familiar home routines is, however, but one of the tasks. At times it was even harder for the surviving parent to give the child emotional support because his or her own reactions to the spouse's death were only to a limited extent within conscious control. In all our work with parents, however, we were impressed that they could often realize their own difficulties and exercise sufficient control over them in order to help their children. Sometimes parents could not alter their attitudes but could recognize their personal idiosyncrasies and did not want their children to react similarly. It proved helpful when the parent told his child, for example, that he found it very difficult to think about coffins and could not bear to visit a grave, but that most people had much less trouble with this and he hoped his child would be able to deal with these matters better. The parent could then either brace himself to answer some of the child's questions or refer him for the necessary assistance to another member of the family or to the therapist when the child was in treatment.

The younger children especially needed much help in understanding the realities of death and in learning to differentiate themselves from the dead, so they could feel sure that they themselves and the surviving family members would not die in the wake of the parent's death. Visits to the grave were always important milestones in the children's struggles to come to terms with these concerns. When these visits were well prepared for and timed according to the child's ability to integrate them, they were helpful. We return to this topic later.

When we worked with children during their first weeks without the dead parent we noted that their daily lives reminded them of the loss so constantly and intensified their longing and frustration so greatly that they either needed to resort to temporary defenses or felt overwhelmed in their despair. Parents who were in tune with their children could gauge when to let them be, when to show their empathy by a silent hug, when to put the children's missing into words, when to share their own memories and feelings and encourage the children to do likewise.

Some of the inevitable barriers that arose from the parent's and child's different relationship with the deceased are described in later chapters. Their memories were different or the same memory evoked different responses. Moreover, young children, especially, sometimes longed and remembered in different ways, for example through actions. Adults varied in how much importance they attached to the concrete objects associated with the dead loved one. The dead parent's clothes and possessions were usually very meaningful to the children because they represented both the parent and their own past with him or her. They found these belongings helpful during their mourning and kept some of them indefinitely as a necessary bridge between their past and future lives. Photographs, displayed in the home or readily accessible in albums, were another link to the dead parent. With many of our patients they proved helpful at different stages in their development. At times of great anger they reminded the youngest children of their own love for the parent. At a later time, pictures served as a guide to selective identifications. The report on Lucy poignantly illustrates this point.

The child needed his own recollections of the deceased parent in order to mourn him, and he also required the surviving parent's help in confirming the objective truth of his memories, of positive and negative aspects of the dead parent's personality and behavior. He also needed further knowledge about the dead parent at each new stage of his development so that he could include the parent in his own growing personality as well as differentiate himself from him. When the surviving parent could understand and assist his child's different ways and needs in mourning, the child, in turn, could appreciate the parent's manner of mourning and understand that only some of it could be borne together.

Young children especially needed help in tolerating their sad and angry feelings and in distinguishing the objective reality of the parent's death from their own fantasies. Defenses against painful affects and confusion of developmental conflicts with the actual tragic events tended to interfere with some children's mourning. In some instances parents could intuitively understand the working of their children's minds and assist them in coming to terms with their concerns.

Bess, three and a half years old, was well aware of the finality of her mother's death but one evening announced, "Mommy called and said she'd have dinner with us." Her father replied gently, "I think you wish mommy would call and have dinner with us. When we miss mommy so very much we'd like to think that she is not really dead. I guess it will be a sad dinner for both of us.''

Another area in which children often needed help was when they identified with some aspects of the dead parent. The important role of identification in mourning is explored later in considerable detail. It also forms a part of all case reports. At this point it must suffice to mention some of the implications for practical handling. With many bereaved young children, identifications with the dead parent were superficial and temporary. They usually served the children to remember the lost loved one and to express, in action, their longing for him or her. Four-year-old Jeremy often remembered his father by playing with the father's things and by putting on father's hat and tie. Sometimes children identified with unhelpful aspects, such as the parent's sickness, or they feared so much that the parent's fate would befall them that they avoided all forms of identification. When parents know that identification is an integral part of mourning and is especially important for the child's personality development, they can help clarify for the child in which ways it is all right to be like mommy or daddy and in which ways the child can be different.

Five-year-old Jennifer played lovingly with her dolls but claimed that she did not want to be a mommy. She could be assured that she would not be a mommy for a long time but when she grew up she could safely be one. She could be nice to her children, as her own mommy used to be, and she would not die like her because most mommies live for a much longer time and get to be grandmothers.

One of the hardest phases is the end of mourning when a new love object is sought and the child needs to accommodate within him the new relationship alongside the remaining residual cathexis of the deceased-parent image. Except in later adolescence when object removal coincides with this step, the child's needs usually have to be subordinated to the parent's and to the limitations of a reality he cannot change. Our younger patients were sometimes ready for a new parent long before one was available, or they were offered a new parent before they were ready to accept one. In both instances the interaction was difficult for all concerned and tended to lead to friction. Surviving parents who could not remarry felt the brunt of the child's need and sometimes reproach. Those who remarried before their children were ready were equally reproached, though for different reasons. The problems of children in different age groups and circumstances of mourning are explored in later chapters in several contexts.

Even when the timing seemed right, the old and new parent's consideration for the child's feelings was of utmost importance. Sometimes the child's concern centered around specific things or plans, such as changes in the home routines, arrival of new siblings, adoption procedures. It was a time of comparing the new parent with the deceased, which revived painful memories and feelings and aroused conflicts of loyalty. It also reintroduced into the child's life the normal concerns that come with having two living parents and the need to adapt to their adult relationship. Thus gain and loss were interwoven in a complex way and required much patience and mutual understanding. Whereas the love for the deceased parent sometimes appeared as an obstacle, ultimately the wholesomeness of that lost relationship provided the best basis for the child's ability to build his new relationship.

The surviving parent's task is so difficult, and the child's behavior can be so perplexing or respond so little to the parent's help, that professional advice may be indicated. It is usually easier to assist a child in mastering his conflicts when they arise and before they invade other aspects of his functioning and impair his emotional development. Many parents have approached us for help at the time of one parent's terminal illness or immediately after the death. Often their children showed no pathology, but the parent felt that they were facing a supremely difficult period and wished to discuss their handling of it with a professional person. Both the parents and the children benefited from such work.[1]

While our emphasis is on helping children as soon as possible it must be remembered that the experience of a parent's death always remains a very troubling part of a child's life. The difference lies in whether it remains an unmasterable emotional burden and interferes in the development of the child's personality or whether it becomes a stress that he can cope with and integrate. Under favorable circumstances even very young children can be helped to succeed in this difficult task.

---

1. Parents may also find it helpful to read books on assisting children with their questions and feelings about death and bereavement. In chapter 9 many such publications are reviewed.

KEN
by Elizabeth Daunton

Thirteen-year-old Ken was able to mourn his father. Several factors helped him—his phase of development, the nature of his personality, the circumstances accompanying and following his father's death, and the support of his family and therapist [E. F.]

When his father died suddenly of a coronary infarction Ken was thirteen years and two months old and had been in analysis for two years. He is an identical twin and one of a large family. In the three preceding years there had been three deaths in Ken's wider family. When he was ten a grandmother had died. During his twelfth year an uncle suffering from a terminal illness had lived in Ken's home for several months and had died there. Some months later a grandfather died.

As Ken was in analysis during the stressful time of his uncle's illness and death, it was possible to see how these realities were handled by parents and patient. The mother, although burdened by many responsibilities and worries, was sensitive to her children's feelings and gave them appropriate explanations of the uncle's illness and death. After the death, the mother apologized to her family for having had less time to talk individually in the previous months. Ken attended the funeral with the older members of the family. He shared his parents' religious beliefs in a life after death but made a distinction between bodily and spiritual survival.

His inner conflicts led him to react in a similar way to the illness and death of his three relatives. In each case the deaths were preceded by illnesses which involved Ken's mother, either in visiting the hospital or providing nursing care. Ken was a boy who customarily warded off painful feelings of loneliness and anger by partial identifications and passive-into-active mechanisms. These modes of defense stemmed from experiences in Ken's third and fourth years when the mother had been preoccupied with a new baby and then with the serious illness of Ken's twin.

During his uncle's illness Ken dealt with his unconscious resentment about his mother's preoccupation by identifying with her and at times being too solicitous toward the uncle himself. However, Ken had also a true compassion and empathy for his uncle and could view him rather realistically. Suffering often made the uncle irritable; Ken recalled that he had been nicer before he became ill. His uncle had some distressing physical symptoms. Ken's concerns about these remained isolated until after his uncle's death; he then could speak of his fear when he saw his uncle bleeding from nose and mouth. While Ken had a realistic understanding of the uncle's illness, his unconscious guilt feelings about masturbation led him to link the illness with "bad habits" like smoking.

Ken's grandmother had died several months before he began treatment. I was unclear about his relationship with her and the nature of his mourning. Her death was recalled for the first time at its first anniversary when Ken visited the cemetery to put flowers on her grave. This visit followed a vacation from treatment and preceded a missed appointment. During our discussion Ken became very confused about the time of year when his grandmother had died; he became sleepy and repeatedly closed his eyes as he struggled to remember. The confusion and his unconscious identification with the dead grandmother, shown by closing his eyes, stemmed from a conflict between his love for her and a resentment that her hospitalization had taken his mother away from him. The transference meaning became clear when Ken expressed the thought that I had become sick during the vacation. His fear that people he cared for could become sick, because of his anger about being left, was discussed with him.

Ken and his family saw his grandfather infrequently so that his illness and death had less feelingful impact on him. He was more conscious at this time of his resentment about mother's absences when grandfather was in the hospital. The current reality of having an absent, worried mother was painful in itself; it was made more so for Ken in reviving the distressing feelings of loss and anger when, at age three, mother had been preoccupied with his sick twin.

At the time of his father's sudden death, Ken was in church. On returning home he found his mother telling the shocking news to his elder sister. In recalling this the next day, Ken said his sister had collapsed on the couch; he couldn't quite hear what his mother was saying and thought, "It can't be that my father has died." The mother then shared the sad news with Ken. When he called me shortly after, he was already experiencing a terrible grief and broke into sobs as he told of his shock. I offered to see him if he thought it would help; he said he preferred to stay with the family.

When we met the following day, Ken told of the events leading to his father's death. Father wasn't feeling well and went upstairs to rest; later mother heard a noise and found him lying on the floor. He was still breathing; mother called the police but in the short interval before their arrival father died. Ken cried as he talked and said it was such a terrible shock he just couldn't believe it. He apologized for "breaking down" when he called me. I said it is usual and right to cry at times of great shock and sadness. He said he had also "felt awful" for crying in school when the teachers sympathized with him about his father's death.

Ken described how he had spent the previous afternoon. The family had been invited to a neighbor's house; another neighbor had offered to care for his baby sister; he had decided to accompany her so she wouldn't be lonely. At the neighbor's house he had played ping-pong; at first he had done poorly but then improved his score. He felt badly about playing when his father was dead. I said he had such intensely sad feelings that "it would be too hard to think about them all the time." I added that I did not think he was running away from his feelings.

Later Ken cried again and said he just couldn't believe that his father was dead. Although he hadn't always done what Ken liked, "He was a good father." Ken had sensitively observed how some other family members responded to father's death. His observations allowed him to deduce their underlying feelings. He related that his two-year-old brother was bewildered by seeing grownups cry. He kept looking "wonderingly" at his mother's face. His father's mother, Ken said, had cried once and then had "a sad face." His apology for crying stemmed in part from a fear of upsetting me, perhaps in identification with the grandmother who had controlled her tears to spare the children pain.

Ken reported on the provision father had made for his sons' education and said that his brothers and he were planning a memorial service. I saw Ken next three days later. In the meantime he had shared fully with his family in the rites for his father. He described the difficult experience with feeling, impressing me with the bewildering variety of affects he had to contend with. Ken said he had spent some time at the funeral home and had kissed his father on the forehead before the coffin was closed. He was pleased by the large number of friends who had paid respects to his father but disturbed by the crowds and by the preoccupation of mother and grandmother. After the funeral the house was so full that there was no room for the children to sit down. Ken looked forward to the time when they would have the house to themselves again.

In describing the journey to the cemetery and the burial ceremony,

Ken spoke of a number of shocks he had received. For instance, a military salute was given and the firing of the guns had startled him. Ken's stress on these lesser shocks seemed to help him assimilate the greater shock of the death and burial of his father.

Ken conveyed a feeling of strong mutual support when he described how he and his elder brother had walked to the graveside with mother, each holding her by the hand. In speaking of the funeral procession Ken revealed his sensitivity to the feelings of others, as well as his preconscious recognition of the long task of mourning. The many cars in the cortege had to pass over a railroad track. While the car he was riding in was stationary he had noticed a woman waiting in her car for the long procession to pass. Ken had thought how much patience she would need. I related this to the treatment, and to Ken's mourning task. I said that he, like any boy whose father had died, would need much time to feel his sadness and to get used to being without the father he loved; this was not something he could hurry over or that I should feel impatient about.

In the following months, treatment was concerned mainly with difficult current realities in Ken's life as well as inner conflicts relating to his father. He could proceed with the task of mourning in spite of some temporary interferences and the many pressures upon him.

At this time Ken's mother was burdened with her own feelings of loss as well as most demanding family responsibilities. Shortly after her husband's death her baby had to undergo surgery. She needed the help of her older children; her anxiety also led her for a time to restrict her sons' usual activities. The situation became easier after a few weeks when a relative came to live in the home.

Ken felt keenly his mother's preoccupation as well as his father's absence. He began to worry that his mother too would die. He showed here the realistic fear of every child left with one parent. Another cause of his fear was his unconscious anger with his mother for her preoccupation and the demands she made on him. A third important motive for his anxiety about his mother was the suddenness of his father's death, which allowed Ken no chance to anticipate and to use anxiety as a signal; hence his feelings of shock and unbelief and the tremendous upsurge of grief. Thoughts of his mother's possible death, therefore, served the purpose of the anticipation denied him when his father died.

Ken and his twin, Jack, supported each other immediately after father's death, for example in making plans together for a service for their father. Subsequently, Ken's course of mourning seemed to be little affected by his current relationship with his twin. When Ken began treatment he had, at times, difficulty in differentiating himself from his twin. By now he had a stronger sense of his own identity and shared little of his inner life with his brother. Each boy appeared to experience mourning in his own individual way.

In the weeks after father's death, Ken began to sort out some conflicting feelings about him. Many verbal tributes had been paid by relatives and friends; these aroused feelings of bewilderment, pride, and envy in Ken. He was bewildered because the tributes suggested that father had been perfect, while he was aware that father had some faults. He thought that one of these was father's habit of swearing in a lighthearted way. He was relieved when I agreed with him that dying does not make anyone perfect. I further suggested that father's friends were remembering what they had most liked about him and were also showing their regard for mother and her children in speaking well of father.

Ken did not identify with his father in death as he had done in the case of his grandmother. His identifications were now of a more active kind. Some served as temporary interferences because they caused guilt, while others promoted the task of mourning. Ken had felt guilty about joining in some bantering talk at the funeral parlor; he recalled that his father had also behaved in a joking way at a previous family funeral.

During this period we discussed several times the part played by identification following a death. I suggested that being like a person who has died is one way of remembering him. We recognized Ken's wish to find out which parts of his father's personality he wished to remember in this way.

Ken's guilt feelings presented the greatest threat to the work of mourning. His previous relationship with his father and some of the ways in which it had been complicated by Ken's relationship with his twin were contributing factors.

Ken's relationship with father had been colored by a resentful feeling that he could not compete with his more active twin for his father's interest and admiration. Father had in fact felt that he had more in common with Jack than Ken, and had enjoyed and encouraged Jack's prowess in sports. Ken excelled only in swimming, where he had a woman instructor and was not a member of a team. His feelings that he could not compete with his twin for father's regard were preceded by similar feelings in his pre-oedipal relationship with his mother. His main defense against his unconscious furious resentment was a withdrawal which led to a restriction of ego functioning. Several times in his first two years of treatment Ken gave up an activity because he felt slighted by male instructors who, Ken said, gave more attention to other students. Before father's death our attention had been focused on this problem. Ken had begun to recognize his underlying feelings and his defense of withdrawal. He had already begun to play football and did not give up, although his performance was affected by his ambivalence and his rivalry with his twin.

In the year following father's death, Ken became more actively involved in football and played with a different spirit. His persistence was in part based on an identification with his father. Ken expressed his sadness that his father couldn't see his progress, because he would have been proud of him.

Several weeks after his father's death, Ken reported the frequent sensation of "seeing something out of the corner of my eye." This something, he thought, would be a lock of his hair which, however, he couldn't see when he looked up. When I asked for Ken's further thoughts about something that seemed to be there but wasn't, he connected this with his father. He elaborated that when he looked at his dad's picture he felt he was there and when he did something wrong he thought father was watching him and felt guilty. The wrong actions he felt guilty about were looking at another boy's answer in math class and swearing. Consequently, Ken revealed his fear that his father might still be paying the penalty for his own lapses into swearing. Ken also began to express concern that his father's heart condition might be hereditary and that he might die from the same cause.

As we explored this material further, several aspects of Ken's conflict could be clarified. In part, his fear of being watched and punished by death related to his guilt over masturbation and his unconscious oedipal fantasies; the latter were brought into sharper focus by his father's death. Ken's belief that his father was being punished served to externalize the punishment he felt he deserved himself for his oedipal wishes. Some of Ken's guilt feelings stemmed from the recognition that he could still enjoy life while his father could not. He also felt unconscious guilt because in some respects his standards of conduct were higher than his father's.

Ken maintained a clear memory of his father, with his strengths and limitations. In the summer a number of families met for a picnic at which the fathers played ball with the children. Ken said he had walked about feeling lonely and realized "that something was missing." As we talked he soon recognized that he had missed his father, who had always been popular and in good form at parties. He recalled that another boy's father had made a slip of the tongue, addressing another man by the name of Ken's father. Ken thought this slip indicated that the man who made it was missing his father too. During this time Ken became more sociable himself. For the first time he could be at ease in the company of other boys. He joined a group of neighborhood boys who held parties every few weeks.

At home Ken undertook some of the household tasks previously performed by father. At Christmas he installed the lights along the roof of the house; here he allowed himself to do better than father, who, he said, had usually postponed this job until the last minute. Ken also took an interest in maintaining the yard, consulting a neighbor about the care of the roses. In turning to the neighbor for help and advice, Ken showed his ability to relate to male adults; this marked the beginning of his gradual decathexis of his father. In the second year after the father's death, he was able to extend his positive relationships with male relatives and teachers.

Ken's previous experience of death, which had on the whole been handled realistically and sympathetically by his parents, apparently helped him to face the difficult task of mourning for his father, which was made more difficult by the circumstances of the death and by its distressing effect on every family member, especially the mother. The mother's great strength was that she recognized that each child had feelings in his own right and that each had a need to mourn. An initial impediment to Ken's mourning had been his loneliness and resentment, followed by feelings of guilt. The analytic work in these areas freed Ken to maintain the necessary hypercathexis of his father, followed by a gradual decathexis, and thus to carry out his mourning. After some months Ken began to make relationships with men outside the family. This was a sign of his beginning decathexis of his father and adolescent object removal.

3. Grief and Mourning

We had little difficulty in agreeing about the concept of grief and accepted the dictionary definition of it (Random House 1967) as a feeling of deep sorrow.

The definition of mourning proved to be much more complicated. Common usage of the term, according to the same dictionary, may denote (1) the act of lamenting for the dead, (2) expressing sorrow over misfortune, loss, or anything regretted, (3) the conventional manifestations or outward tokens of such sorrow, for example, rituals, black clothes. A similar overlapping of meanings occurs in German. According to the editor's footnote in Sigmund Freud's *Mourning and Melancholia* (1915, p. 243), "The German 'Trauer,' like the English 'mourning,' can mean both the affect of grief and its outward manifestations." None of these meanings coincides fully with the psychoanalytic concept of mourning which we understood to connote a series of intrapsychic processes, of which the affect of grief and its outward manifestations are but a part. This psychoanalytic emphasis derives from Freud's early formulations on this subject (1915).

We agreed to define mourning as the mental work following the loss of a love object through death. At once two main questions arose: Does it have to be the loss of a love object? Must the loss occur through death?

Some of us felt that mourning indeed follows only the loss of a love object. Others felt that mourning could follow the loss of a highly cathected inanimate object, for example a home. Several examples were given from the analyses of children showing "mourning reactions" following a move. We asked ourselves if this is especially true of children because they tend to personify objects. There were many instances where children had grieved for a lost teddy or favorite toy. How far, however, should one extend this? Would the loss of a beloved comfortable pair of shoes be followed by mourning? A similar problem was posed for us by the "abstraction which has taken the place of one [a loved person], such as one's country, liberty, an ideal, and so on" (S. Freud 1915, p. 243). Can we consider the loss of youthful ideals due to maturation or the loss of a favorite field due to urban development the "exciting cause" for a mourning process? These are not inanimate objects personified by the child but resemble them in that they are not actual love objects.

Further, does mourning follow the loss of self-representations and of parts of one's own body? Many examples were given, ranging from the painful decathexis of a person's earlier image of himself to the excruciating inner struggles of patients in the wake of the loss of a limb or a body function. In these cases a long period of hyper-cathexis and gradual decathexis were most striking.

We also considered the reaction to the many partial losses during maturation, the loss of the oral-libidinal relationship with the mother, the relinquishing of the oedipal attachments, the adolescent object removal which Anna Freud (1958) likens to mourning. Such losses relate to objects but represent only parts of an important relationship. Are such losses mourned in the same way as total losses of love objects? This would also include such partial losses as occur when a parent withdraws from his child or rejects him. Can a rejection be followed by mourning and, if so, at what point?

We found it necessary to consider those earliest losses in either the need-fulfillment phase or the beginnings of object constancy when loss of the love object primarily represents serious narcissistic deple-tion or is impossible to distinguish from it. From our own experi-ences and from the knowledge of the work of others we realized how difficult an area this was to understand in terms of loss and mourning.

Our discussion of the question, "Must the loss occur through death?" led to similar problems. Some felt that the reality of death was the sine qua non of mourning because it implied a special final-ity. Others thought that a love object could be irretrievably lost through circumstances other than death, for example divorce or a broken engagement, in which case the identical process of mourning would take place. Examples were quoted from the analyses of chil-dren who had been adopted at a later age from foster homes. Are these total and irretrievable losses comparable to loss through death? Are children of divorced parents in an identical or different position as far as mourning is concerned? Thinking particularly of young children with limited reality testing, would not a long-term separation present a reality comparable to death?

The group could not decide any of these questions at once. We felt there were both important similarities and differences among these instances. We asked ourselves whether the various forms of loss involved differences in quantity or in quality or in both. It also was not clear whether allowance should be made for differences in developmental stages (levels of ego functioning, differentiation in mental representations, etc.) or whether we could find criteria applicable to all phases of life. We were not sure whether different love objects would be mourned in different ways.

We noted that psychoanalytic authors disagree widely on these subjects. S. Freud (1915) includes the loss of abstractions which have taken the place of a loved person as a cause for mourning. Anna Freud, who defines mourning more strictly as following the acceptance of the loss of the cathected object in the external world (1960, p. 58), likens some aspects of adolescent development to mourning. She says in this context, "Some mourning [by the adolescent] for the objects of the past is inevitable" (1958, p. 263). Members of our group who had published papers on mourning had dealt with the subject specifically in relation to the loss of a love object through death and had considered other forms of loss as related but not identical (R. A. Furman 1964, 1964a, 1967, 1968, 1970, 1973; Barnes 1964).

In discussion after discussion we examined these concepts on the basis of our available analytic material. In many instances we found that we needed to digress to other related topics, such as the concept of object constancy, questions of primary and secondary narcissism, the nature of self and object representations, in order to gain further understanding. For the purpose of clarity, the following conclusions are presented in summary form and do not attempt to follow all aspects of the group's thinking.

Does mourning follow only the loss of a love object?

Loss of parts of the body or of body functions. We considered clinical material of patients who had lost a body part through amputation or who had lost bodily functions through polio. In these cases a painful slow process of longing and renunciation (hypercathexis and decathexis) of the lost part or function occurred, akin to the mourning process. It was pointed out however, that neither limb nor function "loves you back" and that it was impossible to become like the lost limb or function; that is, identification did not and could not occur along with decathexis. We found that in these purely narcissistic in-stances—losses of parts of a person's own body—the decathexis led to a redistribution of the narcissistic libido and an alteration of the self-representation. The self-love which had been invested in the lost body part or function was directed to other body parts or functions and the patient's image of himself changed correspondingly. The in-ternal processes did not involve the decathexis of an object represen-tation and the alteration in the self-representation was not the out-come of a withdrawal of object libido. The mental work in no way involved the relinquishing of a loved person and of the relationship with him. Any changes in the image of, and love for, himself did not result from the withdrawal of love from another person.

Loss of ideal, or idealized, aspects of the self. We reviewed in-stances of narcissistic losses based on misconceptions about the self that could no longer be maintained. Our clinical material included ex-amples of aging with the renunciation of the youthful self-image, of unrealistic overestimations of the self, of a girl's fantasy of possess-ing a penis. These losses, too, required painful decathexis and alter-ations of the self-representation. The processes were similar to those of mourning, but they differed decidedly in that they involved neither object libido nor object representations.

Loss of "abstraction which has taken the place of one [a loved person], such as one's country, liberty, an ideal, and so on" (S. Freud, 1915). We considered cases in which patients had lost their country in the sense of being forced to emigrate or in the sense of its disappearing as an independent political unit. In some of these cases ideals such as liberty, honesty, and justice were lost at the same time or independently of the loss of the country. During the Nazi period preceding World War II some people lost their country under trau-matic circumstances; they were also deprived of liberty and their ideals of honesty and justice were destroyed. The material showed that such abstractions were mental representations of concepts invested with both narcissistic and object libido and represented extensions or dis-placements of self and object representations. In most instances the narcissistic cathexis prevailed and ideals generally could not be said "to love you back." When these ideals were narcissistically invested, their loss was followed by decathexis and alteration of the self-representation but excluded the important aspects of object libido and object representation. When the ideals were invested with object libido, they represented either displacements or extensions from a love object. The reaction to their loss then depended on, and constituted a part of, the way in which the loss of the love object itself was dealt with. It was the original person, not the displaced or extended abstraction, to whom the mourning process really applied. For example, when love of country was primarily a displacement from love of mother, the significant mourning process applied to the loss of the mother, and love of country was but an aspect of it. Where the displacement or extension occurred without the loss of the original love object, the reaction to the mere loss of the abstraction depended on the object's still being available. This differed from a mourning reaction in which the object was lost, the loss in these instances being at best partial. A modification rather than a decathexis of the cathected object representation was required.

Loss of highly cathected inanimate objects. In reviewing children's reactions to the "old house" from which they had moved, to the loss of a beloved doll, or to the beloved pair of familiar old shoes, it was evident that many factors entered into the child's reactions, such as intense displeasure at the unfamiliar or loyalty conflicts stemming from ambivalence: "Can I keep my love for the old house if I like the new one too much?" Nevertheless, the clinical examples showed painful longing and slow decathexis in addition to the factors mentioned. It appeared that, when inanimate objects were cathected with object libido, the inanimate object represented either an extension of, or a displacement from, the real love object. The loss of such inanimate objects was experienced as similar to the loss of the love object itself. There was a big difference, however, between losing the real love object and losing something that was only its extension or displacement while the main love object was still available. When the child's "old house" was an extension of his mother, in moving he lost the house but not his mother. The intrapsychic processes involved changes in the total composite nature of the cathected object representation of mother but did not require a decathexis of, or identification with, that object representation. The situation was different when the old house was loved as a displacement from a lost mother, as sometimes happened when a family moved from their old house after the death of the parent. Then the intrapsychic reaction merely appeared to belong to the inanimate object, the house, but actually constituted a part of the reaction to the loss of the loved parent.

In most instances of highly cathected inanimate objects, however, our examples showed that they represented mixtures of narcissistic and object libido, the former often prevailing. To the extent that narcissistic investment was involved, the reaction to the loss led to alterations in the narcissistic cathexis and in the self-representation but differed clearly from the reactions to object loss.

Loss of parts of object relationships in normal or pathological development. We first discussed normal developmental losses, for example the oral-dependent relationship of babyhood, the sadomasochistic relationship of the anal phase, oedipal relationships, and adolescent object removal. Clinical examples showed that the ending of these phase-adequate relationships was not experienced as a painful loss when the intensity of the cathexis was allowed to lessen in the course of maturation and the child was ready for a new type of relationship from which he gained gratification. We did see considerable grief, longing, painful decathexis, and inability to relate in another form when a partial drive relationship had sustained a developmental interference and the normal maturational progression was impeded. We found further that, in the healthy maturational course, the loss of early phases of relationships was largely dealt with by identification processes in one form or another. This led to the building up of the personality, with secondary narcissistic investment, development of ego attitudes, and emergence of super ego (Jacobson 1954). These processes went on while the constancy and reality of the love object assured adequate narcissistic supplies and offered alternative modes of object relationship.

We noted next that similar processes occur in some forms of pathological development. Even when the phase-adequate relationship was developmentally interfered with, when the healthy identification processes were impeded, and when the real object did not offer adequate alternative forms of relationship, the experience of loss and grief, and the intrapsychic work following it, were tempered and modified by the real existence of the love object. This happened in children with partially withdrawn or depressed mothers, or in cases where the child's mother could sustain only a pathological relationship. In such situations of partial loss of object relationships, either normal or pathological, the real love object, at least by his mere presence, offered a modified though inadequate or pathological relationship. Further, aggression continued to be turned outward against the object;

the object representation was not likely to be obliterated by aggression because the continued perception of the love object helped to reestablish it or to keep it intact. One patient who was often disappointed in his dependent infantile relationship with his mother vividly expressed the main point, "But what would I do if she really died?"

We agreed that losses of partial object relationships were similar to complete loss of a love object in that changes in object libidinal cathexis were involved which included identification and partial decathexis. They differed, however, essentially from the total loss of a love object in that they effected only modifications of the object libidinal cathexis and of the object representation. These processes were made possible through the continuing perception of and interaction with the real love object. At no point was there a complete or nearly complete decathexis of the love object. On the contrary, the original love object remained important.

On the basis of these discussions we concluded that mourning as "the mental work following the *loss of a love object*" was indeed substantially different from (1) the mental work which followed the loss of narcissistically cathected objects, such as parts of the body and its functions, and extensions of the self either in the form of inanimate objects or in the form of abstractions or ideals; in these instances of loss, changes in object libido and decathexis of the object representation were not involved. (2) the mental work which followed the loss of parts of object relationships (for example, oral-dependent relationship, oedipal relationship, partial withdrawal of love object), and the loss of objects representing extensions of or displacements from the love object (country, toys, houses, clothes). In these instances of loss the intrapsychic work included, and was affected by, the continuing perception of and interaction with the love object. Changes were effected in the nature of the object cathexis and in the corresponding object representation, but the object representation was at no point completely or almost completely decathected. On the contrary, its continuity was assured by the perception of the love object and it, in turn, affected the outcome of the internal processes.

Losses in the earliest phases of development. We considered losses that occur in that phase of early development when the self and object are either not differentiated at all or when the beginning differentiation is so tenuous and labile that the loss of the love object represents primarily a serious narcissistic depletion.

We knew from the work of others as well as from our own experience that a baby a few weeks old will become extremely distressed if his needs are not met adequately and consistently, but we agreed that we had no grounds for assuming that his distress in any way relates to his subjective experience of loss. At a later time, when the baby has only achieved the stage of the need-fulfilling object relationship, that is when the mother's image is cathected only at periods of tensions arising from unfulfilled needs, the loss of the mother would constitute a narcissistic depletion. This would lead to severe subjective distress and to potential harmful interference with the basic narcissistic investment of the body image and the development of object relationships.

Lucy was ten weeks old when her mother died suddenly (see analyst's report, p. 219). Throughout Lucy's childhood and adolescence she suffered from obesity, and from recurring abdominal pains at times of stress.

Feeding herself was intimately connected with being loved, and food had become a substitute for narcissistic supplies from people. When she felt cared for by her stepmother, Lucy could diet, but she resorted to stuffing herself and stealing food when the care of another person was not forthcoming. Eating gave her a feeling of contentment, and food was the consistently available comfort which she could administer to herself, without depending on the "feeder" who could change or become inconsistent.

Another aspect of Lucy's difficulty with dieting was her concern with her body image. Whenever she imagined herself thin she feared she would not be herself. Although conflicts from later developmental levels played their part, the early shifts in the need-fulfilling person seemed to have predisposed Lucy to react with bodily feelings to mental stresses.

In order to remember with longing that he experienced the loss of a love object, a child must have reached the beginning of the stage of object constancy.[1] At this stage the mental object representation is

1. Our concept of object constancy is based on our correspondence with A. Freud in 1963 and is as follows: Object constancy begins after the stage of need fulfillment and forms the basis for all subsequent levels of object relationships but does not represent a circumscribed stage as such. Rather, object constancy continues to solidify, becomes more stable in the face of frustration, and less affected by stresses from within and without, all through the maturing years till, hopefully, it reaches an optimum level in adulthood. We utilized this concept of object constancy in our follow-up work published in *The Therapeutic Nursery School* (R. A. Furman and A. Katan, eds., 1969).

cathected even at times when tensions from unfulfilled needs are not present or are frustrated to an extent. Chronologically the child usually reaches this stage in the second half of his first year of life. We felt that at this stage the total loss of the love object would be conceived as such, setting the stage for intrapsychic reactions affecting object cathexis and object representations.

We discussed our own clinical examples and compared them with some described in the literature. In one case an infant almost one year old was seen after a week's separation from the mother. He was listless, pale, unresponsive, and regressed both in level of object relationship and ego functions. In another case an almost identical picture was observed in an eleven-month-old who had at no time been separated from his mother but had just experienced an operation followed by several days of hospitalization. The impression of narcissistic depletion, accompanied by regression in relationship and ego functions, resulted in one instance primarily from the loss of the mother, in the other mainly from gross interference with the body and its narcissistic investment. In many instances, of course, hospitalization and separation coincided and made it even harder to compare the relative impact of each. (See the analyst's report on Danny, p. 198.)

To the infant in early object constancy, the loss of the mother is a threat in terms of need fulfillment as well as a loss of essential narcissistic supplies, leading to enormous inner-need tensions and to gross narcissistic depletion. Even allowing for this, something must happen to the object representation of the mother that resembles the hypercathexis and decathexis in mourning. Isn't this included in the well-known description of the clinical manifestations following separation from the mother, namely "protest, despair, withdrawal"? (A. Freud 1960, p. 57.) A one-year-old baby was described who had lost his older brother through death. This baby searched for the brother around the house and expected his appearance at the door. At one point the baby's older sister had dinner with a neighbor. The baby was most upset, inconsolable, refused to eat. The mother guessed that the baby feared his sister would also leave for good. She took him to the neighbor's to see the sister, which at once calmed the upset baby. In the discussion it was thought that with this loss, which does not imply unfulfilled needs or withdrawal of narcissistic supplies, we could better see the fate of the object constancy of the representation of the dead brother, the intensity of the longing for him—in short, the bases for the intrapsychic processes of mourning.

We agreed that in this early phase of object constancy, the intrapsychic work of mourning would be approximated much more closely in cases where the loss of the love object did not also constitute an interference with need fulfillment and depletion of essential narcissistic supplies. In instances, however, where the baby at this stage lost his main love object, namely his mother or mother substitute, such double loss was unavoidable and the child's reaction complicated.

We concluded that mourning of a love object, in the sense in which we use the term, could begin to be considered theoretically only after the bereaved had reached the stage of object constancy as defined above.

We asked ourselves when, and to what extent, object love was ever free of narcissistic elements, in the sense of the object playing a part in need fulfillment and furnishing narcissistic supplies. When does the loss of the loved person involve no interference with need fulfillment or narcissistic depletion so that "the ego . . . is persuaded by the sum of the narcissistic satisfactions it derives from being alive to sever its attachment to the object that has been abolished"? (S. Freud 1915, p. 255.) We thought that in this regard there was a continuous maturational line represented at one extreme by the baby's total dependence on the mother as a need-fulfilling object and, at the other extreme, by the adult independent self-love and ability to supply his own needs. The baby would experience the loss of the need-fulfilling mother as an intolerable rise in tensions and as a narcissistic depletion. To the adult the loss of the loved person would imply minimal withdrawal of narcissistic supplies. We felt, however, that this latter extreme was a theoretical ideal, never really reached or reachable. The adult object cathexis includes not only love for the object but also the need to be loved by the object, so that the loss of a love object, even for the adult, represents to a certain degree a loss of narcissistic supplies. In some adult relationships, for example in marriage, need fulfillment and narcissistic supplies from the love object constitute an important aspect. The loss of the love object includes both loss of love and narcissistic deprivation. Similarly, we noted that there are losses of love object for the one-year-old child which involve little narcissistic deprivation, for example the baby whose brother died. Still, there is a considerable difference in the quantity and quality of the normal adult's and very young child's cathexis of an object representation in terms of narcissistic investment and need for narcissistic supplies.

Along this maturational line all gradations might exist, depending on the following factors: (1) the relative quantity and quality to which the lost love object was also a source of narcissistic supplies; (2) the extent to which these supplies would be taken over by the self; or (3) the extent to which they could be effectively provided by others without endangering the mental work that follows the loss of the loved person and the continuity of the self-representation.

In the youngest children, at the beginning of object constancy, even those ego functions and activities necessary for basic self-preservation and continuity of basic self-representation still depend on narcissistic supplies from the love object and libidinization by her. If this main love object is lost, these functions become depleted and tend to be impeded or lost. The clinical manifestations, such as loss of appetite, lack of interest in the environment, susceptibility to somatic diseases, were well described by Spitz (1945, 1946).

Beginning with the toddler we observed that the ego functions and activities most interfered with are those which still depend on the libidinization by the lost love object (walking, talking, bladder control, early sublimitory activities). Whereas the longer-established functions and activities are more effectively and stably cathected with narcissistic and neutral energy, the most recently acquired ones depend on the narcissistic supplies furnished by the love object.

Compared with the one- or two-year-old, the child at the phallic object-centered stage of development can fulfill some needs for himself (bodily independence in eating, toileting, dressing). Primary and secondary narcissistic investments have taken place to a considerable degree. Needs are met more readily by others because the unique form in which they are met by the mother figure is of less importance. At the same time, object constancy has reached a considerable degree of stability, and object representations are rather clearly differentiated and composite. In other areas—for example adequacy and assurance of need fulfillment, control of drive expression, inner and outer reality testing—the four-year-old still relies on the love object. He also is yet unable independently to recognize and verbalize affects, especially painful ones, for some years to come. He therefore requires "support," that is, narcissistic supplies from a loved person, to maintain and exercise these functions following bereavement. R. A. Furman's patient (1964a) used the analyst in just such a way. The analyst, as well as the father, prized feelings and libidinized the patient's ability to experience and express them. We noted this with a number of young patients.

The more mature the ego, the more are its functions and activities independently invested with narcissistic and neutralized cathexis and less endangered by depletion through loss of narcissistic supplies. We concluded that crucial points exist in the stages of neutral ego development which make the processes of mourning itself possible. (1) The child must have reached a stage when the loss of the love object does not interfere with the cathexis of those functions and activities that are required for mourning. These include memory, perception, and object constancy. (2) The child's basic self-investment must be sufficiently autonomous and independent of the love object that he can survive mentally as a person and can, in some areas, accept a substitute for the continuing partial supply of needs. At this stage the fulfillment of such needs and gratifications is no longer the major aspect of the object relationship. When another person provides such needs, he does not take the place of the loved person in the child's affection but on the contrary enables him to "survive" narcissistically while he performs the mental work of mourning.

In the youngest children, object constancy itself may be overtaken by regression in the absence of the love object, thus curtailing even limited work on decathexis. Adults, by contrast, may give up those activities, at least temporarily, when enjoyment of them depends on the participation by the lost love object. Their major autonomous and neutral functions and activities as well as their basic self-investment will not suffer.

The question of whether all cathected object representations include the need for narcissistic supplies from the object can be answered only in a complex way: Yes, insofar as children and adults need not only to love but to be loved back. Yes also, insofar as all relationships at all stages tend to include some form of narcissistic supplies and need fulfillment. There are, however, vast differences in the quantity of these narcissistic elements, so that at the most primitive stages of development narcissistic gratifications actually constitute the major part of the main object relationships. There are also vast differences in quality. At certain levels of development the bereaved personality cannot continue to maintain itself and its basic functions without the love object's narcissistic supplies. At later stages these supplies are increasingly supplanted by narcissistic self-investment and autonomy of functions. They may also be supplied by others because they no longer constitute the major aspect of the relationship with the love object. The loss of the love object thus increasingly constitutes less of a threat to the integrity of the bereaved individual's personality.

On the basis of this discussion we understood better an important factor. The nature of the relationship with the lost love object greatly determines the effect on the bereaved, whether a child at different stages of development or an adult. At all stages some relationships are bound to include more narcissistic elements than others; for example an invalided adult who loses his long-term nurse may suffer a greater narcissistic stress than a child who loses his sibling. Age and developmental stage are not the only determinants of the narcissistic elements in a relationship, nor are they the only determinants in mourning in general.

Does Mourning Follow only a Loss Through Death?

Loss of parts of object relationship in normal or pathological development. We had already explored this category of loss in the discussion of whether mourning follows only on the loss of a love object. We came to the same conclusion under the present heading: partial losses of the love object, whether through developmental progression (for example, loss of oral-dependent relationship, adolescent object removal) or through pathological interference (for example, emotional withdrawal of the love object) differ essentially from the total loss of a love object. Such losses effect only modifications of the object libidinal cathexis and of the object representation, not its decathexis. The continuing perception of, and interaction with, the real love object is an important factor determining the nature of these processes.

Loss of the love object through permanent separation, without perception of or communication with the love object. We studied material from work with several children who had lost their beloved foster mothers when they were adopted. One boy was moved from his foster home at eighteen months, then again at twenty months, at which time he was adopted. He grieved desperately and continued to be subject to severe periods of grief up to his sixth year. The drawn-out nature of his mourning and difficulty in sufficient decathexis appeared to be due in part to the fact that his foster mother had not really died. Another child was two when she was adopted from her foster home. Her mourning proceeded differently but was also characterized by its lack of completion by the time she was in her sixth year. Again, the fact that the foster mother had not died was of importance in her reaction.

These and similar cases differed greatly from others where the parent had died and the child had perceived and acknowledged this fact. Particularly illuminating in this respect were those children who had suffered both types of losses, through death and through other separations.[2] We felt that the continued total separation from the love object appeared to evoke a mourning process, but its course was considerably affected by the ambiguous nature of the reality: "I do not see him, but he is alive somewhere." Other factors, such as feelings of rejection and guilt, further complicated the picture.

Loss of the love object through permanent separation with intermittent perception of the love object and/or communication with him. Among our cases were several children who lost one parent through death and another through desertion. The whereabouts of the deserting parent were periodically known—an occasional letter or gift would serve as his indirect representative, and there were visits in some cases. The situation was similar to that of some children of divorced parents. In these instances the children underwent psychic reactions akin to mourning in that hypercathexis and partial decathexis of the cathected object representation occurred along with identification. There were also marked differences. Sufficient decathexis could not be achieved, or was much harder to achieve. The process was greatly prolonged and the repeated cyclic experiences of aroused hope, partial gratification, severe frustration, and anger complicated the intrapsychic work.

We considered cases of adults who experienced separations not unlike those of our children discussed above, for example a deserting spouse, a broken engagement. We felt that for the adult, as for the child, the mourning process was inevitably and significantly complicated by the knowledge that the loved person lived: "While there is

2. The analysts' reports on Geraldine, Sally, and Addie illustrate this point.

life there is hope.'' Later in our discussions we came to understand better that the actual evidence of death was a very important factor— the mourning, both of adults and of children, could be greatly handicapped if they did not have concrete knowledge and confirmation of the death of the loved person (if the child never saw the grave, if the adult was notified only of "missing in action").

Loss of the love object through permanent separation, without perception of or communication with important persons whom the child never knew as love objects. Several children with whom we had worked in analyses were adopted at birth, within the first weeks of life, or were children whose parent died before or shortly after they were born. It goes without saying that such circumstances had a profound and often distressing effect on the children's emotional development. Our data, however, showed that the lack of personal contact, the resulting lack of an object representation based on real sensory perceptions, the fact that he "never loved me back," precluded mourning in our sense of the word. Both the cathexis and the decathexis of such object representations stemmed from sources other than the love of that particular lost person and therefore had to be understood in a context other than mourning for that person.

Gary's father died in the war overseas shortly before Gary's birth. The mother, grandmother, and Gary spent the first five years of his life in an isolated village. From the start the mother told Gary about his handsome and gifted father whom she had loved so much and who would have loved Gary as much as she did. In this way the father became an indirect source of narcissistic supplies for Gary as well as a model for identification. Instead of representing a rival, the father formed a special bond between mother and child. When the mother remarried, Gary had to adapt to a real father. During his analysis he could be helped to work through his oedipal conflicts. His eventual fond relationship with his stepfather did not require his mourning and decathexis of his first father. Gary had not maintained a real object relationship with him.

It seemed noteworthy that some adoptive parents had told the children that the natural parents had died, in the hope that this would not only avoid difficult questions from the children but would also prevent the children's cathexis of the "lost" parents and possible later search for them. None of the adopted children ultimately believed this information except when concrete evidence of the natural parents' death was available.

Loss of the love object with children who do not have a concept of death and are too immature to be helped to develop such a concept. This concerns young toddlers and babies who have achieved the beginnings of object constancy. Some of the aspects of their reactions were discussed earlier. Reviewing our data now from a different point of view, it appeared to us that these children's initial reactions were identical, irrespective of whether their loss occurred through separation or death. There was, however, a very different subsequent course, for the loss of a love object, important enough to such young children, continued to play a part in their lives throughout their maturation. It therefore inevitably concerned them at a later time when they began to understand the reason for the separation. If the separation is due to the death of the loved person, a child integrates his experience differently than if the separation is due to other causes. If the separation turns out to be temporary, and the object is later restored, the psychic work proceeds on still different lines.

We concluded that the reality of death was the sine qua non of mourning because this reality implied a special finality. For the bereaved person the full work of mourning became possible only when such a reality could be perceived, comprehended, and acknowledged.

At this point we reaffirmed and accepted our definition of mourning as the mental work following the loss of a love object through death. In our discussions we had, by this time, covered most of the work of mourning.

4. The Process of Mourning

Understanding Death

The indispensable first step of the mourning process is the individual's awareness, comprehension, and acknowledgment of the death of his loved one. Our clinical material showed that the special finality of death represents an external reality that differs considerably from situations in which the love object has become unavailable through withdrawal, maturation, separation, rejection. Death is unique as an external reality but has to be conceived and understood as such by the bereaved person. At which stage of development does it become possible for a child to conceive of death?

An infant or very young toddler is unable to differentiate between death and other causes for the unavailability of his loved one. His age-appropriate response to the loved person's continued absence would be the same at the time of the loss, whatever the cause. The effect on the eventual course and outcome of his mourning would differ, however, if his love object had actually died and he grasped this fact during his subsequent development. Infants of about one year of age whose loved one died would begin to understand this fact within their next twelve to eighteen months under optimal circumstances.

In our experience, normally developed children above the age of two years could achieve a basic understanding of "dead" if they had been helped to utilize their daily experiences with this goal in mind. This was not only true with youngsters who lived in wartime, as recorded by Burlingham and A. Freud (1942), but also with toddlers reared in this country in recent years (McDonald 1963; R. A. Furman 1964, 1973). Many children we knew had been spared experiences with the death of people, both of loved ones and strangers. None, however, had escaped encounters with dead birds, squirrels, or other animals; and flies, wasps, and ants either found dead or killed in the house. These incidents had aroused their curiosity and, at times, their sadism or pity. In all instances we knew of, it was much easier for the child to comprehend death factually when it was not initially associated with the loss of a loved person and, by the same token, it was easier to understand the death of a loved one when the child already had a concept of death.

Susie was barely three years old when her mother died. After being told this sad news, Susie soon asked, "Where is mommy?" Her father reminded her of the dead bird they had found and buried not too long ago. He explained that mommy, too, had died and had to be buried. He would show her where whenever Susie wished. One month later Susie reported to her father, "Jimmy [the neighbor's six-year-old son] told me that my mommy would come back soon because his mommy said so. I told him that's not true because my mommy is dead, and when you're dead you can't ever come back. That's right, daddy, isn't it?"

Our case material illustrated a number of ways in which children attempted to come to terms with the reality of their loved one's death and how meaningful and helpful concrete evidence of death was to them at certain points. By contrast, we learned how difficult this task was for them when the adults in their environment wittingly or unwittingly misrepresented or obscured the objective facts.

Knowing and understanding that his loved person is dead is not the same as accepting it. Clinical examples showed that people of all ages grappled, for varying periods of time and for different reasons, with the task of integrating the reality. S. Freud (1915) drew attention to the tendency of the bereaved to deny the death of the loved one, at least temporarily. Knowledge and comprehension of the external facts are, however, indispensable as a basis for accepting the death of the love object and for effecting the appropriate psychic adaptation to it. "Mourning occurs under the influence of reality testing" (S. Freud 1926, p. 172).

Withdrawal of Attachments—Decathexis

According to S. Freud's earliest statements (1915, p. 244), the principal task of mourning consists of decathexis. "Reality testing has shown that the loved object no longer exists, and it proceeds to demand that all libido shall be withdrawn from its attachments to that object"; and "the ego, confronted as it were with the question whether it shall share this fate [extinction], is persuaded by the sum of the narcissistic satisfactions it derives from being alive to sever its attachment to the object that has been abolished" (p. 255). The imperatives for decathexis come, according to him, on one hand from the demands of reality testing; on the other hand, from the need to survive and to maintain the pleasures inherent in living.

We, too, feel that decathexis of the mental representation of the love object is an important task of mourning. Our experiences with adults and children, however, suggest that mourning never does, nor necessarily should, succeed in the withdrawal of all investment. The mental representation of the lost love object retains some cathexis. The amount varies and depends on many factors.

Our previous discussion of the concept of death led to the conclusion that the normal adult's and adolescent's reality testing is adequate to the task of "demanding" that he sever his attachment to the dead loved one. Younger children, from about two years, need help in developing their concept of death and in maintaining it, because their reality testing is immature and depends on that of the adult. When three-year-old Susie, in the example above, struggled to keep her sense of reality about her mother's death in face of the older boy's contradiction, she needed to turn to her father for reassurance. Latency children require less assistance, but our clinical material demonstrates that it is extremely difficult for them to rely on their own reality testing when their most important love objects contradict them either consciously or unconsciously.

Regarding the second imperative for decathexis, the wish to live and to enjoy the pleasures of living, there appear to be considerable differences between the developmental levels. In our earlier discussion of the narcissistic elements in relationships at different stages, we concluded that even the infant in the first stage of object constancy can maintain some relationships which contain a minimum of narcissistic elements in terms of need fulfillment (for example, sibling); but the infant's most important early relationships are closely tied to the integrity and functioning of his own personality. The adult personality is independently assured of primary and secondary narcissistic investment and of autonomous functioning. The loss of the love object may endanger his need fulfillment but not the integrity of his personality. In the mature personality "the sum of narcissistic satisfactions it derives from being alive" is never basically threatened.

By the time an infant reaches the beginning stage of object constancy, his primary bodily narcissistic investment is established to a considerable extent so that he can enjoy the gratification of needs sufficiently to "want" to survive, both to relieve the rising inner tensions and to experience some of the pleasures associated with their gratification. Already at this stage, and increasingly during the next few years of early childhood, fulfillment of bodily needs forms only a part of the child's narcissistic satisfactions. The development of self-esteem, the investment of ego functions and activities, depend to a considerable degree on the libidinization by the most important love object. Further, the progression of the instinctual phases and structuralization of the child's personality interrelates with the appropriate object relationships at each phase. The loss of the vital love object endangers both the building up of the personality and the varied narcissistic satisfactions derived from its functioning. For the mature personality, decathexis of the dead love object preserves the narcissistic satisfactions of living. For the young child, decathexis of the mental representation of the love object can diminish or even abolish these satisfactions and prevent their further development. In the pre-latency child particularly, the "sum of narcissistic gratifications" may therefore not exercise a demand for withdrawing his attachments but rather for clinging to the representation of the dead love object.

Kathy was three years ten months old when her father died suddenly. She had always been especially fond of him and he had openly favored her over her older and younger brothers (see the analyst's report, p. 154). From the time of her father's death Kathy remained closely attached to her memories of him. She recounted over and over her experiences with him and imagined how nice he would be with her if he were alive. She never ceased to long for him with deep sadness and he remained her most important oedipal object. It appeared that her continued intense cathexis of him helped Kathy to soften the hardships in her life and enabled her to sustain her phallic oedipal development. When she was six years old, her resolution of the Oedipus complex was accompanied by an appropriate decathexis of the object representation of the father and by a completion of her mourning.

The latency child, following the resolution of the oedipal conflict, finds himself less threatened by decathexis and this is even more true of the adolescent.

Remembering and Longing—Hypercathexis

Sigmund Freud (1915) noted that attachments to a love object were
never withdrawn easily. The unavailability of the loved person calls
forth longing. The closer, more frequent, and more meaningful the
interaction with the love object has been, the more continuous and intense is the longing. In his discussion of longing Freud (1926, p.
171) described it as the intense cathexis of the mental representation
of an unavailable love object, a process which the individual experiences as mental pain: "the intense cathexis of longing which is concentrated on the missed or lost object—creates the same economic
conditions as are created by the cathexis of pain which is concentrated on the injured part of the body." In the mourning process
"each single one of the memories and expectations in which the
libido is bound to the object is brought up and hypercathected, and
detachment of the libido is accomplished in respect of it" (1915, p.
245). This process of hypercathexis and eventual decathexis is extremely painful and consumes a great amount of energy (1915,
1926).

At different developmental stages the nature of the cathected object
representation varies greatly. The infant's and toddler's object representations are less differentiated, less stable, less in accord with external reality. In addition to the effect of the loss of the love object on
the narcissistic investment of the self-image, the pain and frustration
inherent in longing without gratification can readily evoke so much
aggression that the cathected representation of the love object has to
be destroyed. This is not an inevitable outcome at this stage of development. Among our child patients, although many had maintained
ambivalent relationships with their deceased parent, and their aggression caused them great difficulty in coming to terms with their bereavement, we did not find one in whom the mental representation of
the dead parent was destructively obliterated.

It seemed to us that the complexity of the mental representation
can also have an effect on the time it takes to hypercathect all its
aspects, but it does not necessarily determine the amount of pain. The
more mature the personality and the more long-standing the relationship, the more composite is the mental representation, consisting
of a myriad of memories of different experiences. In the very young
child, by contrast, the memories are fewer but all the more intensely

cathected. On that basis it appeared that the process of hypercathexis and decathexis may well last longer in some instances (older person, longer relationship) but some memories may be less intensely cathected and therefore perhaps less painful.

Charles, aged eleven at the time of his father's death, described how painful the evenings were when he longed for his father to return from work as he had always done. Eventually "I got used to having different evenings." One and a half years later Charles visited an art museum and felt himself overwhelmed by a sudden pain and sadness. He realized that the last visit to the museum had been with his father. On this occasion Charles had been confronted with a memory which he had not yet hypercathected and decathected because there had been no occasion to do so.

A very young child more often encounters such a memory within the framework of daily routines. Our material showed, however, that, in some respects, the young child's longing extends far into the future. He misses the love object in situations in which gratification occurred in the past. Throughout his later development he longs for him in each new situation that is meaningful to him and would customarily have been shared with the love object. Such situations range from attending a school function with parents to beginning menses.

The process of remembering shows variation in different age groups. In the adolescent and latency child, as in the adult, remembering consists primarily of thinking, feelings and, at times, verbalization. In the younger and youngest children, remembering is, age-appropriately, accompanied by physical activity.

Clive was just two years old when his father died. Thanks to his mother's help he soon understood the difference between death and temporary separation. It was quite difficult, however, for his mother to tolerate the overt signs of Clive's longing and sadness. For weeks he spent much of his time repeating the daily play activities that had constituted the essence of his relationship with his father. He also insisted, over and over, on taking the walks he had taken with his father, stopping at the stores where his father had shopped and recalling specific items. Denial and identification entered into this behavior but appeared to serve the process of hypercathected remembering rather than to hinder it.

In different forms and at different times other young patients showed a similar tendency to remember with action.

We noted that the content of the memories reflects individual and developmental differences in the handling of ambivalence. When S. Freud discussed mourning reactions among primitive peoples and obsessional neurotics he stressed the universal "ambivalence of human emotions" (1913, p. 60) and its role in the mourning process. He stated that, whereas a high degree of unconscious ambivalence to the dead may be warded off by projections (resulting in a fear of ghosts) or by obsessional self-reproaches, this is not usually the case with normal civilized adults. "It is now quite easy to keep down the unconscious hostility to the dead (though its existence can still be traced) without any particular expenditure of psychical energy. Where, in earlier times satisfied hatred and pained affection fought each other, we now find that a kind of scar has been formed in the shape of piety, which declares 'de mortuis nil nisi bonum' " (p. 66).

As we noted earlier, none of the bereaved children we worked with aggressively destroyed his mental image of the love object. Some harbored a good deal of unconscious hostility which they warded off by projections and other mechanisms. At different times this facilitated or hindered their mourning process. In several instances, particularly among the prelatency children, anger and reproaches to the dead parent were preconscious and conscious. The children directed their hostility not only at the death itself but at the love object's shortcomings prior to his death; it was a necessary part of the mourning process for them that the surviving love object accept their verbal expressions of anger and, in some instances, acknowledge the objective reality of their cause for complaint. This proved to be particularly difficult for many of the surviving parents who needed their own "de mortuis nil nisi bonum" defense and could not allow, much less support or encourage, their children's different reaction.

We assumed theoretically that the older child and particularly the adult would have a much greater tolerance for mental pain, both in terms of its intensity and duration. In addition there would be some inherent differences between individuals in this regard. Our clinical material showed however that some children, at all ages, were capable of tolerating much pain for long periods of time.

One father described his son, three and a half years old, several months after the mother's sudden death. "Bobby is still the saddest human being I've ever seen. He is the sadder because he does not cry and wail, but because it fills all of him. His face is drawn and his eyes are so deep and dark. It hurts even to know how sad he is.'' This father, like those who have empathized with their bereaved patients in treatment, knew that this silent sadness often contained the child's strongest pain.

For some children tears represented the beginning of relief. In others, however, repeated and prolonged inconsolable sobbing was also observed. Some young children's pain was so poignant that adults could not allow themselves to observe it. Sometimes this was due to the surviving parent's being unable to mourn; the inability of other adults to observe the child's sadness was harder to understand. While adults may deny the child's ability to comprehend death because they fear the child's sadism (A. Freud in Nagera 1970, p. 379) they may also ward off recognition of the child's suffering for reasons of their own. Could their parents have considered them as without feelings in their own childhood? Might the intensity of the child's feelings represent a threat to their adult defenses?

Some children could bear an astonishing amount of pain alone. Most needed a loved person who could either share their grief or empathize with them and support their tolerance and expression of affect. This was an important function of the analyst with several children in latency and early puberty. The youngest children required more directly the assistance and "permission" of the surviving parent.[1] We thought that adults, too, were helped when they had a sympathetic person to mourn with but, as noted earlier, children under five years of age and through their early years of latency still needed a love-object's help in recognizing, verbalizing, and tolerating affects.

The greatest interference in the bereaved person's affective experiences did not appear to stem from the expected age-adequate differences in their ability to tolerate pain. Rather, it could be attributed to individual defense mechanisms which had been established prior to the bereavement and in identification with the dead or the surviving love object. The main task of the treatments was to help the patients to become aware of these defenses so that they could experience their feelings.

It was surprising to find how few of the adults we worked with

---

1. This aspect is illustrated by the analysts' reports of Geraldine, Jim, Hank, and Kathy.

could allow themselves to tolerate sufficiently their own distress in order to mourn. A number of surviving parents could not mourn at all. Others cut it short prematurely. For some, by contrast, the process was greatly drawn out because they feared being overwhelmed by feeling. Some parents warded off aspects of their own sadness by being unable to recognize their child's feelings. Others excluded the child from their sadness in an attempt to prevent him from being sad. When the surviving parent could not mourn adequately or could not empathize with his child's feelings of loss, the child sometimes experienced the barrier as a partial loss of the living parent. This further complicated his emotional stress. The surviving parent's difficulties in mourning represented an important interference in some of the children's mourning, either directly or through identification.

Arnold's parents had not recognized that any of their children had feelings about some important events. His mother especially tended to rationalize and make explanations when the expression of a feeling would have been appropriate. When his father died suddenly, Arnold, five and a half years old, did not verbally express any feeling about it. Neither he nor his mother could mourn. Instead, Arnold became very active and would tolerate no mention of the death nor would he stay in the house when a family member cried. Following his father's death, he began to absent himself from home for long periods and at unexpected times. His explanations were lengthy and involved but, like his mother's, not to the point.

It appeared that no parent who had lost his spouse fully conformed to the model of adult mourning portrayed by S. Freud (1915). Those parents who bore the pain of mourning or who could be helped to do so did not altogether withdraw into their grief. They continued to work and to care for their children, usually carrying an added burden in both these areas with admirable strength. Their distress, like their children's, was greatest at certain times of the day or week. At other times they continued their busy lives—to meet the demands made upon them, to gain necessary respite from pain, and to experience some of the "narcissistic satisfactions inherent in living."

The Role of Identification

Through the continuous and often arduous analysis of our patients' defenses and pathological identifications, we became aware of the important role of identification in the mourning process. Initially we were struck with the obstacles which identification put in the path of decathexis, of further maturation, and of healthy personality functioning. In several children, identification with the dead parent led to severe symptomatology and contributed to an arrest at the developmental level reached at the time of the parent's death. Although good substitute love objects were available, these children were unable to resume their emotional development until treatment had helped them undo the identifications and achieve a sufficient degree of decathexis. Several adults were cited who had lost a parent at different periods in their childhood. Important aspects of their pathology in object relations could be traced to the fact that they had identified with the dead parent. With them, too, the analysis of identifications facilitated a belated decathexis and progression in personality development. Other adults whose spouse had died had identified with the lost love object in many areas of functioning. For some the result was a difficulty in adapting to reality.

As our discussion proceeded, we became aware of instances of identification that had been helpful to the bereaved person in the process of mourning and in personality functioning and adaptation. In one example, a late-latency child reacted to the death of her mother by becoming motherly to her younger siblings for a limited but crucial period. One boy, who had lost his mother at twenty months, identified with her special speech intonation. It appeared that this identification helped him to keep up his good early speech development. A latency girl who functioned poorly had one reality-adapted sublimation, an interest in spelling and words. In her analysis this interest could be traced to her identification with a beloved grandmother who had died when the patient was about four years old. The grandmother had involved the patient in her hobby of word games. A case of an adult woman was mentioned who identified successfully with the career of her deceased husband, which helped her mourning and healthy adaptation.

These examples led us to decide that we needed to examine in each of our cases the nature and effects of identification following loss of a love object. On the basis of this detailed study we then discussed whether particular identifications with the dead love object led to difficulty for the bereaved; whether identifications in general, even of an adaptive nature, impeded the mourning process; whether identifications, in some form and to some extent, were an integral part of the mourning process.

S. Freud stated that narcissistic identifications were a characteristic aspect of the reaction to object loss in melancholia, in contrast to normal mourning which consists of decathexis. He postulated that these narcissistic identifications occur as a result of regression from object cathexis to the narcissistic oral phase of libido, "the disposition to fall ill of melancholia (or some part of that disposition) lies in the predominance of the narcissistic type of object choice" (1915, p. 250). "The love for the object—a love which cannot be given up though the object itself is given up—takes refuge in narcissistic identification" (p. 251).

Freud later restated his views. "We succeeded in explaining the painful disorder of melancholia by supposing that (in those suffering from it) an object which was lost has been set up again inside the ego—that is, that an object cathexis has been replaced by an identification. At that time, however, we did not appreciate the full significance of this process and did not know how common and how typical it is. Since then we have come to understand that this kind of substitution is important in determining the form taken by the ego and that it makes an essential contribution towards building up what is called its 'character.' " . . . "When it happens that a person has to give up a sexual object, there quite often ensues an alteration of his ego which can only be described as a setting up of the object inside of the ego, as it occurs in melancholia; the exact nature of this substitution is as yet unknown to us. It may be that by this introjection, which is a kind of regression to the mechanism of the oral phase, the ego makes it easier for the object to be given up or renders that process possible. It may be that this identification is the sole condition under which the id can give up its objects" (1923, pp. 28, 29).

Anna Freud in 1960 included identification in her definition of mourning: "The process of mourning taken in its analytic sense means to us the individual's effort to accept a fact in the external world (the loss of the cathected object) and to effect corresponding changes in the inner world (withdrawal of libido from the lost object, identification with the lost object)." (1960, p. 58).

We have already discussed the importance of identification in the normal development of the personality. In comparing such developmental identifications with those that take place in bereavement, we traced their many positive aspects from the material of our cases. Identification is an economical mechanism and one best suited to conserve the lost object. It eliminates the painful process of hypercathexis (longing) and decathexis. It builds the ego and thereby contributes to the enrichment of the personality. Identification helps the ego to integrate past and future, to bridge the gap between the loss of one love object and the formation of a new object relationship. In many instances it actually facilitates the painful hypercathexis and decathexis by temporarily and partially preserving the love object. Such helpful identifications can be seen to lessen with time in extent and intensity.

On the negative side we found that even adaptive identifications tend to prevent the cathexis of new objects and can interfere with age-adequate object-libidinal ties. For the developing child, new object relationships are necessary for further maturation. For the adult they are necessary for healthy marital and parental functioning.

In some cases of bereavement, identification played a predominantly positive part, in others, a negative part. In several instances the children's personalities struggled against their identifications with the dead parent because these identifications carried the threat of death itself: "If you become like your mommy, you will die like her." [2]

We found that none of us knew of an instance in which at least a minimal amount of identification did not play a part in mourning. We therefore decided to include identification, with decathexis, in our working definition of the mourning process.

The questions then before us were: How much and what kinds of identifications in mourning contributed to the eventual healthy realignment of the personality? Under what circumstances could the basically appropriate mechanism of identification bring about pathological results?

Types of Identification According to Developmental Level

If identification is a part of mourning, mourning can only take place at a point in the child's development when he becomes capable

2. This aspect is illustrated by the analysts' reports of Geraldine, Addie, and Seth.

of identifying. In order to clarify this, we turned to a discussion of the various types of developmental identifications.

S. Freud (1923) discussed two types, the primitive "narcissistic identifications" of earliest infancy and the later ego identifications accompanied by neutralization of instinctual energy. Jacobson's (1954) and A. Freud's (1965) more recent descriptions of the various stages and characteristics of identifications augmented S. Freud's work within a theoretical framework with which we were familiar and which we utilized to understand our own clinical experiences.

The earliest form of identification is a merging of the object and self-representations, a reestablishment of the unit between self and mother (the first love object).

As the infant's reality testing increases and enables him to perceive the differences between himself and his parents, and as the cathexes of object and self-images become established and differentiated, new forms of early identification become possible. These include imitations (affecto-motor identifications) and pre-oedipal identifications. During this period, from the latter part of the first year through the anal-sadistic phase of development, secondary narcissistic investment takes place. This lays the foundations of self-regard, self-esteem, and a sense of well-being. In one sense, these developments point to strides in object and self-differentiation and increased reality testing. In another sense they still typify the immaturity of the child's ego and its dependence on the drives. Pre-oedipal identifications are achieved by primitive mechanisms of introjection or projection, based on instinctual fantasies of incorporation. They correspond to fusions of object and self-images which disregard the realistic differences between the object and self. They are characterized by total rather than partial identification, by magic rather than real alteration of the ego (Jacobson 1954, p. 102).

When the first reaction formations become established, usually around two years of age, they mark the beginning of ego identification. These are lasting ego attitudes and character traits taken over from the parents (Jacobson 1954, p. 106). They presuppose a transition from the desire for a complete union with the mother to strivings to become only "like" her. They depend on the ability to perceive single mental characteristics in the love object and to effect appropriate changes in the self-representation and in the ego in accord with objective reality. These new ego identifications are therefore partial in nature and utilize more neutral than instinctual energy. With the resolution of the Oedipus complex and the establishment of the super ego, the advanced forms of identification predominate. They become largely independent of the ongoing relationship with the love object and are integrated into the total functioning of the personality. They enrich it in the form of character traits, ego activities, interests, and sublimations.

The role of identification in normal development differs from its use in mourning in many respects; these include the situation which brings about identification, the function served by it, and the extent to which it needs to be used. Among our bereaved patients we found identifications from all levels of development, depending in part on their age, in part on their personality makeup and individual strengths and weaknesses. The more advanced partial integrated identifications tended to contribute to a healthy outcome of mourning and subsequent adaptation. The primitive, instinctual, poorly integrated identifications, by contrast, tended to lead to pathology.

Proportion between Identification and Decathexis

On the basis of case discussions, it seemed to us that different amounts of identification would be appropriate for different forms of loss. For example, when an adult loses a parent, a considerable amount of identification would seem appropriate. When an adult loses a marriage partner, varying degrees of identification can be used since both permanent widowhood and remarriage are open to him within the wide range of normality. When a parent loses a young child, very little or no identification is expected. In this connection the case of a mother was quoted whose five-year-old son had died a year before. She had recently observed in herself a tendency to be meek and mild and saw that this interfered with her handling of her living children. She recognized her ineffective attitude as an identification with her dead child's traits during his illness. Her identification had become manifest in her period of mourning and was now no longer necessary to her.

With children of all ages beyond the earliest level of need-fulfilling relationship, identification with the parent plays its part in normal development. This mechanism is enhanced by the threat of loss. In the case of children whose parent had died, we found that identification assumed pathological proportions when it was employed so exclusively that it prevented decathexis. In all children it was important that the proportion between decathexis and identification be such that sufficient object libido becomes ultimately available for the cathexis of new love objects, so that the child's personality development was not impeded.

Content of Identification

With a number of our children the pathological outcome of identification with the dead parent was due to the pathology of the "model." In some cases the deceased parent had actually been bodily or mentally sick for a considerable time, and the manifestations of his illness had formed an important aspect of the child's object representation.

At times the child's immature ego had inadequately perceived and consequently misconstrued the parent's affliction and personality. The identification did not reflect an objective reality but rather the child's concept of it. The example of Addie, below, illustrates this.

There were some situations in which the dead parent had revealed a special aspect of himself in the relationship with the child, which had not been evident in relationships with others. The child's identification singled out such intimate parts of his relationship with the lost love object.

> Billy's mother maintained a mutually exciting sado-masochistic relationship with her boy. Her other relationships were essentially free of such elements. After the mother's death, Billy, who was then in his latency years, identified with this inappropriate but gratifying aspect of the mother in their relationship. Adults who remembered the mother from their own relationship with her could not link Billy's symptomatic behavior to an identification with his mother. (R. A. Furman 1967)

In observing a bereaved child, such behavior could easily be mistaken for a regression in object relationships. Similarly, many young children's remembering through action could look like a regression. The true psychic determinants could be traced only through the work of psychoanalytic treatment.

In some instances the difficulty lay not merely in the nature of the model or in the child's perception of it, but stemmed from factors within the child's personality. The instinctual conflicts of the developmental phase, current at the time of the love-object's death, sometimes determined which aspects of the deceased person's image were most intensely cathected by the child and "selected" for identification.

Addie's phallic-sadistic impulses in the beginning of the phallic-oedipal phase lent special significance to her observations of her father's attacks upon her mother, of their sexual relations, and of the mother's symptomatic bleeding prior to her death. Being a woman was understood to mean "attacked, injured, dead." It was appropriate for Addie, at this stage, to perceive the mother's role as wife and mother as all-important, and to wish to become like her. When these aspects became a part of her behavior and showed themselves in an excited wish to be hurt, they became pathological.

The degree of ambivalence in the relationship with the dead loved one was particularly important in this respect. In some cases it led to identifications based on idealizations; in others—or even simultaneously—to self-punitive or self-damaging identifications or to overtly aggressive behavior.

In the cases we studied, the intensity and degree of inadequately fused aggression did not appear to be necessarily characteristic of the normal anal-sadistic phase of development, but rather of the individual children's personalities. It appeared that the bereaved person's capacity for integration and adaptation helped him, to a certain extent, to "choose" and maintain those identifications which fitted smoothly into his functioning and to give up those which were ego alien. An ability to do this depends on the maturity of the personality and on general mental health.

In most instances, identifications with the healthy aspects of the deceased love object's personality were present alongside the pathological ones. Sometimes it was possible to single them out and understand them in their genetic context. More frequently they formed an integral part of the healthy functioning of the child's personality.

Hank was four and a half years old at the time of his father's sudden death (see the analyst's report on p. 129). The father had been a keen amateur actor and singer. By the time Hank was six he had developed a persistent interest in the theater. He organized many shows successfully within the family and with friends. Singing became a favorite activity for him as it had been for his father. Hank maintained these hobbies in later years. They brought him personal enjoyment and appreciation from adults and peers.

Some Other Means of Coping with Bereavement

In most cases we found that the bereaved person employed a variety of defenses to help him deal with the great stress of his situation. With some, defensive measures were prominent during the initial period following the love-object's death, with others it occurred during later difficult stages of the mourning process. Denial could be seen as a necessary mechanism which helped to "cushion" the ego at a time of extreme shock and allowed it to come to terms with the bereavement at a later date without jeopardizing the ego's adjustment to a new situation at the time. Other defenses could similarly help with the stress, depending on the individual's personality makeup.

A four-year-old boy stated repeatedly and matter-of-factly that his father had been killed and was dead, but he showed no affect. At other times he indicated that he denied the finality of death. Here isolation and denial, as well as an identification with his mother's response were seen as defensive measures. In another case a two-year-old temporarily appeared to use denial and displacement during the first several months following his mother's death. At times he related to his familiar nanny as he had to his mother and called her mommy. His sleep, however, was increasingly interrupted by spells of anguished crying.

It appeared to us that defense mechanisms, when adaptive, precede mourning and do not form an essential part of the mourning process. In some patients the use of defensive measures did not serve as a temporary cushioning and did not, in this way, aid the individual's ultimate ability to mourn. Rather, they impeded the process while shielding the ego from unbearable anxieties.

Seth was four years old when his mother died and his kindly grandparents assumed his care (see the analyst's report on p. 149). He warded off his thoughts and feelings about his mother with an overall restriction of ego functions. He conformed to educational demands but lost all spontaneity, showing no affects or active interests. Under the impact of new stress in his sixth year, Seth's defenses gave way and he developed serious symptoms.

In our work with patients who had suffered object losses other than through death, we had sometimes encountered psychic adaptations very different from mourning. This was particularly so at the developmental levels of early object constancy and the anal-sadistic phase. Some of these children were primarily affected in the area of libido distribution. For example, object love was depleted in favor of inflated self-love; libido was diminished, resulting both in inadequately invested object relationships and in impoverished secondary narcissism; libidinal cathexis was withdrawn both from objects and from the self and concentrated on partial or inanimate objects. Although there were traces of such adaptations among our bereaved patients, none showed them to any major extent. This may be due to the fact that our patients of toddler age had maintained sufficiently strong and positive relationships before the loss of the love object and, in some though not all instances, retained another love object following the loss, that is, usually the other parent.

Establishing New Relationships—Recathexis

S. Freud stated that "when the work of mourning is completed the ego becomes free and uninhibited again" (1915, p. 245). We understood this to mean that the normal completion of mourning enabled the individual to resume age-adequate functioning and to continue his maturational course unimpeded by the loss he had suffered.

In our earlier discussion of the proportion between decathexis and identification in mourning, we had realized there was a wide range of normality. In some instances of bereavement it was necessary for the individual to form attachments to a new love object in order to function age adequately and to continue his maturational course. In other instances this was not essential or was even contraindicated. For example, after the adult had mourned the death of his parent, it would be unnecessary for him to cathect a new parent. In this case a certain amount of remaining cathexis, together with advanced forms of identification and attendant sublimations, would be the most usual outcome. The adult could mourn the death of spouse or friends in a similar manner; or he could mourn them in such a way as to free an adequate amount of object libido for new attachments. Either outcome would be within the normal range. For the child, at different stages in his development, there are also some object losses which do not require replacements for age-adequate functioning, for example the death of a grandparent or sibling.

In some respects, however, there is a difference between child and adult. The adult no longer requires a major love object for the full structuralization of his personality. Adult sexual relations and parenthood represent further developments for him but they are not essential to the normal functioning of the adult personality. The child, by contrast, needs parental love objects, not only for the fulfillment of needs but also for the phase-adequate development of object libido and for the building up of his personality. Without parental love objects, the child cannot progress adequately in his relationships, and both ego and super ego developments can be endangered.

We discussed the stage at which a child no longer requires a new parental cathexis. Our data suggested that the earliest time a child could make do with less intensely cathected substitutes was the phase of early adolescence. In some cases it appeared that the young adolescent's development would have been facilitated if he had had an opportunity to cathect a new parental love object. In practice, such love objects were usually not available. When they were, there often was not enough time for the child in the early adolescent phase to mourn and then to recathect, because the maturational trend against intensive investment of a parent was already under way.

In the prelatency years the need for a parental figure is particularly great. In this period of development it is especially important that the young child mourn his parent in such a way as to free his object love for a new investment. It is equally important that a potential love object be available to him.

We noted in several instances that the mere availability of a new parent figure did not assure the child's cathexis of him. If his mourning was not complete, if its completion did not free sufficient object libido, if he feared a repetition of the loss too much to invest himself fully again, the child was unable to form a new relationship with a parent.

In addition to the child's internal handicaps, the difficulty sometimes lay in part with the new parent's ability to help the child integrate his past with his present. For example, the new parent might not make allowance for the child's residual ties to the dead parent.

The following reports on the analyses of Geraldine and Jim illustrate the struggles of two latency children, each coping with the death of the mother. Their developmental capacities for mourning were initially foiled by individual personality difficulties which predated the bereavement, by severe stresses accompanying and following the mother's death, and by the absence of support from surviving loved ones. Analytic treatment succeeded in facilitating a belated mourning.

GERALDINE   by Marie E. McCann

Geraldine [1] was eleven years and eight months of age when I first met her and it had been three years and eight months since the death of her mother. She was a child who had not been capable of mourning her mother's death, which occurred just one week before her eighth birthday. Geraldine had the developmental readiness for mourning in that she had entered latency at the time of her loss, but she could not accomplish mourning because of characterological difficulties which predated her bereavement and because of a lack of help. She was never helped to understand the realities of the terminal illness, she lacked the assurance of her needs being met after her mother's death, and her environment failed to offer her any of the support necessary for a child to mourn. I shall attempt to show in the treatment of Geraldine how mourning the death of her mother was made possible via the transference.

During her mother's terminal illness and following her death, Geraldine had utilized defenses of denial of all affects and denial in action, by being good instead of bad. Eleven months before she began treatment she developed amnesia, and repression blotted out not only the affects but also the actual reality of her mother's terminal illness, death, and her life in the two years and nine months subsequent to the loss of her mother. Geraldine began analysis with no real memory of her mother's death, thus eliminating reality testing by which memories are assigned to the past. Her analysis continued for six and a half years and ended when she was a little over eighteen years of age, a week after her graduation from high school.

From the analytic work, which extended from prepuberty into late

1. Adapted from "Mourning Accomplished by Way of the Transference" by Marie E. McCann, THE ANALYST AND THE ADOLESCENT AT WORK, edited by Marjorie Harley. Copyright © 1974 by Marjorie Harley. Reprinted by permission of Quadrangle/The New York Times Book Co.

adolescence, I have selected the work related to the analysis of defenses which had prevented her mourning, the shifting and lifting of mechanisms, and the working through the relationship with her mother with facilitation of her mourning via the transference. This thread is the focal aspect of her analysis and weaves through the entire period of her treatment.

Geraldine was the only child of her parents. She had a half-brother seventeen years older than she and a half-sister fourteen years older, who were the children of the mother's first marriage. The mother married a second time and separated but had not yet obtained a divorce from her second husband when she began her relationship with Geraldine's father and Geraldine was conceived. Actually there were further delays in the mother's obtaining her divorce so that Geraldine was about three years old when her parents married.

Geraldine's father, now in his late sixties, worked as an independent waiter in a rather sporadic manner, earned minimal wages and constantly was heavily in debt. His history of chronic alcoholism and severe pathology (on occasion involving hallucinations and paranoid ideations) interfered with his functioning as a father, as a husband, and as a contributing member of society.

Geraldine's mother died of cancer at the age of forty-eight, one week before Geraldine's eighth birthday. Verified history reveals the mother's pregnancy with Geraldine as very difficult due to the presence of many uterine tumors. She was hospitalized six days prior to Geraldine's birth, which was by Caesarean section. She also had a hysterectomy at that time, with a history of multiple fibroid tumors for several years. The mother had excision of papilloma, left breast, when Geraldine was about four and a half. Cancer was first diagnosed when Geraldine was almost seven years old; the mother had a right mastectomy, at which time a marked involvement of axillary glands was discovered. She was again hospitalized for X-ray therapy, came home briefly, then was hospitalized for a left mastectomy. She had a rapidly metastasizing growth, with weight loss (her top weight had been 275 pounds), anorexia, vomiting, weakness, shortness of breath, and severe chest pain. She was admitted to the emergency ward four months after her last surgery and died one day later.

The mother was described as having been extremely bright and a whiz at math; she was employed in the accounting departments of several government offices. In personality she was portrayed as a difficult, demanding, domineering, and stubborn woman. She was volatile and at times had an uncontrollable temper.

Early history is almost totally lacking due to the father's hazy and unreliable memory. The mother stayed at home to care for Geraldine and tried to alleviate dire financial problems by caring for other babies and by sewing. She returned to full-time employment when Geraldine entered nursery school. The parents had violent fights, with many separations. The fights also involved Geraldine's half-brother, who left when she was quite young, and her half-sister who remained in the home. The wild fights were always very upsetting to Geraldine, who is described as clapping her hands over her ears and running out of the house.

After the mother's death Geraldine stayed with her half-sister one week, went to an aunt's for another week, and then moved to the home of a neighbor who had often cared for her when the mother was either working or ill. She remained at the neighbor's for a little over a year. She spent the following summer with maternal relatives on a farm and then went at the age of nine and a half to live with her maternal aunt and uncle. She remained there until her treatment began, which was when she was placed at the Children's Aid Society, a residential treatment center for emotionally disturbed children. Residential placement during analytic treatment was considered essential to ensure continuation of her treatment by offering her controls and stability which her relatives could not provide because, against Geraldine's wishes, her father would occasionally take her for visits with him. Neither Geraldine nor the father described what occurred on the visits but they became increasingly upsetting to her and she eventually asked her aunt not to allow the father to take her away from the aunt's home. She also needed protection in the event that there was further exacerbation of the amnesia.

The causative factors about the onset of the amnesia are still only partially understood. The initial knowledge was that the amnesia followed her deception in changing D grades in music to B's (she was an excellent student), being reprimanded for the deception which was followed by a runaway of several hours, threats by her father of being sent away to a "bad girls' " school, going to school the following day and failing to return home at the close of school that day. Only during the subsequent years were other factors learned which doubtless related to the grossly overdetermined causes of the amnesia.

These precipitants include a weakening of her denial of sexuality and of her femininity upon seeing a school film on menses (she had forged her aunt's signature on the permission slip, and felt too guilty to mention it); and a pelvic exam following her runaway after the trouble at school because she described a man following her on that runaway day. Other important events revealed much later in her treatment included her aunt's angina attack, her father's proposal that the two of them move to another state, his telling her at that time of her illegitimate birth, and an untrue report from a friend of her father that her father had suddenly died.

When Geraldine was found wandering in a dazed state, she did not know who she was or where she lived. She stated that she had a severe headache, she realized she was on the wrong bus and she knew that her mother was not with her, and she asked a strange man to take her to a hospital. She was returned to her aunt with the aid of the police. The father had Geraldine hospitalized for complete neurological studies, and no organic basis was found. She was then referred to a child psychiatry clinic. At the onset of the amnesia, Geraldine recognized only her father, then later her half-sister. She had no memory of her mother's terminal illness and death. The eleven-month delay until placement at Children's Aid Society and the beginning of treatment was due to no available analytic opening.

The aunt gave a full description of Geraldine as she had known her. She referred to her being strong-willed and determined, with lots of grit. She felt that the closeness in their relationship developed after the onset of the amnesia when Geraldine remained out of school for the semester. Prior to the amnesia, she was withdrawn and distant. She never cried; she controlled her anger but expressed it in looks of cold fury and in devious ways. She is of very superior intelligence and has artistic and musical talent (her mother played the piano and sang well, often participating in church services). Geraldine was transferred to major work classes (for children of superior intelligence) when she was ten and a half. Her amnesia did not affect her reading but she lost all of her math except simple addition. She had no close friends and she associated only with children she could dominate and rule. She was competitive and jealous. After the amnesia she withdrew from peers completely.

Geraldine at eleven was of average height, slightly stocky in build, with beginning breast development and mild acne. She is a Negro of light brown complexion; her large eyes are intense and were in no way shadowed by her dark-rimmed glasses. Her shoulder-length hair was worn in two braids. She had an air of quaintness about her—in her clothing but even more in her overall appearance. In conversation she spoke voluminously and in a vocabulary far advanced for her age, avoiding slang and with stress on propriety and impressing others. She often used literary references quite aptly and as proof of how well read she was. She presented herself as calm, self-assured and in command of the situation. Her posture had a stiffness and rigidity. Most striking was her lack of true affect, deceptive at times through her effort to portray the affect which she felt was appropriate and expected of her.

Geraldine approached me and treatment with wariness, caution, and a manifest attitude of cooperation; she came promptly and talked incessantly. She set out to impress and to please me. Early in her treatment she offered factual statements about her amnesia, describing its onset or saying, "I know my mother is dead but I cannot remember it." Such statements disappeared as she tried to keep the amnesia hidden from all others—it was a defect, to be concealed and ashamed of. Her most notable qualities in those early months were the lack of any genuine affects, the frozen personality, and the shallowness of her relationships.

The key to her relationship with me initially was clearly a need for my presence, and this was most evident in her reaction to my three absences during that first year. While I was there, all was fine; when I was away, everything seemed very different and her self-control seemed to regress to an alarming degree. The need to have me present was gradually understood as her need to have me there to support her "proper girl" self. The origin of this was her tendency to adopt the behavior which various parent substitutes had expected of her and which, to a great extent, coincided with the ideal of a good daughter which her mother had held up for her (but she had failed to serve as a model).

My first absence resulted in her acting out an identification with her mother in her verbal attack on her father for his neglect, thus displacing her anger toward me to her father. This outburst stunned the father. Geraldine had never spoken to him like that before; it was just as if his wife had returned from the grave. A few months later I was away for a week and she repressed the approaching separation but while I was gone she was depressed, cried frequently, and had serious fights with the other girls in the cottage. These reactions frightened her but the most terrifying aspect was the extent of the emotional impact of my absence. When I returned, all was fine; without affect she described what had occurred and added reproachfully, "I don't understand it at all and I don't know why I'm so certain but I am positive that none of this would have happened if you had been here."

I agreed that such strength of feeling does not make much sense unless we understand that these feelings are not just of the here and now but are feeling memories from earlier times in her life. Then she felt things got out of control when that very important person—her mama—was not with her. She scoffed at such an explanation but thence ensued the first meaningful discussion of her mother and a partial lifting of her amnesia. She told of the week following her mother's death when her sister carried out the plans for Geraldine's eighth birthday party, plans that had been initiated by her mother. She said, "I know my sister Joanne was trying to cheer me up, make me happy," and we could talk of this reversal of affect, the happy, good mood (the affective counterpart of denial), a defense often employed by Geraldine. Further talk of her mother was bland and affectless as she described how unavailable her mother always had been— "She did little for me as she was always either working or ill." However, in her poems and plays Geraldine presented repeated themes of loneliness and having to fend for herself. When we could view the clear loyalty conflict in one of her plays, true affect began to enter the sessions.

The fourth anniversary of her mother's death was near and she told me how she envied her mother who got chocolates Geraldine longed for but never got, and could play the piano beautifully by ear while Geraldine had to learn to read notes laboriously. She was unable to compete with her mother and showed this in her dropping piano lessons. She became openly depressed and self-injury was evident in a fall and a painfully injured knee on the actual anniversary date of the mother's death.

As my summer vacation approached, Geraldine could never remember it, the dates, or the details but negated my reference to her tendency to forget unpleasant things. This repression was accompanied by an intensification of all her other defenses—denial, isolation, denial of affect, and rationalization. During my vacation she became very upset, feared she would crack up, and accused a male staff of trying to kiss her. She wrote me an unmailed letter of reproach. Geraldine was experiencing added internal pressure at this time in that menses had started shortly before I left for vacation. She could not even mention it to me and when I brought it up; her reply "It's a perfectly normal, natural thing that happens to every girl sometime between the ages of 12 and 21" was bereft of any feeling. I asked if she had read this in a book somewhere and her shy reply was, "Sure, that's how I have learned most things." We could then speak of her turning to books, rather than to people, for answers and identified this as her learning through her head and not through her heart (with feelings via a human relationship).

When I returned from vacation she told me of the events but had absolutely no feeling. We could then see how while I was gone she had become terribly anxious and out of control. When I came back the crisis was over; she had lived through it and the anxiety was gone. This pattern was repeated many times—her tremendous anxiety of being overwhelmed, being annihilated, engendered by a fear of needs going unfulfilled.

A new quality of a positive mother–child relationship emerged in the treatment in her reading fairy tales and singing lullabies to me. When I said that her mama must have done such things with her she disagreed with annoyance—her mother was too busy.

President Kennedy's assassination brought forth her initial denial and incredulity of death news, then an appropriate but most intellectual description of her responses. Her only affective reaction was in seeing his casket lowered into the ground. When I spoke of an earlier funeral—her mama's—she vehemently denied that this was so. "I was too young, I knew nothing of mama's funeral, I wasn't even there." The following week she fell in the gym and broke her left leg, requiring a toe-to-thigh cast for ten weeks.

She missed one treatment session, the day of the fracture. She described the trip to the emergency ward, the pains and fears. There was an unrecognized loneliness expressed as she recounted the miserable day. Very soon afterward she began asking me personal questions—where did I live, what was it like. She reminisced how her mother used to take her up "that hill' to the suburb where I live. She recalled that it seemed to her "It was like going into a different world."

At Christmas she spoke of having for the first time in her life a feeling of Christmas—of love—inside her. Within a few days she openly professed her deep love for me but could not bring into treatment her subsequent frustration and anger in receiving no similar reciprocation. It was at this point that a cottage parent's mother died of cancer and Geraldine developed severe abdominal pains and was hospitalized overnight, with no positive physical findings. She told of her desolate loneliness in the hospital, negating that her longing was for me, and proceeded to displace her feelings for me to the resident at the hospital. She developed an open crush on him, wrote him notes, and at times chastised him for his double-talk to her. My attempts to bring this into the treatment were met with vehement disagreement, criticism of me, and the conclusion that I was "a nut."

Through the month of January she showed no anxiety about leaving elementary school. However, she fell twice the first week of February, her first week in the overwhelming junior high school. That was also the week that her cast was removed. I reminded her of this pattern of not permitting anxiety ahead of time, fearing being overwhelmed, having to get through the crisis, and then letting feeling out in some way, as it must have been at the time of her mother's death when she had real needs and no idea of how they would be met. She furiously disagreed, basing this on the fact that her loss was minor in that her mother was never able to do that much for her anyway. This feeling was omnipresent in the transference. However, that night she sobbed inconsolably for hours, and slipped and fell in the hall twice.

She was steadily becoming more upset—her old old defenses were no longer effective. She regressed (was infantile in her play), she isolated herself to her room and withdrew from peers, her schoolwork deteriorated, she was furtive and suspicious, and she talked of seeing a man in a brown suit lurking around. I knew all these things about her but not from her—with me she was angry, clippy, and sarcastic, refusing to discuss anything. She had a wild out-of-control episode one stormy night; she crawled out the music room window, ran around campus, crawled into the senior boys' cottage where she was found sleeping on the floor. Her diary explanation which she sent to my office was that she thought she was going crazy, an adolescent boy Carl made her go out, she felt like she was standing aside watching herself, later realized that Carl was truly part of her.

I can only speculate on precipitants for this acting out of her bisexual conflict, and the data for my speculations came only years later. A few days prior to the episode she saw a sex-education film at school and the science teacher asked for a volunteer in an experiment. Geraldine volunteered and was to lift something from a can. The object proved to be the heart of a cow. She was filled with horror and repulsion and felt ill. It seems clear that Geraldine denied affects and facts regarding sexuality just as she did those regarding illness, surgery, and death. To her, growing up and becoming a woman meant being attacked sexually, being attacked surgically, and dying.

It was very soon after this incident, on the fifth anniversary of her mother's death, that Geraldine truanted, spend the day in a church, and reported taking forty aspirins over a three-day period. She would not discuss any of this with me (the aspirin taking, the trip to the emergency ward, the day spent in church, the truancy, etc.) but soon began to treat me openly like a mother—asking me what her dress size was, and instructing her father to leave her birthday gifts with me. Within a few days her positive feelings toward me were reversed to hate and were then projected to the other girls—they hated her, were out to hurt her, to kill her.

This reached a height one day when she refused to leave school to return to the residential treatment center—she was not safe, was subject to attack, was mistreated, feared her amnesia would return. She was brought home from school by a cottage parent and came to her session looking horrible, drawn, tense, mask-like. Walking in like a robot, she said, "I have taken all I can. I can stand no more." I said this must be exactly how she felt much earlier in her life and she began sobbing, "Yes, but it's five years now since mama died. I should be over it but I'm not. I want more than anything for someone to hold me tight and really mean it." She told in detail and with tremendous affect of her mother's final trip to the hospital, of being told by Joanne of mama's death. Joanne told her that her mother had gone to join Jesus and that Geraldine would join her there one day. Geraldine replied, "Yes, mama is dead." She did not cry until that night at a neighbor's home; she feared crying for twelve hours alone and without comfort or support.

She told of the funeral, the hymns sung, the trip to the cemetery, adults discussing whether she should go to the graveside, and deciding that she was too young. Thus she sat alone in the car. She explained she had not seen mama lowered into the ground, the first time she saw that was with President Kennedy. We talked of her longing for reunion with her mother (a merged relationship), her aspirin taking as such a gesture; yet this is not what mama would have wanted for her; she is now thirteen, her needs for mama are less than at age eight, she has capabilities, can do more for herself. After this, she was better able to deal with her positive feelings toward me, once offering herself to me in her wish to be my cat, to be loyal and loved.

A resistance in form emerged in the treatment. She refused to take in my words, was repulsed by anything I said, yet she showed an oral inhibition in missing meals and an out-of-control orality in eating paper in interviews. I spoke of her inability to eat what she should yet her reaction to my words was as if saying, "Don't feed me that line." She told me of an early experience when she foolishly made a hot dog, using her finger and a piece of paper, bit herself. She looked repulsed as she added, "How can cannibals do it—eat humans? " I equated her affect to her response to my words, as if taking them in was devouring me as well, being cannibalistic. It was after this work that Geraldine for the first time seemed truly allied with me in the treatment. She progressed in many ways—showed increased self-esteem, evidenced a Negro identity which had been steadily denied, looked and dressed more like an adolescent, and was in an overall way more attractive. Her domination of peers shifted to more genuine leadership, with fondness exchanged in the relationships.

There was a difference in her reaction to my summer vacation. There was no repression. She was angry with me, equated my trip to her mother's "trips" to the hospital: her mother always deceived her; she never spoke of cancer and told Geraldine she was going to the hospital for an examination, yet always returned having had surgery. These complaints were voiced with annoyance and irritation, a preamble to later aggression of greater strength toward her mother, yet they were memorable in that they were the first nuance of her direct angry feelings toward her mother. Her own guilt and the defense of undoing she utilized came in her telling how her father drank and worried the mother, as if worry caused cancer. In contrast, she avoided worrying her mother by helping at home and by getting very good grades.

There was a gradual change in her relationship with her father. She became openly glad to see him, was eager to meet some of his relatives visiting from a nearby state. She made her father a birthday card, then quickly and guiltily made one for me. Thus appeared the first oedipal jealousy, guilt, and need to atone in the transference.

Her guilt still made it impossible to identify with her mother but she began to identify with her aunt in her interest in cooking and in working with younger children at church.

Geraldine's progress was interrupted by the very serious and long-undiagnosed illness of her meaningful aunt, the one with whom she had lived. She showed a repetition of her earlier denial of illness by asking friends into the home on one of her regular Sunday visits and thus acted as if her aunt were feeling fine. I pointed out the repetition to her and she acknowledged that she was terrified, her aunt looked like a ghost. She thought, "Here it is again, where will I go, where will they send me." She felt like running away, but where? This led into her recall of events preceding the amnesia—her conviction that her aunt would die when she had an angina attack, her memory of her father's proposal to take her away to live with him in another state, her father then revealing that the parents had not married until she was three years old. She described how she suddenly felt that she didn't care about anything, felt like her head was held on by strings. It was after this patial lifting of the repression that, for the first time, she recognized the woman with whom she lived for that year after her mother's death. Her conclusion about this return of the repressed was, "I am getting help."

Her aunt improved physically then had a relapse the end of December and told Geraldine that she expected to enter the hospital for tests during that week. That same day she also reprimanded Geraldine for wearing lipstick secretly at church and strongly disapproved of Geraldine's forwardness in church with an adolescent boy with whom she was infatuated. Simultaneous with this were two other very upsetting things in Geraldine's life: she visited her father's apartment for the first time in two years and saw evidence of the fact that his lady friend had recently moved in with him. This was a repetition of earlier experiences of being rebuffed by her father. Now he had a lady friend living with him and Geraldine was "out."

Earlier, he had seductively encouraged her ideas of living with him and keeping house for him after her mother's death but clearly offered nothing in reality. Then again, prior to the onset of the amnesia, he had proposed that the two of them move to another state. It seems clear that Geraldine's oedipal guilt increased at the time of rebuffs by her father. In the treatment she was very upset at my news of leaving the residential treatment center even though she knew intellectually that her treatment would be uninterrupted. Again, she could voice no anxiety about any of these things, yet acted it out in running away, taking Sominex and appearing late that night at the hospital emergency ward, asking for a reevaluation. She told of her worry about her aunt's health, her fear of cancer, her feeling that her birth was responsible for her mother's illness and eventual death.

Subsequently she refused to talk with or visit her aunt, explaining that her aunt's heart could stand no more, she had caused her aunt enough trouble already. I interpreted her identification with her aunt, explaining that after she heard of her aunt's expectation that she would go into the hospital, she brought about her own trip to the hospital, as if what happened to her aunt also happened to her. With me, Geraldine excluded me, tried to hurt my feelings—employing again her passive-to-active defense. She feared getting epilepsy, saying good people did not get epilepsy, and equated that illness with going murderously out of control. In her sessions she acted like Jesse James, but refuted her own murderous thoughts and subsequent guilt in relation to me. She was negating all interpretations but tentatively acknowledged the existence of the unconscious (referred to by her as "things in the back part of my mind") in her discussion of her slips of the tongue, described by her as "skid talk," which they were studying in English class.

As she became friendlier toward me, both positive and negative oedipal elements appeared in the transference. She was jealous of me in reference to her father—he always seemed so eager to see me, so hurried to end their visits so he could spend time with me. Then her excitement with me was displaced to the girls at school—she was so embarrassed at their hugging and kissing her after her original song was played in a school program. She wished she could avoid the girls and all that excitement. When she missed her next session with me, I pointed out the displacement and her avoiding excitement with me to which she replied "You're a nut—a real nut."

She reacted strongly to the fact that she was the only Children's Aid Society child I would continue to see after my job change. She was excited and elated at being my "chosen child" yet filled with guilt. We could elaborate her concept of chosen child to its popular equivalent in that an adopted child is often referred to as a chosen child. This stirred up her guilt about eliminating her competitors, the other children, and also stirred up her loyalty conflict. Her wish to be my chosen child meant being disloyal to her mother, her aunt, and ultimately her own race. It also represented in her fantasy being male in that she thought she would literally come with me, fantasied that I would be working with boys in the adolescent residence housed in the same building where I would have my office. She felt she would live there, and would have to cut her hair and wear boys' clothing to be acceptable to me.

As the sixth anniversary of her mother's death approached, I mentioned her failure to say anything about it and her angry retort was, "What do you expect me to do, celebrate?" But once more she brought nursing books and renewed her interest in becoming a nurse—this always occurred as an undoing whenever her aggression toward her mother strengthened. Her father then requested a birthday visit at his home and Geraldine fainted in school the next day. She confirmed my suggestion that there was a connection by telling of many early trips to various churches with her father where wild orgies went on and women were fainting all over the place. That was when she was terrified of her father, but this no longer was true. She wanted a visit but felt attending church with him was not a good idea. The visit went well.

She became increasingly disappointed and frustrated with me at my not doing enough for her, and these feelings were displaced to her young male French teacher. In one session she danced the interpretive dance she had choreographed to the song "Somewhere." She danced the part of Len and treated me as her partner and the dance represented a search for love, love of a mother. The next day in school she had a panic reaction, fell, backed into a corner, felt as though she was being stabbed. I interpreted her reach toward me in the dance as a reach toward a mother, her disappointment, deep frustration and killing (stabbing) wishes. It turned out that her guilt resulted in her feeling that it was she who was being stabbed. This led her to musing about the incident of taking the Sominex and going to the hospital a few months back. She was truly glad that had happened because it brought about a change in her; prior to that she felt like half a person and felt that whatever happened to someone dear to her was happening to her. Suddenly she had realized that she was Geraldine, a separate person, that the Sominex would have hurt her.

Subsequent analytic unfolding included many references to the superiority of males. She wrote a poem as if she were a tall lanky farm lad; she identified herself with the soldiers in Vietnam. Her original songs were songs of love—search, unworthiness, declaration, rebuff, reunion—with a strong male identity showing throughout them. We could discuss her belief that being male meant being first, crowding out all competitors, including her father, with her mother.

Her anger about being female was directed toward her mother and appeared in regard to her sister. Joanne's advanced pregnancy was the impetus for revealing her fantasies regarding conception. She said she knows that the father determines the sex of the baby; she knows that with her brain. Yet she still harks back to her earlier belief that the mother has the baby and controls the baby's body formation: sex, coloring, etc. We could then look at her conviction that it was her mother who denied her "number one status," being male. She often referred to herself in parodying a national car rental ad, "I'm number two but I try harder."

The anger at her mother for her femininity appeared in the transference several months later. We were discussing Joanne's uterine hemorrhaging, or more accurately, I was the verbal one with Geraldine sitting in an icy silence, one of controlled rage. She reproached me for giving her nothing good, only the bad. She wanted nothing from me: no news, no explanations. "Female troubles" were repulsive to her and she wanted to know nothing of Joanne's physical condition. At the end of this session, in scooping up her books and papers, she took my ballpoint pen. She was embarrassed when I inquired the next day and apologized for forgetting to bring it back. She continued to forget it, finally lost it and later replaced mine with a pen she begged from her father. We could see her strong need for something from me, who gave her nothing. I suggested she earlier felt this way about her mother.

Geraldine's aggression to women increased and went in many directions. She was angry with her aunt for not giving her an immediate invitation when Geraldine resumed her relationship with her. She was hurt and furious that Joanne did not tell her directly of her baby son's birth. She was jealous of her eighteen-year-old cousin visiting her aunt for the summer and using her old room. She was angry at her father's lady friend when she saw the robe the woman gave him for his birthday; such an intimate gift seemed to shatter her denial that theirs was a platonic relationship. She proceeded with her requests for visits with her father and her aunt two weeks before my vacation. She was angry with me about the vacation and wished much wrath on my head.

She had the two visits and became very upset. She saw her nephew for the first time and was most offended by her sister's subtly preventing her from holding him. The next day she swallowed three safety pins (my unspoken thoughts were of diaper pins) and one had to be removed surgically from her esophagus. When she returned to treatment, after her two days in the hospital, I interpreted to her her aggression toward the introject. I spoke of how earlier it had seemed that when something happened to someone else, it seemed to be happening to her. This seemed to be the other side of the coin. Her anger toward others was taken out on herself as if it were not happening to her at all but to someone else instead.

She was definite about not wanting any visits while I was away. She felt discouraged about her treatment but was buoyed up by my speaking of how she had gotten through difficult times before and could again. The last day before my vacation she brought her guitar, sang the Beatles' song "Help" and smiled when I said I felt I got the message. She added, "Sometimes I can sing what I cannot say." She managed well as a model citizen while I was away.

I have given some fairly detailed developments during the first two and three-quarter years of Geraldine's analysis to illustrate the quality of object relationship and its development via the transference, thus making mourning possible. The following three and three-quarter years followed more typical analytic unfolding with relatively little acting out—her anxiety more tolerable, and her ego able to involve and ally her in the treatment. Geraldine was the one source of information. She brought material, albeit at times with much resistance. External reality events (illness of her sister and of her father) ushered in regressions for brief periods but never regressions to the point of merging with the object.

Sequentially, the analysis unfolded with many ups and downs. There was a period of resistance, this time anal in form. For a time, Joanne then became a focus for her ambivalence. As her aggression toward women became more conscious and more tolerable she had less need to deny it in action—in being good instead of bad. The origin of this had been to be a very good student so as not to worry her mother. During this work on the aggression toward her mother, her grades slipped markedly. Later they climbed, but this time not as a defensive maneuver.

After more work on her bisexual conflict and on her oedipal rivalry, Geraldine no longer denied her sexuality. She began asking for sexual information, stating that at the age of sixteen she was grossly naive. She produced many of her sexual fantasies, the majority of them emerging more readily after I had given her a bit of factual information.

Primal scene material entered the treatment via dreams, screen memories, and later through transference manifestations. Only after this work was she truly able to learn the details of her mother's illness. She had condensed the two mastectomies into one yet was puzzled, as her recall involved two separate apartments at the time of surgery. She asked for clarification by way of doctor's reports and hospital records. The clarification of the reality was indeed helpful to her as she was then able to recall more details of the timing of surgery and the places where they lived. Thus memory of the two mastectomies returned.

Typically adolescent, she worked at arriving at her standards and choices regarding many things, including the choice of a church, with a period of being an agnostic. As to the type of racial identity that was right for her, she knew she was no Uncle Tom and finally concluded that she was aggressive for black rights, but not revolutionary.

During the process of adolescent object removal (A. Katan 1937) as she moved into dating, she spoke of the conflicting standards in her background. Her mother married twice, lived with her father, had her, then married him only much later. Her identification with this aspect of her mother emerged in her strong identification with a friend who thought she was pregnant. Geraldine told of having morning nausea, adding, "Who ever heard of a pregnant virgin," and it was Geraldine who fainted when the friend found she was not pregnant. When Geraldine first heard of the friend's suspicions of being pregnant she was shocked; she disapproved and spent several days with uncontrolled crying in her sessions.

She could see that her degree of affective reaction was out of proportion to the current reality and she agreed to a connection with her first knowledge that her mother was unmarried when she became pregnant with Geraldine, and Geraldine's illegitimate birth. The tears could then be understood as a piece of her mourning—her mourning the death of her idealized mother when she learned from her father about the circumstance of her conception and birth. This had followed the actual death of the mother by two and a half years and preceded the onset of the amnesia. We could also gain some insight into a major aspect of her symptom of falling as an identification with the "fallen woman"—her mother.

She also talked of her father's double standard—he lectured her to be a "good girl" yet he still failed to marry the woman he had been living with for years: "Just like with mama." Her aunt represented severe morality; she was extremely rigid and considered card playing, dancing, and dating before age eighteen all as evil. Geraldine decided, "I have to look at these standards of others and come up with my own."

Her reactions to separation and loss occurred several times with favorite teachers and the meaningful staff of the residential treatment center when she moved at age seventeen and a half to a group home for twelve adolescent girls. Of course the end of the analysis loomed steadily for the final fifteen months of treatment, even though she predicted that she would be in touch with me in the future (which she has been). The losses were dealt with in feelingful ways, with most appropriate affects. As the treatment end was about four months away she had three brief periods of amnesia (called "lapses" by her). We could discuss their occurrence since two of them happened as she left my office. We could see the old pain of loss, the fear that the feeling was too great, was intolerable, as she not only felt nothing, she knew nothing—the blank of amnesia. The three incidents occurred within two weeks' time and did not reoccur later.

I might conclude with some reflective comments of Geraldine during the final months of her analysis. As to her many struggles with her aggressive feelings and how she dealt with them: "With mama, I was scared to death to step out of line. I saw with my own eyes how she attacked, in words and actions, my dad and sister and after all, I was just a little kid—very powerless." And, "Mama didn't treat dad too well at times. I remember once when I was about three, he was hospitalized with pneumonia. We moved and mama didn't even tell him because she was mad at him." Another description of her dilemma, "How could I ever be mad at mama—she was really the only security I had. You really have to side with the parent who looks after you."

She always knew that her mother was regarded as the black sheep by all her relatives and Geraldine was never thought of as a person, only as "Helen's daughter." The relatives were never around or interested in her early years and her aunt took her after her year with the family friend more out of duty than any genuine love for her. In regard to her aunt, she recalled that backtalk was never tolerated, and she was convinced that her aunt could tell if she even had an angry thought. She was equally in touch with the positives in the relationships. She spoke of her gratitude to her mother for imbuing her with a love for music and reading—both great pleasures in her life. She was realistic about her aunt: "We will always disagree on many things—my aunt is old and won't change and after all she has a right to her own opinions too." Her aunt's husband was always regarded by Geraldine with fondness and admiration; she admired his sensitivity, patience, industriousness.

As to her earlier denial of all affect, again her own statements are more descriptive than any I might make. "You know, I think my treatment, or really my life, has been sort of in three phases. At first, I blotted out all feelings—things happened that were more than I could endure—I had to keep going. If I had really let things hit me, I wouldn't be here. I'd be dead or in a mental hospital. I let myself feel nothing and my thoughts were all involved with fantasies, fairy tales, science fiction. Then the second phase, my feelings took over and ruled me. I did things that were way out. And the third phase, now, is that my feelings are here, I feel them and I have control over them. One of my big assets is that I can experience things with genuine feelings. At times it hurts but the advantages, the happiness, far outweigh the pain."

Her reflection on her relationship with me was expressed when she brought her boyfriend to meet me, several months after ending her analysis. She explained to me that she had told her husband-to-be all about herself, her life, her treatment. She referred to me as her friend, then turning to her boyfriend said, "She never lectured me, blamed me, chastised me, praised me—she let me be me, she helped me to know and to sort of like myself."

Her gains have been notable in this period of adolescence when she had to try to accomplish the developmental tasks as well as the major task of mourning a loss which had to be blotted temporarily from her memory, taking along with it the capacity of feeling herself worthy to live. Her life events will help determine her future as tendencies toward somatization and action under great anxiety remain with her, although under relatively good control. Many aspects of this lengthy analysis have of course been excluded as I have tried to focus on the task of mourning which was accomplished via the transference.

At seven years three months, Jim experienced a traumatic car accident. Jim, his fraternal twin, his brother who was three-and-a-half years younger, his mother, and another family consisting of a mother and four children were returning from a vaction. The car hit a bridge abutment and was demolished. Bodies were hurled in all directions. Both mothers, Jim's fraternal twin, and three of the other family's children were killed. The survivors sustained multiple injuries. Jim himself had a serious head injury and did not recover consciousness for several weeks. For some time after that he showed confusion and hyperactivity which, at least initially, were of organic origin. He remained in a hospital for about three months, in the same room with his younger brother who was casted for limb fractures. Jim and his brother were looked after primarily by a special nurse who was kind and helpful.

Five months after the accident his father brought Jim for a psychiatric evaluation because he was concerned about some of the boy's behavior. Jim showed extreme hyperactivity coupled with such limited attention span that it was impossible to carry on a conversation with him for any length of time. This also interfered with his school adjustment and contributed to his serious difficulty with learning. Whereas in the past Jim had always been the aggressor with his twin and other children, he now reacted with complete passivity to the attacks of others. In particular, he could not stand up to his little brother who had turned into a vicious attacker since his casts had been removed and who singled out Jim as his target. However, the symptom that alarmed the family most was Jim's frequent spells of sitting motionless, staring at an object or out of the window and seemingly losing touch with the world. The father and grandmother described Jim as depressed at these times. When they noticed his withdrawn "depression," they tried desperately "to get him out of it" but with little success as he did not respond to what was going on around him.

In the evaluation interview with the analyst Jim was severely hyperactive. His thinking was confused, his speech disjointed. He was excited and displayed a false happy affect as part of his overall behavior. His appearance and activity suggested an organic involvement, but neurological examinations revealed no evidence of impairment. A psychological test given by a woman showed a different side. Jim was able to relate to her and became calm. He cooperated sufficiently to complete the test and achieved a reasonably valid score of somewhat above average intelligence. The analyst therefore assumed that Jim's behavior with him was mainly due to extreme anxiety. This was verified during Jim's analysis.

Jim very likely learned of his mother's and twin's deaths from his younger brother in the hospital and probably overheard conversations among the nurses and relatives during his hospital stay. He did not however register this knowledge consciously, either because of organic confusion or denial. The father had not wanted Jim to know of the deaths and did not tell him about them until he returned home. Even at that point, however, Jim denied the fact and, for days, searched the house for his mother and twin. Also, immediately after Jim's release from the hospital, his maternal grandfather had died after a few weeks' hospitalization. He had been ailing for some time but the shocking news of the accident had adversely affected his physical condition. Jim had been quite close to this grandfather, who had always admired him for his aggressive "manliness." Jim did not deny this death as he initially denied the other deaths, but he had no affective reaction at the time.

The family was quite secure economically and socially. Jim had an older sister, well adjusted and a good scholar. She had spent the fateful vacation with the grandparents and was subsequently able to mourn appropriately. There was also a baby girl, who had been left at home in the care of a housekeeping couple. This couple had been with the family since Jim was four and a half years old. They were sensible and sensitive people, maintained good relationships with all the children, and were familiar with caring for them. Immediately following the tragedy they were important surviving love objects and provided reasonably consistent fulfillment of needs as well as a good measure of emotional support. Unfortunately, their role was soon seriously interfered with and their stay in the home terminated within a few months.

By the time Jim arrived home from the hospital the father had cut short his mourning and soon remarried. At that time he found it difficult to talk about his recent bereavements, to tolerate his grief, or to visit the cemetery and allow himself memories or reminders of the dead. The stepmother brought her own three children as well as several members of her domestic staff. The new marriage was, from the start, disharmonious. The enlarged family's daily life was in an up-heaval, resulting in neglect of the children's physical needs at times. Emotional support for Jim was especially lacking as the stepmother found it difficult to relate to him.

In view of the unsettled atmosphere in the house and the pressing needs of all the children, it was decided to postpone individual treat-ment for him and to work initially with the father and, to some ex-tent, with the stepmother. The main goals were to help the parents provide consistent care for all the children, enable them to build their relationships with the children so that they could support them emo-tionally, and alter some of their educational methods to further the children's chances of mastering real events. Over a period of two and a half years some progress was made in these areas. The children's needs were met adequately. The father was able to gain considerable understanding of his children and could be helpful to them and sup-port their development. Unfortunately, Jim still lacked an opportunity to relate to a maternal figure but, with the help and cooperation of the father, the maternal grandmother assumed a special role in time. She had always been an interested and active member of the family with whom Jim had a fairly good relationship. During the later years of Jim's analysis she, and to some extent Jim's older sister, were impor-tant love objects who assisted him in his mourning.

Little was known of Jim's life prior to the mother's and twin's death. Most of it was reconstructed during the analysis and could, at times, be confirmed. The father, grandmother, and school provided the following picture. Jim had been a severe problem at school. He had lagged scholastically because he could not apply himself to learn-ing and schoolwork. His behavior had caused concern because he spent so much time beating up and belittling his fraternal twin. Be-fore the tragic car accident, it had therefore been decided to transfer Jim to another school, mainly in order to protect his twin. This plan was dropped after the twin's death and Jim remained in the school he had attended. He had even greater learning difficulties after the ac-cident, but his behavior changed to that of a very passive boy who could not stand up for himself.

At home Jim had always been the dominant aggressive twin whose manliness was enjoyed by the father and maternal grandfather. The mother and maternal grandmother, by contrast, had been concerned about the intensity and dangerous nature of Jim's attacks.

Throughout his earlier years Jim had experienced many separations from his parents. These lasted for several days or weeks at a time and occurred with little preparation. The father and grandmother recalled no reactions to these separations and felt that Jim was quite comfortable since he always had his twin and other siblings to stay with him. The family also often changed homes to spend periods of time at their own or friends' farms. Many dogs and other pets were always a part of the household. Sometimes they were sent to the farm on their own or left in town. Some pets were killed. Several were exchanged because they did not manage satisfactorily within the family.

Around the age of three or four Jim set several fires in and around the house. This frightened the mother and maternal grandmother and they spanked Jim. The mother frequently used spanking as a disciplinary measure but it differed from the father's rigorous spankings. Soon after the mother's death Jim set a minor fire which provoked the father to a loss of temper and he severely spanked Jim. In discussing this incident with the analyst, the father mentioned his tendency to such loss of temper with Jim and recalled a number of similar incidents in the past. This was an aspect of the father's relationship with Jim which the father could control during the later years.

Jim started his analysis at ten years of age, two and three quarter years after his mother's and twin's death. He was seen five times weekly for four and a half years. At the beginning of treatment his presenting difficulties were much the same as they had been at the time of the earlier evaluation. He had been unable to mourn, both because of lack of environmental support and internal difficulties.

The main task of the analysis was to help Jim with his reactions to the deaths of his loved ones and with his enormously heightened castration anxiety which resulted from the injuries he and others had sustained during the fatal car accident. Inevitably, work on these topics was linked with many aspects of Jim's personality disturbance which predated the major tragedy. In the context of this report these earlier difficulties are referred to selectively.

Several of Jim's most pronounced defenses served the double purpose of warding off feelings about the deaths and about the injuries. Denial and confusion were evident already during his hospital stay. It appeared that these mechanisms were at first facilitated by his organic state but were subsequently prolonged and intensified as psychological defenses. Denial and confusion helped to keep at bay the frightening news of death and the experiences of hurt and mutilation which had led to interference in mobility. Jim also used reversal of affect extensively. This showed in his false happy affect and excited hyperactivity. As long as he could be happy and bodily active he could ward off sad memories and counteract fear of bodily damage. Jim claimed that the period in the hospital and the nurse who cared for him were wonderful and that it was his happiest time. Jim's "depressive" spells, which had so greatly concerned his family, also served defensive purposes. When these episodes began to occur in the analysis it was found that Jim was unaware of any feelings or thoughts during these times. He was, in fact, subjectively quite apathetic. Gradually it became clear that this affective and cognitive block set in at moments when a memory of the mother or twin threatened to emerge and bring with it overwhelming sadness. The manifold current and genetic reasons that contributed to Jim's difficulty in tolerating this feeling were traced in the later course of the analysis and through the transference. Initially he was helped to become aware of his defensive measures, and he recovered his ability to feel sufficiently to engage in the process of mourning. The depressive, or rather apathetic, periods subsided as his memories and related sadness became increasingly available to him.

The analyst's emotional support was of great help to Jim, who needed an opportunity to express his feelings to a sympathetic person. Jim also found some help in sharing his grief with his older sister and maternal grandmother. The latter assisted Jim considerably in his mourning in its later stages. When Jim could allow himself feelings about mother and twin he also began to mourn his maternal grandfather, who had died so soon after the car accident. Jim and his grandmother spent much time together reminiscing over photo albums, talking about the past, and visiting the graves.

The transference was an important avenue to understanding Jim's feelings and conflicts. Whereas in the evaluation interview and at periods later in the analysis, the father transference was predominant, for the most part Jim saw in the analyst a love object as the mother had been. His strong, positive feelings in the transference made it possible to reconstruct a healthy, warm, early relationship with the dead mother. Material about weekend and vacation separations led to reconstructions of the impact of the death and to the importance of many earlier separations from the mother and their effect on Jim. For a long period, however, and to some extent to the very end of the analysis, the transference relationship was complicated by the fact that he lacked an adequate mother substitute. Because of this real difficulty, he saw the analyst also as a caring person to whom he could bring his reality hardships and on whom he counted to intercede on his behalf with the father or stepmother to improve his care.

Jim's guilt about the deaths in his family was first reached in relation to his twin, toward whom he had been so aggressive both in action and thought. Jim felt very badly about being the survivor and repeated dejectedly, "It should have happened to me, I was the bad one." A screen memory paved the way toward understanding the origins and vicissitudes of Jim's agression to his twin. Jim recalled from the age of two an incident of almost pushing his twin out of a window and his rescue by their mother in the nick of time. By contrast, he had many memories of being left by his parents when his aggression to his twin was not stopped and when Jim himself was the target of extreme aggression by sitters. It was confirmed by the family that, on some unfortunate occasions, sitters had neglected to care for the children and abused them physically so that marks of beatings were found on the children's bodies. It was understood in the analysis that the mother's earlier spankings of Jim as well as his anger at her contributed to his first consistent attacks on his twin, who served as an object of displacement and of turning passive into action. Later, the father's loss of temper and spankings frightened and excited Jim, who again dealt with his feelings by way of passive into active and identification. In time Jim externalized his passivity and feminity onto the twin, which further contributed to his aggressiveness against him.

Through the analytic work Jim could integrate the knowledge that his guilt over being the survivor was genetically connected with his guilt over his anger to both parents and he was able to recognize his infantile anger at his mother. Jim's last memory prior to the accident played an important part. He had a vivid picture of the two mothers in the front seat, one mother pointing to something and drawing the driving mother's attention away from the road. The children were somewhat excited and rambunctious in the back seats but were not the cause of the distraction. He thought for a long time that it was his mother who was driving although all available evidence suggested that the other mother had been at the wheel. The analysis showed that

Jim's insistence that his mother was driving warded off the idea of her being to blame for the accident. He felt that if his mother drove it was the other mother who had distracted her and was therefore responsible. The mother who protects and the mother who exposes her children to danger was a theme that affected Jim's feelings about his mother throughout his early life and was augmented by the fateful accident. This long-standing conflict was also worked through repeatedly in regard to his feelings about the lost, abandoned, and mistreated dogs, a theme that likewise had always been a part of his life. During the later part of Jim's analysis several of the family's dogs were killed in accidents or sent away. In connection with these incidents the important meaning of the dogs for Jim could be understood and reconstructed for the past. Mourning for them was closely interwoven with his mourning for the mother, twin, and grandfather.

As mentioned earlier, after the car accident Jim's defenses underwent a marked change. There was no overt aggression; on the contrary, he was so passive that he could not defend himself. The manifest picture suggested that Jim had identified with the dead twin in the wake of the tragedy. The analysis, however, revealed that Jim's altered behavior resulted mainly from the fact that his experience of the accident, and all that it entailed, had greatly heightened his castration anxiety. This made Jim much more fearful of the father's retaliation. It was not till the third year of his analysis that Jim could stand up for himself. It was later still when he could recognize a teacher's sadistic excitement and remain uninvolved. Identification also did not appear to play a major part in Jim's mourning for his mother. In its course Jim used one aspect of healthy identification with her. He became warm toward his youngest sister and was thoughtful and protective of her. In this way he recaptured a positive early period in his relationship with his mother as well as a relationship he had been aware of between mother and the baby girl before the mother's death.

Jim was fourteen and a half years old, and in adolescence, when his analysis terminated. By that time he had completed the major parts of his mourning for his mother, twin, and grandfather. As he was finishing his analysis and coping with the impending separation from the analyst, Jim suffered another loss through the death of a friend. Although this death revived memories of his earlier mourning, the losses did not become confused and the feelings were not intensified. Jim dealt with the later bereavement appropriately. He had also mastered the heightened castration anxiety which had resulted from the car accident and contributed so much to his symptomatic behavior and difficulty in standing up for himself appropriately. The aspects of his difficulties that predated the accident and deaths appeared to require further working through but the family's situation at the time made it necessary for Jim to attend a boarding school out of town. Jim and his father were aware of the fact that Jim might need further help at a later date. Follow-up contact with the analyst has been maintained and shows that Jim has utilized his gains and progressed appropriately in his personality maturation.

Jim's initial great difficulty in tolerating affects and anxiety was a major cause of his presenting problems. The overwhelming circumstances of his double bereavement and of his own and his younger brother's severe injuries were of such a nature as to overtax any person's limits of endurance. With Jim there were additional complicating factors. Those from the past had affected his capacity for dealing with stresses; present factors, following the tragedy, had deprived him of the necessary age-appropriate care and support.

Among the affects it was sadness, rather then guilt or anger, that caused him the greatest difficulty. His episodes of apathetic withdrawal were primarily a defense against overwhelming sadness. His fear of his sadness was not due to fear of guilt over ambivalence. There also was no indication of depression, although the family's observations suggested this. His apathy subsided when he could tolerate his sad memories of mother and twin and could express them in the context of his relationships with the analyst and, later, with the sister and grandmother. Jim's difficulty in the present was due to the lack of someone to fulfill his needs consistently, to support him emotionally, and to share his grief. His fear of sadness, however, was so great because of his heightened anxiety at all levels—fear of castration, fear of loss of object, fear of being overwhelmed. In part these anxieties were prominent because of the nature of the deaths and injuries; in part they related to the earlier repeated separations during which Jim had at times suffered mistreatment and lack of need fulfillment. These early experiences had heightened his developmental anxieties and helped to shape his defenses, especially against the helpless feelings of sadness and longing.

5. The Individual Circumstances of Bereavement

Coping with the Fear of Death

Before we can begin the task of mourning we have to come to terms with the impact of death upon ourselves. Young children usually do not know yet that all living beings have to die. Older children and adults do know it but maintain more or less appropriate defenses in their daily lives to deal with the inevitability of death. When we are confronted with death our equilibrium is likely to be shaken. The closer we feel to the one who died, and the more likely it seems that what happened to him could happen to us, the greater is our fear for ourselves. Adults usually feel most threatened when a contemporary dies—when the cause of death is communicable, unavoidable, or unpredictable—or when they are, or expect to be, in a similar fateful situation (fire, airplane). In circumstances that bring us close to the prospect of our own death we search instinctively for aspects that help us distance ourselves from it. If the death occurred in a car crash we think, "I am always a more cautious driver," or, "I never drive that route at night." If the death was caused by an illness, we reassure ourselves with, "I have regular check-ups and such a disease would be detected in its earlier stages"; or, "I would see a better specialist sooner."

One patient's father described his experience.

His wife had been a healthy young woman who had died of an incurable disease within a few days after the first symptoms appeared. At the funeral, friends and relatives took their turn to speak to the father. The deceased wife's contemporaries could not use this moment to express their sympathy but asked anxious questions about the wife's disease: "She did have headaches a few weeks earlier, didn't she?"; "I understand there is a hereditary factor, isn't there?" The father said how sad he was that he could not reassure them because he had to answer no to all their hopes of being immune. He added, "They were so scared for themselves, they could not yet think of me."

We cannot allow ourselves to empathize with the dead person and his bereaved family and cannot mourn until we have sufficiently allayed our anxiety. Hopefully, we find our own middle ground between being too endangered by feeling at one with the deceased and warding off that danger by feeling we have nothing in common with him. This difficult but necessary equilibrium is beautifully expressed in the saying, "There, but for the grace of God, go I." It is a prerequisite for mourning and for helping those who mourn.

In some instances an individual's personality makeup and the particular circumstances of a death may make it especially hard to find the appropriate degree of differentiation. Young children encounter special difficulties in this task for developmental reasons. Their self-differentiation is still incomplete, their defense structure is labile, their reality testing is limited. Phase-specific concerns color their understanding of death: sadism during the anal phase, castration anxiety during the phallic phase, death wishes during the oedipal conflict, harsh, uncompromising guilt feelings in the beginning of latency. The child's ability to differentiate himself effectively from the fate of the dead loved one depends on several factors. Among these are the circumstances of the death, their effect on his developmental concerns, and the extent to which he receives appropriate help in this area from his surviving love objects. Our experiences confirm McDonald's (1963, 1964) observations of nursery school children when a peer lost his mother. She found that the children could empathize with their bereaved classmate and be helped with their own mourning after they could ask, "Can this happen to my mommy?" and, "Can this happen to me?" In that case the answers to both questions could be sufficiently reassuring.

The occurrence of death always entails a specific personal threat to the survivor. It sets the difficult task for him of finding the midway position between excessive identification and lack of empathy. Earlier we stressed the fact that the finality of death represents a unique external reality. The recognition of this finality helps to initiate the mourning process in the bereaved and helps him to complete it. We noted that in this respect the psychological task is different for individuals who suffered the loss of a love object for other reasons, such as separation or divorce. In some instances a loss through death may even have appeared easier to deal with since the person did not need to struggle with repeated frustrated hopes or with feelings of guilt or rejection. At this point we are focusing on another unique aspect of death—that it arouses a special fear with which we need to cope. When a person cannot sufficiently come to terms with his own attitude toward death his mourning process is likely to be interfered with.

When a child's parent dies this task is greatly augmented. The younger the child, the less he is differentiated from his parent. The great wish to regain or join the dead parent may further enhance the child's tendency for merging. This could manifest itself either in playing dead or in excessive fears of dying. In one nursery school, the mother of a girl three and a half years old was killed in a car crash. During the month following this tragedy Mary repeatedly lay on the floor motionless. A little boy commented on this to the teacher, ''Mary is pretending to be dead like her mommy.'' One motive for Mary's behavior was her struggle to understand what dead meant, but the teacher felt that the little boy had correctly guessed the main reason: Mary's wish to be with her mother and like her mother.

The fear of dying like the parent is often an equally important concern for the insufficiently differentiated child. The same behavioral manifestations that express a wish to die may contain a fear of dying. Both wish and fear may be further augmented by instinctual meanings. For example, the conflictual feelings of the phallic-oedipal phase, together with some external circumstances and experiences, may lead children to confuse death with sexuality. Feeling left out of the parents' adult sexual relationship and wishing to take one or the other parent's place then becomes linked to conflicts about dying.

> Arthur, in latency, had repeated pleasurable dreams of dying in violent accidents. In contrast, when awake, he was very sensitive to his own injuries and often sadistically attacked bugs and bees, which he greatly feared. At this time Arthur had not yet been helped to understand his mother's earlier death. His own explanation derived from his observations of parental primal scenes. To some extent his behavior and dreams appeared to represent this mixture of pleasant and terrifying feelings.

The younger the child, the more he needs the surviving parent's help in differentiating himself and his own fate from that of the dead parent. In many ways this runs contrary to the child's tendency to identify himself with his parent, both developmentally and as a part of the mourning process. The conflict over such an identification is an almost never-ending process, as the child needs to grapple with it on each subsequent developmental level, long after the parent's death and even into adulthood. In working with parents we have frequently noted instances of such a struggle. When the parent had lost a mother or father through death in childhood his parental development and functioning could be interfered with by his conflict over assuming this role.

For many adults the concrete facts of death itself are so frightening that they wish to keep them from their children, both to protect them and to protect themselves. Quite often children are told that the deceased went to heaven. Some parents gave this explanation although they frankly stated they did not believe in heaven or were not sure about it. Some parents who did maintain religious beliefs distorted them in talking with their children. They did not explain the difference between bodily death and spiritual afterlife but conveyed the impression of bodily assumption. They forgot that their children needed to develop a concrete concept of death in order to come to terms with their anxieties. Avoidance of the realities tended to shift, rather than decrease, the children's fears. Sometimes it also created a conflict in the children and a barrier between themselves and the parents when they found that some of their observations did not tally with the parents' information. In some instances it proved easier for the child than for the adult to view the stark reality.

> Wendy was almost four years old when her mother died. Through discussions with the therapist the father was able to help her to understand death and to assist her in her mourning reactions. A year after the mother's death, a distant relative died. When the father was talking about the death with Wendy, a discussion followed about the burial in the ground. The father, anticipating some pain on Wendy's part, added that the deceased would be comfortable in the ground because he would be protected by a box. Wendy's response to this was, "But if he is really dead, why does he have to be comfortable?" (Barnes 1964, p. 350)

Unfortunately, the avoidance of the concrete facts of death often extends to the ceremonies and places that focus on them: the burial service, the cemetery, the grave and gravestone. These concrete evidences and reminders of the bodily death are an important part of the acceptance of death and of the child's ability to differentiate himself appropriately from the dead. The parent who is able to be in tune with his child can best gauge when and how much his child can integrate in this respect. Overwhelming the child helps as little as avoidance.

Addie's mother died from a blood disease just before Addie's fourth birthday (see the analyst's report on p. 140). Addie was staying with her grandmother during the mother's terminal hospitalization and was not told of her mother's death. She learned about it later from a playmate. In her analysis Addie struggled for years with the concept of death and finally asked to visit her mother's grave. The grandmother had never been to her daughter's grave herself and she resisted Addie's request; when the visit to the grave finally materialized, the grandmother had a severe angry outburst over a minor detail. Addie, by this time, could understand somewhat the defensive nature of the grandmother's anger. For Addie the visit was a turning point in coming to terms with the concept of death, though not yet with her feelings of sadness.

Ronald was two and a half years old when his mother died of a blood disease. His father had not explained either the cause of her death or the concrete realities of death but, in line with his own religious beliefs, had stressed that the deserving go to heaven. Ronald had not attended the funeral and the family never visited the mother's grave. In his analysis during his latency years Ronald showed his confusion. He professed to believe that his mother was in heaven and that he, if he were dead, would join her there. Heaven, as well as God, were concrete concepts for him. He also spoke guiltily of two cemeteries near his home, "where dead people are buried naked." He liked to "snoop" in these cemeteries as well as in and around funeral homes. He was preoccupied with killing bugs and observing the changes death produced in them.

Fred was five when his mother died of leukemia. According to the family's tradition, the mother's body was displayed in an open casket and all the members of the family kissed her. Fred's concept of death prior to this time stemmed mainly from the dead animals he had seen on hunting expeditions with his grandfather. He found both the dead animals and the funeral customs overwhelmingly upsetting.

Jenny was barely three years old when her mother died of an acute hemorrhage. She did not attend the closed-casket funeral service with her father and older brother and sister, but her father told her where they were and what was happening. Since she already had some understanding of death from her appropriately handled experiences with dead animals, her father gradually helped her to extend and deepen her concept and to relate it to her mother. It took several months before he felt she could cope with, and profit from, a visit to mother's grave. When it took place, after due preparation, Jenny's struggles to differentiate herself intensified. She questioned anxiously whether her father, siblings, and she herself would die and would they die together. She was able to integrate the answers and gain considerable mastery. Some days later she stated soberly, "Most mommies don't die. I'll get big and I'll be a mommy and a grandma and then I'll wear a shawl like Mrs. M.", a very old lady Jenny knew and liked.

A child is helped to develop a concept of death and to differentiate himself from the dead when he is able, age-appropriately, to share in his family's knowledge of the concrete aspects of death and in their personal and social observances of the death of the loved one.

The Significance of the Form of Death

The difficulty in differentiating from the dead parent and, later, the difficulty encountered in identifying with him, is greatly heightened by the circumstances of a parent's death. Unlike grandparents or other older people, the parent of a child is usually in the prime of his life. The death is always untimely, whether violent or due to disease. Some of the parents of the children we worked with died violent deaths in traffic accidents, or by murder or suicide. Others had long-term illnesses which were accompanied by physical deterioration and mutilation, such as cancer, or led to increasing loss of functioning, such as leukemia. Still other parents died of such sudden overwhelming afflictions as heart attacks or viral pneumonia. Each form of death entailed its own frightening, frustrating, overwhelming experiences for the family.

Ricky was seven years old when his mother was killed in a plane crash. One of Ricky's siblings and the pilot suffered serious injuries. Ricky himself did not recover consciousness for some weeks.

Seth was just over four years old when his mother died of a blood disease which was diagnosed only from the autopsy (see the analyst's report on p. 149). Since Seth's early second year his mother had suffered from fatigue and weakness. It was suggested that the mother be hospitalized for tests. Seth said good-bye to his mother when his father drove her to the hospital. She died the day after admission.

Steven was six years old when his mother died of cancer. During the preceding fifteen months she had undergone a radical mastectomy, repeated surgery in other parts of her body, and X-ray treatments. Her bodily appearance and countenance deteriorated till, during the final weeks, she was but a distorted shadow of her former self. Steven last spoke to her on the phone several days before her death.

Jack was three and a half years old when his mother shot herself. He came upon her disfigured body in a pool of blood. The police drove her off, accompanied by the father, while Jack stayed with a neighbor. The mother had suffered from severe depressions, had received hospital care, and had recently shown considerable improvement. She had been glad to be able to look after her children again.

There are no peaceful deaths for parents of young children. Whenever we merely say "his parent died" we leave out the inevitable horror and tragedy that such a death entails.

The form of the parent's death arouses special anxiety in the child when the circumstances coincide with and give apparent reality to developmental concerns (sadism, castration anxiety). Sometimes the nature and sequence of events are so complex that the child, with his limited reality testing, is unable to grasp them. Frequently the impact of the parent's dying and death causes so much anxiety that the adults cannot cope with it. They are either overwhelmed or need to resort to extensive defensive measures.

It is not surprising that the child's surviving parent and other adults close to him find it difficult to help the child with his anxieties. They may not yet have mastered their own anxieties or may hope to shield the child from a similar dread. This sometimes leads a parent to deny to his child the real events and the concreteness of death. In some cases the parent attempts to alter the facts by presenting the child with an untruthful but more palatable version of what happened. Other parents show or tell their children every detail in the hope that intellectual knowledge will enable them to master the terrible reality. In the process the parent often misjudges the child's ability to integrate sensory and verbal information and, instead of helping him, further overwhelms him.

Surgical and medical procedures are frequently a difficult part of the parent's terminal illness.

When five-year-old Ted's mother was hospitalized for a mastectomy his father told Ted that mommy's breast would be cut off. In answer to Ted's questions, he explained about surgical instruments and procedures. Ted, who already suffered from severe fears of bodily harm, could not integrate this information at this time. He dealt with his anxiety by becoming the sadistic attacking doctor both in fantasy and in his behavior with peers.

Billy, aged four, had received no verbal explanation of his mother's mastectomy. Driven by her own anxiety, however, his mother subsequently exposed him unwittingly to her operative site. Billy was deeply shocked and unable to master his anxiety, until, during his later analysis, verbal explanations helped him to integrate this experience. (R. A. Furman 1964a)

Greg was only three and a half years old when his mother underwent the same surgery. She told him that the doctor needed to take out a lump which had grown at the side of her breast but did not belong there. In reply to Greg's questions as to how the doctor would do that, the mother replied, "I do not know exactly how he does it but I know that he is a kind man, that he learned very well how do such things and will do a very good job." Greg's concerned but contained reaction showed that the mother had sensed correctly how much he could integrate at this point. In time she took up other aspects with him.

By the time the ill parent dies, the child has often had to grapple with the knowledge of a series of surgical and medical interventions.

This may have aroused his anxieties to such an intolerable extent that death itself is seen as a final bodily assault.

Sudden deaths impose a different stress on the bereaved. The overwhelming surprise affords him no chance to prepare himself and sometimes heightens the feeling of potential danger to the survivor.

Nine-year-old Erin's mother suffered a sudden heart attack and was found dead in bed by Erin. For weeks Erin at times was in a daze. When her father spoke with her about this she related how she repeated to herself mentally the swift chain of events. Later she said over and over, "But I did not even know this could happen."

Suicides are particularly hard to understand and therefore apt to arouse fear, anger, and guilt in the bereaved. In some cases they also raise a concern with heredity.

Kenny was only two years old when his father killed himself by throwing himself under a train. The father had been mentally ill for some time but lived at home and maintained a close relationship with his little boy. The mother, upset, guilty, but also somewhat relieved after the trials of the preceding months, spent a hectic time attending to the many official investigations and formalities. She told Kenny that his daddy had died of a sickness. Kenny indicated at the time as well as at many points later in his development that he knew some details concerning the nature of his father's death. His mother was unable to bring herself to discuss the facts with him, fearing that this might lead to his becoming like his father. Devoted and concerned, she sought analytic treatment for Kenny later when he developed symptoms. She hoped that anlaysis might prevent his becoming mentally ill. The analysis had to be cut short however when it began to focus on Kenny's concerns about the causes of his father's death, and the mother once again could not permit exploration and discussion of this topic. Although Kenny had begun to mourn his father he could not complete the process. The conscious and unconscious concerns about the nature of the death were one of the important interferences.

George's mother jumped to her death when he was five and a half years old. She had been severely depressed when George was younger but had apparently improved during the previous year. Her suicide came unexpectedly. George was told that she had killed herself because she had a special sickness of thinking and feeling. This helped George to begin to comprehend his mother's death and to initiate a mourning process. Unfortunately, the family could not allow themselves or George to work this through and to bear the accompanying feelings. The mere information proved insufficient in helping George to come to terms with the impact of the tragedy.

Mark was a little over four years old when his father took his life with an overdose of pills. He had been only mildly depressed, and the mother was shocked and distraught when the police called her during the night to identify her husband's body. She told Mark right away that his daddy had died. A private cremation service was arranged which the child did not attend. For several months the mother was too upset and angry to discuss the events with her son although she realized that he looked to her for help and information. "How can I tell Mark that his father loved us when he left us so helpless and uncared for?" It was of great help to the mother and enabled her to feel sad when she understood that the father had suffered from a special sickness of the mind. Its nature and extent unfortunately had not been evident and therefore he could not get psychiatric help in time. She was then able to share this information with Mark and address herself to helping him with his concerns and feelings. She realized how many clues he had picked up and how confusing and frightening they had been for him. Among other things Mark wanted to know how the police could know it was his daddy and whether mommy had believed the police. He was greatly relieved to learn that his mother had seen daddy's body and had attended the cremation. He confessed that he thought there might have been a mistake since, as far as he knew, there had been no concrete evidence for his father's death. Mark decided to place a plaque with his father's name on it in his yard so that he would have a special place to go and think of him. Mark's intense mourning extended over the next eighteen months.

Each death brings with it its specific anxiety-arousing impressions, sometimes different ones for each member of the family.

Stressful Events Preceding and Following the Bereavement

As though the death of a loved one were not stressful enough, it is sometimes associated with additional upsetting events. Some of these coincide with the death accidentally; for example a man's parent may die when he himself undergoes an operation or when his child is very ill. In other instances the additional stresses are related to the death: a woman's husband may die in a car accident in which she herself is badly injured and, due to her prolonged incapacity, loses her job and needs to sell her house.

When a child's parent dies, there are almost always attendant stresses. Sometimes they are so great, and the total impact so overwhelming, that the child's ability to cope with his bereavement is delayed, interfered with, or jeopardized. Among the children we worked with, such circumstantial events were at times so upsetting that they overshadowed the loss of the parent for a long period. Sometimes they produced such a cumulative effect that the reaction to the death itself became intertwined with the child's mental efforts to deal with the other events. A similar point was made by A. Freud (1960) in discussing studies of the effects of separation from the mother on young children. When the young child is observed in the hospital, institution, or foster home, other stresses combine with those of separation from the mother and distort the child's actual reaction to the separation. She mentioned the importance of studying the reactions of young children who remain in their homes with the rest of their families.

The following vignettes illustrate two divergent situations facing children at the time of the parent's death.

Geraldine was almost eight years old when her mother died of cancer after many operations, hospitalizations, and years of debilitating illness (see the analyst's report on p. 69). She had lived in poverty and turmoil. Although Geraldine had witnessed all the mother's physical distress, she was given no explanation of her mother's illness and was subsequently only told that her mother had gone to heaven. The father, though separated from the mother, had maintained frequent contacts with Geraldine but disappeared following the mother's death. An almost adult sister who had lived in the home refused to care for Geraldine and moved away. Geraldine was taken in by a neighbor who cared for several foster children. She was later moved temporarily to distant unsympathetic relatives, and one and a half years later ended up in a permanent home with an aunt and uncle.

Jane was eight years old when her mother died in the hospital of a rare circulatory disease shortly after the first symptoms appeared. Jane's father kept her and her siblings honestly abreast of the developments and appropriately arranged for them to participate in the funeral ceremonies. The mother's home duties were taken over partly by a loving nanny who had lived with the family since before Jane's birth. The grandmother, who had always been close to the family, helped out daily. Untroubled by financial worries or other upheavals, the family remained in their comfortable home and mourned together.

Most children fare neither so badly nor so well. The death of the father as breadwinner often brings with it financial stress, necessitating loss of home and even partial loss of the mother if she goes out to work. The mother's death usually presents the family with the difficult, almost impossible task of finding a full-time homemaker who, at best, is a stranger to the children and unfamiliar with their routines.
Fate also introduces unexpected hardships:

Ellen was fifteen months old when her nurse became ill and could not be with her for four weeks. Within a few days of her return Ellen's mother died suddenly and unexpectedly. The nurse took over full-time care of Ellen. During the following month however the nurse fell ill again and had to be hospitalized for two weeks. During the nurse's first illness the mother had mitigated the separation, during the second illness several people helped out.

In some instances the additional stresses for the bereaved child are not objectively unavoidable but stem from clashes between the child's and the adult's emotional needs. After the death of the spouse, some mothers or fathers leave the city, move to another house, change the furniture, go to work, or shortly remarry because they cannot bear to be reminded constantly of the past. Their children experience such changes as stressful losses and find it difficult to meet the demand for new adaptations. To them the change represents another loss. The concrete familiar environment is essential to the stable continuity of their own lives and forms a helpful link to the past.

Peter was a little over four years old when his father died suddenly of a heart attack. His mother had great difficulty in coping with her bereavement. Taking Peter with her she spent all weekends away from home in the company of friends and planned to move in with relatives. It relieved her loneliness and distracted her from her anguish. She was surprised when Peter told her and showed her by his behavior that he needed his home and its many reminders of his daddy to help him in his mourning. The frequent visits with other families were painful and frustrating to him and did not cheer him up. It was a mark of the soundness of the mother–child relationship that Peter could express his thoughts and feelings and that his mother could not only listen to him but respond in action. They did not move and compromised in other areas on their different needs.

Sometimes the child's additional losses are not limited to house and home but include a separation from the surviving parent. With several of our child patients the death of the mother precipitated the desertion of the father, and the loss of older siblings who moved away. In some cases the loss was partial, caused by the emotional withdrawal of the parent or by his need to work longer hours away from home.

Additional losses are not the only stressful events. Within the home, routines may be changed so drastically that the child experiences turmoil.

Susan, John, Linda, and Debbie ranged in age from two to fourteen years when their mother died in a car crash. Numerous relatives converged upon the home, each doing a little for the children during their brief visits. Some decided suddenly to take one or the other child out for a meal or for an overnight stay, others duplicated chores or unwittingly undid each other's activities. One night three dinners were brought in but no one had attended to the washing of clothes. Maids came and went and further complicated the family situation. It is always difficult to fill in for the work of a full-time mother. In this family however the chaos also reflected the adults' need to distract themselves with activity. This burdened the children with excessive upheaval and anxiety.

Needless to say, an attempt to change absolutely nothing can be equally unhelpful if it conveys a defensive denial: "He did not die, everything is the same." In each case the child's ability to deal with the task of mourning is related to his experience of the circumstances surrounding the parental death. Sometimes these are optimally helpful, more often they are detrimental.

The Role of the Surviving Love Objects

With all bereavements and at all ages, a person's ability to devote himself to the task of mourning generally depends on two factors: the assurance that his needs will be met consistently, and the continuation of his other relationships.

Several aspects of this topic have been touched upon. Our discussion here is therefore in part a review and serves to highlight some points. Its relative brevity does not reflect its lack of importance. Our experience showed that the surviving love objects play a crucial part in the life of the bereaved person and contribute much to the manner in which he deals with his loss.

Even at times when no object loss has occurred, a person's basic narcissistic investment demands that he first concern himself with the danger that threatens him when his bodily needs are inadequately or inconsistently gratified. If he is an adult he may focus on securing a financial income for himself, on finding someone to assist him in providing his personal comforts, or on taking over himself more of the work involved in meeting his own needs. If he is a child his basic aims would be the same but, depending on the stage of his development, he would pursue them in a different manner. An eleven-year-old may concentrate on doing things for himself, a four-year-old may seek gratification from other people. Because of his immaturity, however, the child is more likely to fail in finding ways of caring for himself and in tolerating the ensuing frustrations and tensions. His failure exposes him to increasing anxiety and he then employs the defensive measures at his disposal or becomes overwhelmed.

At a time of bereavement a person's adequate need fulfillment is quite often endangered. His resulting concern with his own needs, his anxiety and his ego's measures to deal with it, may appear egocentric and lacking in thought and feeling for the dead loved one. Actually, the opposite is closer to the truth. An individual has to want to live and assure himself of his continued chance to live in order to differentiate himself from the dead and to ready himself for the mourning process. The concern with need fulfillment becomes pathological only in instances where it is unwarranted or greatly exaggerated. In such cases the bereaved person's preoccupation with himself may not represent a response to his threatened self-preservation. Rather, it may be the manifestation of a change in the nature and distribution of his libido; that is, object libido may be withdrawn from the object representation and narcissistically invested in the self-representation. A permanent change of this type precludes mourning and jeopardizes the further development of object relationships. We sometimes observed such processes in the analyses of children who had suffered other losses, such as a depressed mother's withdrawal. None of our bereaved children, however, showed this reaction.

When the loved person who dies is not a source of need fulfillment, the bereaved can devote himself more immediately to the task of mourning. Sometimes a death may actually benefit a bereaved person in terms of need fulfillment. For example, when an adult's parent dies an inheritance may free the surviving son or daughter from financial worries or, when a young child's sick sibling dies his mother may be able to devote herself more appropriately to her surviving boy or girl. Such situations may give rise to conflicting feelings and may interfere with the mourning process in their own way.

To the extent, however, that the deceased did fulfill a bereaved person's needs, his death always represents a danger to the survivor. When a child's parent dies this is most strikingly the case, although even here there are many variations. In very young children, before and at the beginning of object constancy, love and fulfillment of bodily needs largely coincide. The loss of the main need-fulfilling person may then constitute primarily a narcissistic depletion and weaken the narcissistic investment of the body image to such an extent that the infant does not seek or accept fulfillment of his needs. If this state persists beyond a certain period, the child's primitive personality disintegrates and he may succumb to physical disease and die (Spitz 1945, 1946).

Beyond earliest infancy the young child tends to maintain more than one relationship, and the relationships are not so closely tied to bodily need fulfillment. Toddlers may lose an important love object without suffering impaired need fulfillment. For a toddler twenty months old his father's death may not directly represent the loss of a need-fulfilling person if he has mostly been cared for by his mother; his mother's death may not represent the loss of a main need-fulfilling person if a toddler has mostly been cared for by a nanny. Even if his main need-fulfilling person dies he may be able to utilize his other love objects for the fulfillment of needs without unmasterable stress. The youngster's trust in the surviving loved person, the latter's love for the child as well as familiarity with the ways in which he has been cared for, can help to bridge the gap and assure sufficient consistency and satisfaction. By contrast, if the toddler's needs remain unfulfilled, or if a stranger can fulfill them only inadequately, severe stress may be engendered. The child's anxiety would not be allayed; his personality functioning could falter and foil his attempts at mourning.

The older the child, the more he is able to fulfill his own bodily needs. The parent cooks the meal but the child feeds himself; the parent prepares the bath but the child washes himself. As direct bodily care contributes less to the parent–child relationship, the manner of bodily-need fulfillment by others becomes less important. The child in the phallic-oedipal phase, in latency, and even in adolescence, still depends on adults to provide for him, but this function no longer forms the essence of the relationship. Since the child realizes his dependence on others, he feels assured of need fulfillment most readily when he can count on people whom he knows, loves, and trusts. The surviving love objects are, in his mind, best suited to the task.

Need fulfillment sometimes constitutes an important aspect of adult relationships. Advance provisions for the possibility of a loved one's death are often made—insurance policies, wills. When such arrangements are not made or are inadequate in meeting the survivor's needs, the adult also needs to concentrate first on the task of caring for himself or finding someone to care for him. Like the child, the adult prefers to depend on such established relationships as relatives and friends. As long as the adult cannot feel assured of the fulfillment of his needs he, like the child, cannot fully devote himself to his mourning.

In addition to bodily comforts every person needs to be loved—to receive a sufficient amount of narcissistic supplies from his love objects. The adult is usually fortunate in that he maintains a number of close relationships with his family, relatives, friends, and colleagues. The death of a loved one, however dear, does not deprive him of all love. The younger the child the more he invests all his love in the members of his immediate family, especially his parents. When a parent dies, the child loses a major source of love. He therefore depends all the more on the surviving parent for emotional gratification, for it is difficult to receive and accept love from a stranger.

The parent further represents an essential part of the child's functioning. This is particularly true of the toddler who is still in the process of investing his basic ego functions, such as speech and motility, and of gaining control over his primitive impulses, such as messing and hurting. The nursery school child relies on his parents for the development of reality testing and logical thinking, for tolerance and expression of affects and for behavioral control. The older children use the parents in less basic ways. The latency child needs his parent's support in developing sublimations and mastering his inner and outer conflicts. The adolescent needs the parent as a safe harbor to venture from and to measure himself against. All these functions fall into the hands of the surviving loved ones to some extent and are perhaps even harder to fulfill than the bodily needs. From the child's point of view no one is better suited to fulfill all these tasks than the surviving loved person or persons. A new person is inevitably at a disadvantage and, however loving and skilled he may be, a considerable time may pass before he can effectively supply at least a part of the child's many psychological needs.

Assurance of consistent bodily and psychological need fulfillment, and acceptance of and fondness for the need-fulfilling person do not represent a libidinal shift in the bereaved person's attachments. When he seeks someone to gratify his needs, when he enjoys being cared for and gladly depends on the caring individual, he has not, in doing so, withdrawn his love from the deceased and transferred it to the new person. He has only found respite from tensions and anxieties arising from inadequate need fulfillment. Even very young children, for whom need fulfillment is intimately connected with love, do not accomplish simultaneously the steps of accepting a new person's care and transferring their old love to her.

Our experiences with one-year-olds are too limited to serve as a basis for conclusions. With toddlers from fifteen to twenty-four months of age, however, we observed several instances of a new need-fulfilling person having to take over, or an already loved person having to extend his or her care after the loss of a parent. In each case the young child accepted the newly offered care and related in time to the need-fulfilling person, but his longing for the lost loved one did not cease. On the contrary, it appeared that, once his need fulfillment was assured, he could devote more energy to the efforts of dealing with the loss of the love object.

This course of events could be observed even more clearly with children who had reached the phallic–oedipal level at the time of the parent's death.

Addie was four years old when her mother died (see the analyst's report on p. 140). She was at the time cared for by her grandparents with whom she had a close relationship. When she started her analysis at six years of age it was found that her cathexis of her mother had not diminished and the mother had remained Addie's oedipal object. In her treatment Addie could resolve her conflicts and complete her mourning. Only then could she also love her grandparents as parents and continue her emotional development with them.

Some children not only behaved as though they had transferred their old love but actually attempted to do so as a defensive measure. Such a displacement enabled them to ward off the pain of longing but it was not accompanied by a shift of object libidinal cathexis and did not replace mourning. The outcome manifested itself as an adaptation, but it blocked the chances of a further development of their relationships. Martin explained this process well:

Martin's own father had died suddenly when Martin was four years old. His mother hoped to spare him the ensuing hardship by joining in the lives of a friendly family. Martin had a very nice substitute daddy and was treated like one of his children. At first Martin participated willingly in this extended family but, increasingly, his longing for his own father broke through. The presence and kindness of the substitute father only enhanced Martin's pain and frustration. Martin's mother recognized his feelings, ceased to encourage that displacement and helped Martin with his mourning. The substitute father became merely a friendly familiar adult. Many months later Martin observed another bereaved child in his attempts to attach himself to a new adult. Martin commented, "I used to do that but I don't pretend like that anymore. It hurts too much."

Our experience with these and other cases showed that the relationship with the need-fulfilling person does not indicate a decathexis of the representation of the deceased loved one. Rather, this relationship helps to establish a position of internal and external safety from which, under favorable circumstances, the work of mourning can begin. The younger the child, the more do these favorable circumstances depend on a further function of the surviving love objects, that is, on their support of the child's mourning. When they assist the child with his mourning they offer him a most significant aspect of love—empathy and understanding of feelings. In time this not only helps the child to mourn but paves the way for a new relationship in which the child can invest the love that he has so painfully withdrawn from the image of the dead parent. Bodily and psychological need fulfillment is the prerequisite; help with mourning is the essence of the surviving love object's role.

With the youngest children the task of supporting their mourning includes helping them to understand the concrete aspects of death, furthering their grasp of the specific circumstances and cause of the parent's death, helping them to master their anxiety in connection with it, and assisting them in differentiating themselves appropriately from the deceased. Our experience showed that these are all major painful and upsetting concerns which a child can integrate only gradually and which require repeated working through. The adult's sensitivity is put to a severe test in the process.

While the understanding and acceptance of the parent's death form the basis for the psychic work of remembering and longing, in practice these processes overlap. The routines of daily life and of special events, such as anniversaries, holidays and outings, constantly provoke recall and missing at a time when a young child may not yet have gained an adequate grasp of the reality of death or an older one may not yet have accepted it fully.

Mourning alone is an almost impossible task even for a mature adult. The younger the child, the more difficult it is for him to accomplish it without the feelingful assistance of a loved adult. At all stages of development a child's ability to mourn is greatly facilitated when his surviving love objects also mourn, accept and support the child's reactions, and allow him to mourn with them. We found that prelatency children, especially, encountered severe difficulties when the loved adult on whom they depended for survival failed them in this area.

Craig's mother died when he was two and a half years old. His father allowed himself no emotional reaction and soon forgot all events related to his wife's illness and death. By the time Craig was in latency, no fact or feeling relating to his mother's death had ever been discussed. His concerns, by that time largely unconscious, manifested themselves in symptoms and inappropriately timed breakthroughs of feelings. During his analysis Craig could be helped to recapture his thoughts and affects, to relate them to his dead mother and to integrate them in a belated mourning process.

Kathy's father died when she was three years old (see the analysts' report on p. 154). Her mother mourned in the true sense of the word and was sensitive to Kathy's reactions. The mother's difficulty lay in her fear of being overwhelmed by sadness. Kathy sensed her mother's fear of strong feelings and, for a time, addressed herself to her father's death mainly in remembering him without appropriate affects. At a later point, she expressed her sadness only at school. In her work with the therapist, Kathy's mother could appreciate how her own handling of sorrow affected Kathy. She came to share more of her sad feelings with Kathy and told Kathy that she did not need to hide her sadness. Kathy was greatly helped by this, could allow herself adequate expression of feelings and completed her mourning in due course.

Hank's father died when Hank was almost five years old (see the analyst's report on p. 129). His mother considered Hank a loner but his teachers noted his increased withdrawal from social contacts, his lack of interest in activities and his constantly tear-filled eyes as signs of inner difficulty. In her work of treatment-via-the parent, the mother became aware of Hank's deep sadness about his father's death. She had as yet not mourned at all, but in understanding Hank her own feelings rose to the surface. During the following year both Hank and his mother were able to mourn. Painful though this was, the mother was glad that Hank's difficulty had faced her with the task of her own mourning and that she could help her child with his.

In some instances it is not the surviving parent but the grandparent or other close adult, or even a sibling, who is able to share the child's memories and empathize with his feelings. For prelatency children the participation and model of the surviving parent is particularly helpful. If a child in that age group is in treatment, the analyst needs the parent's cooperation and support when the child's feelings emerge, although the emotional burden for the parent may be lessened by the work of the analysis. For the latency child, and even more so for the adolescent, the analytic work may assume a greater portion of the help with the mourning task. Several factors contribute to this, among them the child's lessened psychological dependence on the surviving parent, his greater ability to understand the parent's characterological patterns, the increased intensity and frequency of transference reactions. From the point of view of the overall parent–child relationship, however, it is always desirable that the surviving parent and his child share their mourning to an extent and understand each other's feelings about the other parent's death.

Mourning together does not imply that parent and child have the same feelings at the same time. Their relationships and experiences with the deceased were quite different. Even a specific memory shared by all members of the family, such as that of a birthday party, may be remembered with loving longing by one and with intense anger or disappointment by another. The parent shares in his child's mourning, and the child, to an extent, shares in the parent's in that they are mutually aware of the other's emotional experience and respect and accept their own and the loved one's feelings and thoughts. The adult is not a model the child imitates, though this can occur for defensive reasons. Rather, the adult, through his own mourning and through his support of the child's, conveys that mourning is an appropriate and masterable response to one of life's great hardships.

Ideally, a child invests his love in a new parent at a time when he has sufficiently completed his mourning and is capable of transferring his parental libidinal cathexis to another person. It is particularly fortunate when the new parent is a person whom the child knew prior to the first parent's death, who participated in the child's care at that time, and who later became the need-fulfilling object and assisted the child with his mourning. In practice this is rarely the case. The stepparent may be a stranger who never knew the child's dead parent. He may not have been active in caring for the child or in assisting him with his mourning. He may come into the child's life long after the child has been ready to invest his love in a new parent or long before the child is able to do so. At best the completion of mourning is a relative matter. When the stepparent permanently and fully assumes the parental role, this reality tends to bring into focus in the child the unworked-through aspects of his mourning and the residual cathexis of the dead parent's object representation. The perception of the stepparent's personality and behavior is contrasted with the memories of the dead parent. Sometimes the new parent is not only unfamiliar but compares unfavorably with the deceased. This may newly enhance the cathexis of the old love. At other times the new parent is seen as better, not only because he is available and can provide real satisfactions but also because he lacks some of the personality difficulties which burdened the first parent's relationship with the child. This may evoke a loyalty conflict. At all times the new parent alters the family's pattern of relationships in directions which seem to the child agreeable in some respects and disagreeable in others. The necessary adjustments inevitably impose a new stress. Before adolescence it is essential for the child's healthy emotional development that he invest his love in a new parent and continue his growth in the setting of a complete family. The work of mourning prepares him for this step, but when he actually takes it the child may encounter considerable inner difficulties.

Being a stepparent is a proverbially trying job. It is not our aim to discuss all aspects of this task for parent and child but to stress the place of the remaining cathexis of the dead parent's image in the context of forming new relationships. The mental representation of a dead parent is never completely decathected. It remains alive in the form of memories and feelings and, indirectly, contributes to the child's identifications and to certain aspects of his personality development. Loving a new parent cannot and should not erase the remaining traces of the earlier relationship. Some parents are able to acknowledge and respect this in their child and help him in his attempts to harmonize his different attachments. A stepparent builds his or her relationship with the child in part by appreciating that a new parent cannot actually take the place of the dead parent and by empathizing with the child's feelings. When both the surviving parent and the new parent can assist the child in working through the old and new attachments, they foster the investment of the new relationship and pave the way for the continued growth of the child's personality. This arduous task completes the role of the surviving love objects when a child's parent dies.

6. Object Loss and Mourning in Children and Adults: Some Differences

So far we have kept developmental factors in the foreground of our thinking. We realized, however, that various factors determine a person's reaction to the loss of a love object and contribute to his ability to master the task of mourning: the individual's mental capacities for dealing with the loss, depending on his age-appropriate development and personality makeup; whom he has lost, i.e. the role the lost object relationship played in his life; and the impact of the circumstances of the loss as well as those preceding and following it. Without understanding the intricate interaction of these factors it was impossible to assess the bereaved prson's developmental capacities for coping with his stress.

In one family the sudden death of the father affected the mother and her three children. The reactions of each seemed, at first, to depend primarily on their very different age-appropriate capacities for mourning. Another determinant was the relationship with the father (and husband), which had been cathected differently by each member of the family, both quantitatively and qualitatively. This relationship had provided each with different object libidinal and narcissistic satisfactions and had received very different amounts of libidinal cathexis. Eleven-month-old Danny (see the analyst's report on p. 198) maintained a special relationship with his father which had apparently reached the beginning stage of object constancy and was characterized by certain playful interactions. It seemed likely however that most of his object libido was invested in his relationship with his mother. For three-year-old Kathy (see the analyst's report on p. 154), in the beginning of the phallic phase, her relationship with the father provided very different satisfactions, and they were different again for five-year-old Ted, at the height of the oedipal phase. Although Kathy and Ted derived their own gratifications from the relationship with the father, their ca-

119

thexes of the relationship were much greater and more intense than Danny's. The mother had maintained a particularly satisfactory and close relationship with her husband but, appropriately, she had distributed her object libido much more widely to include her children, parents, and friends. These great differences in the libido distribution and in the nature of the lost gratifications were brought out sharply when the mother, following her husband's death, decided to live with her parents in another town. In doing so she quite realistically utilized her relationships with her parents, both for object libidinal and narcissistic satisfactions. This made it more possible for her to mourn her husband. Kathy and Ted remembered the grandparents. To Danny they were total strangers. The only object relationships the children could readily utilize were those with their mother and each other. All their object libido was concentrated in these few investments. All their satisfactions had to derive from them. A further factor in their reactions was the difference in circumstances surrounding the father's death for each member of the family. Danny was very ill himself, hospitalized alone, and subjected to many medical procedures. Subsequently he suffered the loss of his familiar home. Kathy and Ted also lost their home but they were healthy, suffered no interference with their bodily narcissism, and remained throughout with each other. They were separated from their mother for a briefer period than Danny. Ted alone carried the special burden of feeling that his behavior could have contributed to the father's death. When the mother joined her parents she returned to a familiar environment. With her adult functioning she was also much better equipped to make the necessary adjustments. The children moved into a strange environment not of their choice and were, developmentally, less capable of mastering the change. Although the mother's predicament was very great, her children's situation was, in some respects, even greater. In any case, all family members faced a very different total situation. Their long struggles could not be compared or evaluated simply on the basis of their different developmental capacities to mourn.

In arriving at our tentative conclusions regarding the definitions of mourning and the process of mourning we considered primarily the developmental factor, the individual's age-appropriate mental capacity to deal with the loss of a love object. We also took into account the nature of the role the lost object played in the bereaved person's life. Later we addressed ourselves to the impact of the reality and circumstances of the death and what preceded it and followed it. In this chapter our aim is to review and explore these factors further, to interrelate them, and to understand their significance for criteria of mourning in childhood.

The Mental Capacity for Mourning at Various Developmental Stages

We have not aimed at a comprehensive study of all areas of the personality but have concentrated on those that were highlighted by our clinical material and accessible to our understanding. We hope that further analytic research will explore in greater detail the relevant areas of functioning and help to validate our conclusions. Since most aspects under this heading were discussed earlier the following is a brief summary.

Object Relationships

A child must have reached at least the beginning stage of object constancy (as defined in chapter 3) in order to long for a lost love object when tensions from unfulfilled needs are not present or are frustrated to some extent. The continuous cathexis of an object representation is achieved at this stage and forms the basis for the process of its decathexis, which we consider an essential part of mourning. Chronologically, the child usually attains this stage in the latter half of his first year.[1]

Nature of object representations

At different developmental stages the nature of the cathected object representations varies greatly. At the beginning of object constancy and throughout the anal-sadistic phase, object representations are not clearly differentiated, are unstable, and are little in accord with external reality. Mental and physical stress can contribute to distortions and changes in the object representations and can lead to their de-

---

1. We consider the loss of the need-fulfilling love object before the stage of object constancy a serious developmental interference for the baby but feel that his reactions to such a loss would not constitute a partial or complete mourning.

struction or fusion with the self-image. The pain and frustration of ungratified longing are so severe that it may be impossible for some youngsters at these levels to maintain sufficient cathexis of the object image to engage in a mourning process. In the children we studied, however, this was not the case with those who lost a parent during the anal-sadistic phase. Their object representations remained relatively stable, as evidenced by cathected memories of experiences with the love object and differentiated object and self-images. With our one-year-olds this was harder to assess and we lacked sufficient case material.

At the object-centered phallic stage, object representations still show some of the earlier characteristics. It appeared, however, that the stability, realistic objectivity, and differentiation of object representations were far enough advanced to withstand the stress of loss and mourning.

Ambivalence

All relationships are ambivalent to a certain extent. The death of a love object tends to heighten the component of hatred. The task of dealing with this is always a part of the mourning process (S. Freud 1913). At the earliest developmental phases, especially during the oral-sadistic and anal-sadistic phases, the admixture of aggression in relationships is particularly strong and inadequately tempered by, or fused with, love. Separation at these stages is characteristically conceived of in terms of mutual anger. The toddler's difficulties in dealing with his aggression may well jeopardize his mourning process. In our experience this was true with some of our patients but not with all. There were some children, bereaved when they were toddlers, whose ambivalence was not of such proportions as to interfere with their mourning. By contrast, there were other patients who were chronologically older at the time of their bereavement whose earlier experiences had prevented phase-adequate instinctual fusion. Their relationships remained intensely ambivalent throughout subsequent maturational levels. Their hostility caused them severe conflicts. When it was heightened by the death of the loved person it constituted an interference in their mourning process.

Narcissistic Gratifications in Object Relationships

Children and adults need to love and be loved. All relationships at all stages tend to include some form and amount of narcissistic gratifications and need fulfillment. At the earliest stages of development, narcissistic gratifications tend to constitute a major part of the parental object relationships. If, at these levels, such a relationship is permanently disrupted, the bereaved personality may not be able to maintain itself and its functions without the love object's narcissistic supplies. Chronologically this would usually apply to the infant and young toddler. At later stages these supplies are increasingly supplanted by narcissistic self-investment, by autonomy of functions, and by the assistance of other love objects. It is necessary that the loss of the love object not interfere with the cathexis of the functions and activities that are required for mourning, e.g. memory, perception, object ·constancy, and recognition and tolerance of affects. These achievements are to some extent a function of maturation; to a large extent, however, they depend on the role of the lost relationship in the life of the child and on the circumstances surrounding the loss. For example, a young toddler's loss of his mother has a very different effect from his loss of a sibling. Even the loss of the mother will be coped with differently if the mothering has been shared by a nanny who continues to live with the child, if he remains in his familiar surroundings with the rest of his family, and if he is assisted in understanding the mother's death. It is also important to note that, beyond the baby's earliest relationship, a child's attachment to a loved person includes aspects other than need fulfillment. The gratification of mental needs increasingly supersedes that of bodily needs. The relationship with love objects serves other purposes and focuses on different forms of interaction.

We found repeatedly that the cathexis of the deceased parent's object representation was not simply transferred to the need-fulfilling substitute. Rather, assurance of adequate need fulfillment enabled the young child to address himself to the task of mourning and, at best, paved the way toward the later establishment of a new relationship.

Remembering, Longing, and Detachment

Toddlers and older children remembered their lost loved ones and their experiences with them. In the latency years and in adolescence, remembering occurred in the form of thinking, feeling and, at times, verbalizing. In the younger children it was often accompanied by the repetition of such physical activities as had been part of the lost relationship (see example of Clive, p. 55). It seemed important for the prelatency children in particular that the surviving love object support and share their remembering and allow them to recall both good and bad aspects of the dead loved one. In the older children the ego and super ego identifications with the lost person also determined their attitudes in this respect. For example Lena, aged eleven years when her mother died, had great difficulty in allowing herself to remember her mother and especially to share her feelings about it. Some years prior to her death the mother had shown quite similar reactions when she mourned an important love object. It could be understood that Lena reacted like her mother.

We assumed considerable age-adequate differences in the ability to tolerate the pain and anguish of longing but found great individual variations in this respect, due both to differences in endowment and in defensive structure. Some very young children were able to bear and express deep sadness repeatedly over a long period of time. Some adults could not do so. As with remembering, however, the youngest children usually required the direct assistance and "permission" of the surviving parent. The older ones needed a loved person, though not necessarily a parent, who could either share their grief or empathize with them and support their tolerance and expression of affect.

Children could achieve the necessary amount of decathexis when remembering and longing had taken place sufficiently. In developmentally important relationships, decathexis was particularly difficult for prelatency children when there was no opportunity for an appropriate new relationship. The mere availability of a new love object, however, did not bring about a detachment from the lost one. The child also could not effectively cathect a new person unless the latter allowed for a residual attachment to the dead loved one and helped with the working through. This is to a considerable extent also true of the adolescent and adult, but certain types of object relationships are not so essential for their own further development. The adolescent and adult are more capable of seeking out new relationships independently.

Identification

Identification plays an essential part in the mourning process, along with decathexis. In children, identifications in different forms are developmentally important and widely used mechanisms. In mourning they are "favored" because of their great psychological advantages for the bereaved. It appears important in certain childhood relationships that identification not altogether supplant decathexis, so that the child's object relationships have a chance to mature further. For the purposes of mourning the young child in the oral-sadistic and anal-sadistic phases is handicapped by being capable largely of only primitive instinctual identifications. The more advanced partial integrated identifications tend more readily to contribute to a healthy outcome of mourning and subsequent adaptation. We found that some such ego identifications occurred in youngsters as early as the second half of their second year. By contrast, primitive forms of identification were also present in much older children because of their personality makeup. In several cases the pathology resulting from identification was not only due to its primitive form but also to other factors such as the child's limited reality testing and the nature of the model.

The reports on Geraldine, Addie, and Seth portray the analytic understanding of primitive and pathological forms of identification. Ken, Jim, Hank, and Kathy illustrate advanced and helpful forms of identification. Several case vignettes show how certain interferences in mourning and adaptation were rooted in identification with the deceased parent's personality difficulties. Some of the clinical material highlights the fear of identification with the dead love object (e.g. Danny) and the obstacles to developmental identification caused by lack of knowledge about the dead parent (e.g. Lucy).

The Concept and Acceptance of Death

We considered the individual's awareness, comprehension, and acknowledgment of the death of his loved one as a sine qua non of mourning. In our experience normally developed children from the age of two years on could attain a sufficient understanding if it had been discussed with them around common encounters with death. Such young children could apply this concept to the loss of a loved person when realistic and continuous help in understanding facts and feelings was available from surviving love objects. The concept and acceptance of death were much harder to acquire when they had to be learned in connection with the death of a loved one and when the child was not given consistent realistic information. With the death of a parent the child experienced numerous special obstacles. Among these were the difficulty in differentiating himself appropriately from the parent and in coping with the great stress engendered by the particular form of the parent's death, for example, if it was sudden or violent, or a death preceded by bodily or mental deterioration. In addition, the child was sometimes affected directly, not only by disruption of personal care and loss of other relationships but also by incurring injury in the same accident that killed the parent.

We enlarge on this important topic of the child's concept of death, and the adults' role in helping him to develop it, in several contexts. The individual child's ability to mourn does not depend only on these developmental steps and their interaction within his personality. At several points in the above review it was impossible to pinpoint the developmental criteria without taking into account the variable of "who died," that is, the meaning and nature of the lost object relationship. Comparisons between adults and children at different levels are not meaningful unless the enormous differences between their object libidinal cathexes are taken into account.

Object Libidinal Cathexes at Different Developmental Levels

In discussing the effect of this factor on the bereaved person's reactions we also do not intend to explore fully all sides of this complex topic. We discuss only those that were brought out clearly by our clinical material and on which our studies focused.

The developmental role of object relationships, so crucial to the understanding of a child's parental bereavement, has already been considered at some length. The young child maintains a special type of relationship in which the love object forms an essential part of the child's personality and is instrumental in the building up of his basic personality structure. When the child is deprived of such a love object the integrity of his personality may be disrupted, and the further maturation of his personality structure may be endangered. The toddler maintains this type of relationship mainly with his mother and, to some extent, with his father. The phallic-oedipal child relates in this way to both parents. The latency child has already completed his basic personality structure but needs his parents to solidify, harmonize, and enrich his mental development. At different stages the parental love objects complete the child's personality in different ways. Bodily-need fulfillment plays an important part in the young toddler's relationship with his mother. The older prelatency child can to a considerable extent care for his own body or accept the help of nonparental love objects. For him the parents are essential in other areas such as impulse control, inner and outer reality testing and, above all, as models for identification. In the latency period, the child increasingly takes over these functions and can utilize love objects outside the immediate family to a greater extent. In the early years of adolescence the parents are helpful but not essential as the realistic fortress against which, and from which, the child can effect his object removal and form new identifications with their adult sexual roles. Adults and normal adolescents after object removal do not maintain any relationships comparable to the parental cathexes of childhood.

When his parent dies the child at any stage copes with a unique situation that has no counterpart in later life. His reaction to a parent's death cannot be understood solely in terms of his developmental capacity for mourning but must be considered also in terms of the effect of the loss on his personality and its maturation. There are great variations in this respect between children, depending on their developmental level and on the specific circumstances surrounding the loss. The mourning of children and adults can be compared in regard to the loss of certain love objects but not in regard to the loss of a parent.

At all levels of development, some object relationships fulfill mainly the need to love and be loved. These relationships usually contain a greater or lesser measure of need fulfillment and narcissistic gratification but are not an essential part of the individual's personality functioning. The young toddler may maintain such relationships with older siblings. The nursery school child may relate in this manner to grandparents, uncles, and aunts. The number and variety of these relationships tend to increase until, at the time of adolescent object removal, all object relationships come to be of this nature. From then on the functioning of the personality depends on no one relationship.

The distribution of object libido at different developmental levels is another area of great difference between children and adults. During his first two years the child's object libido is vested largely in one person, the mother. During the phallic–oedipal phase the father becomes a second major love object. Siblings, relatives, and such outsiders as teachers and peers gradually assume a greater share of the child's love. Increasingly, a wider distribution of object libido takes place but, until the time of object removal, the parents remain the chief love objects. We all know how difficult it is for young children to grasp the idea that adults can love more than one person and can love each differently. In young children the greatest amount of libidinal cathexis concentrates on one or two persons. In the adult personality we do not expect an even distribution of libido between family and outsiders such as friends, but we expect outsiders to be cathected more intensively than in childhood. Further, the adult's attachments to family members are much more widely distributed. Spouse and children are loved along with parents and siblings. There are considerable variations within the normal range of the strengths and weaknesses of these family relationships.

The differences between children and adults are not due to a greater amount of object libido in the adult but to a basic difference in the distribution of object libidinal cathexes. The death of a parent therefore means something very different in various phases of childhood than any loss means in adulthood, be it parent, child, spouse, sibling, or close friend. To the adult, the loss of any one love object does not represent an almost total loss of object love. During his mourning the adult can usually rely on his other relationships and later does not need to attach himself to new love objects to the same extent. When an adult focuses all object love on one or two persons and suffers a bereavement, we readily empathize with his special tragedy. Theodora Kroeber's story, *Ishi, Last of His Tribe* (1964), portrays such an extreme event. The young child who loses a parent as a rule finds himself in just such a situation.

These considerations of developmental differences in the role of certain object relationships and in the distribution of object libido made us realize that the death of a parent has a special psychological impact on the child. There are great individual variations between children, according to developmental level and life circumstances, but any child's actual task of mourning a parent differs fundamentally from an adult's mourning task.

For these reasons we decided to limit our study to the death of a parent in childhood.

This sequence of five reports shows that all children who lose a parent through death during the phallic–oedipal phase face some similar problems. More striking, however, are the great differences in their mastery of the task of mourning. To an extent this is because some of them suffered the death of a mother, others that of a father, during a period of emotional development in which the parent's sex is particularly significant. Other causes, however, may be traced in individual aspects of each child's personality and past experiences, in the impact of the circumstances of the parent's death and the child's comprehension of it, and in the role played by the surviving parent or parent substitute.

HANK AND SALLY   by Arthur L. Rosenbaum, M.D.

A variety of factors influenced Hank's and Sally's reactions to the death of their father. One was that the children were adopted; neither of them had dealt with the special realities of their adoption at the time of bereavement. Hank, the older child, although adopted in the first weeks of life, had to adapt to the entrance into his family of his younger sister when she was a toddler. Younger Sally had to work through the earlier now-isolated loss of her foster mother before it became possible to even consider the later death of her father. Both of them, unfortunately, had not been able to verbalize their feelings about these earlier events because the adoptive parents were unable to help them do so. These parents, loving and kind, found that interferences from their own early experiences made the children's verbalization of anger and sadness intolerable to them. This then also determined the mother's initial handling of the father's death. She could fully mourn only when she was working to help Hank with his feelings and thoughts. The developmental stage in which the loss of their father occurred influenced the nature of their individual responses. Both had apparently already entered the phallic–oedipal phase at the time of their father's death. Hank's appearance of depression had been, prior to our work, viewed as characteristic of his personality. The interferences in his ego development, part of his "depression," contributed to the nature of his mourning, and provided a dramatic contrast when relief came, once the work was underway.

Both Hank and Sally were treated via their mother. This treatment depended for its observations largely on the mother and on the teachers in the Hanna Perkins Kindergarten. It depended solely on the mother for her ability to be sensitive to her children's need and readiness for interpretation of the unconscious meaning of their thoughts, verbal productions, and behavior. To expect a mother to participate in such a process, which is often tedious and painful, always presents difficulties. These may come from, among other sources, her own neurotic resolution to the conflicts of her past. When one considers in addition the amount of guilt that a parent actively engaged in such work must experience and tolerate, one realizes the strength of personality integration and health that is required to be successful. When one then adds to this already difficult burden the recent death of a spouse, the expectations become enormous.

HANK

Hank's mother applied to the kindergarten for his entrance when he was five years and two months old, three months after his father's sudden death. Hank had attended a neighborhood nursery school and was completing his second year there. His teacher had suggested that Hank was not prepared to enter a public kindergarten. He spent all of his time in nursery school alone; he refused to participate in any activity at all. He presented no disciplinary problem unless he was pressed to join the group or to play with another child. Then he complained and whined in a most pathetic manner. He did not use scissors, crayons, paste, or paint. He was clumsy, slow, and unsafe in his large muscle activity. He often sought out a visiting mother but formed no appropriate relationship. He had her do something or play with something for him. When the Hanna Perkins Kindergarten teacher and later the Director of Education visited Hank in his nursery school, they were impressed by his abject appearance and his large blue eyes that seemed filled with tears. They noted the reluctance of those around him to expect his participation in activities. He appeared depressed to them.

His mother agreed with the teacher. She stressed that he had a problem in talking about the way he felt. She and her husband had regarded Hank as a "loner" because he preferred his own company to that of his brother and sister. She reported that they said more about the way they felt than Hank did. Yet his parents were always surprised that it was Hank who recalled past events more sharply than the others. It was partly recognized that he only appeared to be isolated and inattentive to events around him. For example, when his sister was adopted at twenty-two months, her name was changed. Hank, with feeling, continued to call her by the old name in contrast to his brother who quickly adopted the new name.

Hank was four years eleven months when his father died. His mother's memory of the circumstances of the father's death was, we later learned, incomplete. She reported then that he had been in good health but was struggling with an important decision about whether or not he should accept his employer's offer of another job, with a commitment to travel extensively, that would require the family to move. So that he could decide better, he had accepted a similar position and had traveled for weeks with only two brief visits home. He had returned home feeling fatigued and irritable. Although these symptoms were attributed to the necessity of making the difficult decision, they persisted, and after two months he saw his physician. A cursory examination revealed no physical problems, but a repeat visit shortly after, with further testing, raised a suspicion of coronary artery disease. He was admitted to the hospital for further tests. During the night following the test, which confirmed that he had heart disease, he died suddenly.

Hank and his brother and sister had spent that evening with their maternal grandmother and slept at her house so that the mother could visit the father in the hospital. When the children were told by the mother, the next day, of their father's death, Hank's behavior was characteristic. His brother and sister seemed appropriately sad, with crying and questions. Hank, however, looked sad, said little, but became physically active in a quiet but disturbing way. He engaged in methodical, repetitive, rhythmic activity, jumping, rolling about, swinging on furniture. Remnants of this behavior persisted and reminded the mother of his reaction on that day. It was not the kind of behavior that irritates adults, but a quiet, isolated activity, distressing to watch.

In the weeks following, Hank, who had never had a sleep problem, delayed sleep, with many questions and requests for one more story. His mother understood this trouble as the father had been the one to help the children prepare for bed in the evening. Hank did not appear changed in school after his loss, but he spent more time alone in his room at home, playing with two dolls that had been gifts from his father.

His mother had made explanations of the reality of the funeral and burial and of the subsequent changes in their lives. The children did not attend the funeral but stayed with a neighbor. At the time of Hank's acceptance to the Hanna Perkins Kindergarten, his mother felt that they had all adjusted to the loss. Hank's difficulties were regarded by her as more characterological or inherited traits than as symptoms or reactions to events.

It is the requirement of the school that the mother be available for a period of time so that the manner in which the separation of the child from mother is handled can be observed. It is also a requirement that the mother bring her child to and pick him up from school. Hank's mother wished to make other arrangements. She felt the need to return to work and would have preferred a car pool. However, she complied with the requirements with an intellectual understanding of the reasons.

She was unable to verbalize any of her complaints about me or the school. Nor could she complain to Hank about the way he treated her. Instead, she handled her painful feeling by making factual, detailed, prolonged explanations that often resulted in a feeling of confusion, a sudden running out of words and a breathless, distressing silence. Consequently, we had great difficulty in working together. She could neither tell me how she felt about the school's demands nor feel good about them. This difficulty, for a time, necessarily became the focus of our talks. As we together understood that her behavior substituted for the expression of her feelings, we could gradually shift our attention to the way Hank handled his entry into the new school. He had already adapted to the earlier separations and maintained his defenses during his entrance to the new school. Consequently, his worries about it were not available to our work. In school, Hank was a very unhappy boy. He refused to participate in anything; he had no fun at all. All activity was painfully tedious and he could not bear it. He whined and complained bitterly. He did not talk to his mother during the ride to and from school. Although he quietly played or sang or talked to himself, he shared nothing of his new school experience with her. He soon asked her if he could like his teacher as much as he liked her, and without hesitating, she answered yes. She was able to tell me how badly she really felt but she could not tell Hank.

As the mother became more aware of her sadness and anger, she reported that Hank had done a very unusual thing. He told her that I had not visited him in school on my usual day. Without another thought, she told him that I'd "probably" be there tomorrow and that

I was "probably" ill. She became frightened at this idea and corrected her statement saying that I probably had car trouble. She suggested that Hank, in any case, should ask his teacher about my absence. He revealed to her the next morning that he had been "fooling" her and that I had really visited as usual. She felt foolish, was very puzzled, and reported that Hank was a storyteller and that he had frightened her. At home she was often aware that he told her things that couldn't be true. She reported that on her way to school with him she often saw a man walking who resembled me and, on many occasions, pointed out the resemblance to Hank. Hank never responded to her remarks. She added that she knew my office was in another part of the city and it couldn't be me. When I compared Hank's "storytelling" with her own explanation, she realized how it must seem to Hank. When she said he could like the teacher as much as he liked her, or that I was ill or had car trouble, or that it looked like me walking when it couldn't be, she was telling him a story. She recalled how often her reasonable, factual explanations had in reality been fantasy. Soon after, Hank became angry at her and called her a bad mother over a minor frustration in the car on the way home from school. Instead of guiltily agreeing with him, as she had before, she criticized him in turn for not being such a good son, for refusing to share with her his feelings and experiences at school. They made an agreement: if he expected her to comply with his wish, he'd have to tell her something about school each day. The work around his loyalty conflict continued as he made his daily reports. Soon Hank began to ask many questions about his father's death, all with appropriate feeling: what was he wearing when he was dead, were his eyes open or closed, what were his last words, did he say his usual "See you later," who carried him to the grave, who buried him, did he have pain, did he die in his sleep, did he dream.

Once his mother had been able to tolerate her own anger, without resorting to the denial and intellectualized explanations, Hank was able to begin his mourning, which lasted with great intensity for the following several months. It was clear to his mother that her own difficulties with feelings were of long standing and had inhibited her in her encouragement of the children's expression of feeling. She began to view her other children's adjustment with a more critical eye and realized what had to be done. How she helped her daughter Sally is a story in itself. Her older son eventually required analytic treatment.

The immediate effect of this outpouring of feeling and questions from Hank was to challenge his mother's own denial about other aspects of the father's illness. She now recalled that both of her husband's parents had died of heart disease in their middle age. Her husband had long been concerned that he too might develop heart disease early. On his return from his business trip two months before his death, he had experienced numbness and tingling of his left arm, a feeling of pressure in the chest, pain in the chest radiating to the scapula whenever he walked or climbed stairs, but he attributed his symptoms to the job decision.

Again, a lessening of his mother's denial enabled Hank to deal more directly with his loss. He began to play a favorite recording repeatedly. He knew all the songs and sang them at home and at school. His father had been interested in the theater and had acted in the musical that Hank now was so interested in. He cried desperately over minor incidents at school, literally leaving puddles of tears on the floor. He was soon able to relate these episodes to specific memories of his father that he had just recalled. At these times he sought out his teacher to be with her as he sobbed long and hard. He brought a picture of his father to school and talked about him often.

As the first anniversary of his father's death approached, Hank developed an interest in the assassination of President Lincoln. The date of his father's death and Lincoln's birthday were only days apart. He talked to everyone about Lincoln's assassination and was convinced that it was Lincoln's successor, Andrew Jackson, who had killed him. Neither is a fact—that Jackson was the murderer or the successor—but Hank could not be told otherwise. He became excited with his teacher and at home. He developed a sleep disturbance that had as its content his wish to sleep with his mother as his father had. He awoke at night crying, "I don't want to die." He became very particular about his clothing, avoiding things that resembled what his father had worn. He also told me and his mother that I would be a suitable successor to his father. It appeared that with his ability to express his feeling, to obtain some new facts, his development proceeded. His oedipal fantasies revealed how his father's death intensified his conflicts by imposing a frightening and sad reality. His mother was able to handle this with delicate sensitivity. Later, on the occasion of his first visit to his father's grave, he said that his interest in Lincoln really had been about his father.

Another striking change occurred in school following the outpouring of grief and the step forward in development. He became interested in everything. He was eager to learn and he learned well. His appetite for new experiences was insatiable and he attempted and mastered activities he had previously avoided. Throughout, he often retold the story of the death, making sense of things that had formerly been confusing. He used scrapbooks to help himself until he finally seemed to integrate his feelings and memories.

As he did so, he began to talk about another important event. Hank could not figure out how it was that his sister could be bigger than he and older than he when she was born. In a sense, his puzzlement was understandable. His sister, when she came into the family, was certainly bigger and older than he was when he came to the family. It was a very long time before he could understand it. His mother, however, understood that the handling of his sister's arrival, with the characteristic explanations that said nothing and the denial of feeling, had not only confused Hank, but also set the stage for his handling of the next important event of his life, his father's death. The inhibition of the expression of his sadness and his aggression began then. For a time, the adoption and the death were confused. He wondered if one can buy a new father as one "bought" a new child.

Hank's preparation for leaving the school to attend public school was very difficult in that it brought up again his sadness at his earlier loss. He worked hard at differentiating separation and death. He wrote letters to me and has visited me in my office. His mother suspects that some of his letters didn't reach me as he merely dropped them unaddressed into the mailbox. During the next years he developed a relationship with the father of a neighboring family through his interest in handcraft. This has been a continuous though not intense relationship. In keeping with his latency adjustment, Hank has progressed satisfactorily in school. An awkwardness in his gross motor activity and the ease with which he can be overwhelmed with sadness recall for his mother his intensely depressed appearance of the past. He has a continuing interest in reading about the lives of the presidents. He identifies with his father in his enjoyment of records and often sings songs from musicals.

SALLY

Sally came to our attention because she was doing so well. The mother's defenses against feelings had inhibited her own and Hank's mourning. During the first part of our work, I simply heard that Sally was a very feminine and capable child. She had attended a nursery school before, and was now in the process of adjusting to a new one. She seemed to do so without difficulty. The story of the important events in her life made us wonder about this apparently good adjustment.

Sally lived in a foster home until she was twenty-two months old. Her adoptive parents visited her there on several occasions and then she was brought to her new home. She was given a new name. All of this occurred within a matter of days. She visited her foster home once, and her foster mother visited her once about a month later. From that time there had been only a few snapshots and a few toys to remind her of her earlier life. Her new parents regarded her apparent lack of interest in her foster mother on the occasions of the visits as evidence that Sally preferred them. No attempt was made to help Sally recall the old home. She soon outgrew the clothes she brought with her and they were discarded. An interest in snacking on sweets that was part of her behavior in the foster home was discouraged early. Sally behaved as though she very much wanted to please her new parents. She attended nursery school at three and a half years. At four years, her adoptive father died suddenly.

Of the children, Sally was the one who clearly understood and accepted the meaning of death. She was appropriately sad and asked many questions. She handled the facts in a realistic manner, much to the distress of her older brother. For example, soon after the death, a salesman came to the door and the children answered his ring. When he asked, "Is your daddy at home?" Sally answered "My daddy is dead." Her oldest brother Jerry was furious with her, demanding that she keep quiet.

During the work with the mother that led to her own and Hank's mourning, Sally's very placid adjustment began to be questioned. It took only a little investigation on the mother's part to learn that Sally was having stomachaches at school each day. The mother became increasingly aware of Sally's interest in her baby pictures. More questioning on the mother's part led to some angry outbursts from Sally. Convinced of the need for Sally to discuss further her earlier loss, the mother made arrangements for her to attend Hanna Perkins Kindergarten. She began when she was five and a half years old, in the year immediately following Hank's admission.

During the early part of the school year Sally seemed to follow, in her play, a boy who behaved at times in a scary manner. She often found herself the target of a sudden and unexpected outburst of an aggressive nature. When her mother spoke to her about her need to take better care of herself, she did so. In this as in other things, Sally seemed too compliant. She seemed to anticipate each demand and expectation and did all that she should do before being asked. She avoided any mistake or wrongdoing. Things were not so at home, however. There she complained loudly that her mother was a bad mother. When reprimanded or when displeased, she threatened to leave and, on occasion, packed a few of her things. She would get as far as the porch and then return. At other times she insisted that she didn't like her home and wished to live elsewhere.

Her mother, as she had with Hank, did not question or contradict the remarks. The initial work was involved with helping the mother look beyond Sally's behavior and complaints, and to wonder about the feelings behind them. As she did so, two incidents clarified a great many things.

The mother had seen Sally and a friend eating a snack in the yard. Shortly after, Sally came in and yelled to her mother, "I want a snack." Sally usually obtained her own snacks and, since she had just had one, the mother thought it was a strange and unusually forceful demand. She refused saying, "You just had one." Sally stormed out but the mother insisted that she return to try to explain her behavior. She suggested to Sally that she became so angry because she was avoiding another feeling. Although Sally was able to add nothing to this, the mother recalled her disapproval of the way the foster mother had served Sally's meals. A variety of foods was prepared and Sally was allowed to choose what she wished. The mother was reminded of her efforts to change this. In discussing it now with a relative, the relative recalled how the mother objected to Sally's taking a grandmotherly visitor by the hand and asking for a cookie. She reminded the mother of her words: "That is the influence of the foster home and it must stop." The foster mother had been an older woman. The mother became convinced that Sally's outbursts over the snack did have to do with her memories of her foster home. She sensitively and gradually introduced the topic of her former home to Sally. Sally's response was not a verbal one. Instead she crawled into doll buggies in the neighborhood and played baby at school.

Shortly after, mother and daughter went shopping. Sally was allowed to go off alone for a few moments. When they arrived home, the mother noticed how Sally walked about clutching her tummy in a conspicuous manner. Sally denied that there was anything wrong but repeated the behavior. Mother followed Sally and found a candy bar on the floor. Sally eventually admitted to having taken it from the store. Mother helped Sally return it and began to find many little things around the house that had been missing for months or even years, that she had assumed were lost: pens, lipsticks, eye makeup, perfume. When she asked Sally about it, Sally revealed a purse full of such things. Mother interpreted over a period of time that Sally was stealing from the mother just as she felt the mother had stolen Sally's memories and feelings about her old foster home.

Mother gradually helped Sally to link her symptomatic actions and isolated recollections with verbal memories of her earlier life. Eventually they planned to call her foster mother and then to arrange a visit. Sally began to act cute and charming to everyone, talking compulsively about her past. The mother recalled how she and her husband had told Sally she was adopted because she was so cute and charming, and she interpreted Sally's behavior to her as due to her fear that she might be sent back. Sally consented to the visit when she could clarify that it would be her "decision" as to when she would go and when she would end the visit. This work coincided with the anniversary of her father's death. She played dead, wished to be dead to be with him, and wished that he had not died. She asked me how many were in my family, contrasting it to the number now in her family since her father had died. She told me that she thought of him always. She added, "I had another mother." Although previously realistic about death, she now revealed a confusion between her adoption and his death by asking if the father was now too big for his clothes. She had become too big for the ones she brought from the foster home.

The visit itself brought some important insights. Sally, soon after her reunion with her foster mother, asked, "Can I play with your cosmetics?" and correctly recalled their location. The foster mother pleasantly recalled how Sally had always loved to play with her lipsticks. Sally, with much interest, toured her old home and was alarmed to hear someone typing on the third floor. She accepted the explanation that the foster mother now had a college girl rooming there. Later, Sally was angry at her mother for taking her from the foster home since obviously there was room there for her. Her mother realized that Sally needed to know that her foster mother was not her real mother and had not been able to adopt her. Although very hard for her to explain, she did so and Sally was able to accept it, giving evidence that she had suspected as much.

Sally's reaction for a long time centered around her anger at her mother for taking her away from the foster home. She arranged a conference to tell her teachers about her three mothers. When she met with them, she burst into tears, and talked of her father's death and of her scary feelings about her foster mother and the original mother.

After this work, and as the end of the year approached, there were many phone calls and visits to her foster mother. These have continued with decreasing frequency. She seems to need the contact less as time goes on. In school, she is a bright, pretty, appealing girl who learns easily and well.

It appeared that Sally dealt with her two losses simultaneously. Although she has been able to decathect the memories of the earlier lost mother, the memories of her father have not been fully decathected. During the year she became happier and less restricted and completed the transition into latency. The work accomplished the recovery for her of the important earlier loss of the foster mother. The handling of this loss by the adoptive parents, with denial of feeling, had left Sally with a sadness and longing that could be expressed only in her symptoms. It is hoped that the opportunity to work through the experience of the earlier loss will enable future decathexis of the object representation of her dead father. Currently, her developmental need for a father is still great. Her wish to make gifts to place on her father's grave on the occasion of his birthday or on Father's Day are an expression of this as well as of her painful wish that he, like her foster mother, could be recovered.

ADDIE

by Myron W. Goldman

Addie's mother died just before her fourth birthday. Addie started her analysis when she was almost six years old and was seen five times weekly for six years and four months, until she was twelve years and four months of age. At this writing, follow-up contact is still being maintained.

At her mother's death Addie was living with her two sisters at the home of her maternal grandparents, who also had with them two of their own sons, seven and nine years older than Addie. The young children had been staying with the grandparents for a few days following their mother's hospitalization for bleeding from the nose, mouth, and ears—a symptom heralding the terminal stage of the mother's blood disease. There had been several earlier hospitalizations, without similar symptoms. Each time the children had stayed with the grandparents, with whom they had always been close. The mother's illness and previous hospitalizations had never been explained to Addie nor was there any discussion about the mother's related symptoms of fatigue and other problems. It was characteristic of the grandmother to maintain an atmosphere of secrecy about what had happened to Addie and her family. There was no discussion about the mother's illness and death, about the fact that the father did not want to take responsibility for his children, or about the father's jail term and periodic alcoholism. The grandmother did not want to acknowledge or discuss these realities because she saw them in light of her own guilt—she had felt very responsible for her daughter's fatal illness. It was her idea that the blood disease began during her daughter's adolescence and had not been given serious enough attention.

Between hospitalizations the mother had been symptom-free and able to take adequate care of her children. The father, a handsome and intelligent man, had lived at home only intermittently. The grandmother did not tell Addie about her mother's death. Two weeks later a neighbor child told Addie that she had attended the mother's funeral service, and the grandmother then confirmed the mother's death to Addie and her sisters, the latter then aged three, and one and a half years old. At the mother's funeral Addie's father informed the grandmother that he would not care for the children and that they should permanently live with her. The grandmother did not share this news with the children either but told them that their father was out of town, which indeed was true as he had left the city at once. One year after the mother's death and father's desertion the neighbor child again told Addie in graphic terms of seeing her mother dead. Addie at this point developed a rigidly stiff neck. Medical examination showed no organic cause and Addie's stiff neck subsided considerably after an interview with the evaluating psychiatrist, who talked with her about her mother's death and suggested that she must be very angry at her father for leaving her. Addie was enrolled at the local day care center several months later and, at the insistence of the grandmother, the nursery staff consulted with a child analyst regarding treatment. Psychoanalysis was arranged, with my seeing Addie in an office at the day care center. I continued to see her there for many years after Addie stopped attending the center and entered public school.

Addie's family lived in extremely cramped quarters in a black ghetto area. The family's income consisted of the grandfather's social security and welfare payments. There were many times of acute hardship within the family as well as violence and sexual acting out around the family in its immediate environment. Nevertheless, the grandparents maintained a solid, decent family life, with close-knit warm relationships and adequate need fulfillment for the children. Legal adoption by the maternal grandparents was implemented one year after start of analysis.

Addie's mother had married early and died in her mid-twenties. The father, only two years her senior, was handsome and charming, also artistically gifted, but in moral outlook quite unlike the mother's family. He was often drunk, abusive, and delinquent. He spent one year in the reformatory when Addie was a toddler and he never supported his family. There were seven moves during Addie's life with her father and mother, usually because there was no money for rent. During Addie's fourth year the father often was not home but would force his way into the house, then leave again unpredictably. During Addie's treatment he lived in different cities and continued to be in difficulties. She saw him briefly a couple of times until he returned to live in her home town when Addie was just over ten years old. Addie's paternal grandmother maintained some contact with Addie and her sisters throughout, and kept alive her belief that her son would settle down, marry again, and care for his children.

The major symptoms which led to the referral for analysis were the tendency to stiff neck; bossiness with sisters and willfulness or disobedience with the grandmother; withdrawal at school; difficulty in falling asleep; and confusion regarding her mother's death, with a belief that she was alive and would come back.

In the second to third month of treatment Addie had many questions about my family. When this was related to her own first family she stated that her father had killed her mother, later correcting herself that the mother was sick and died. Shortly after, anticipating the summer vacation, Addie feared that the analyst would die, killed by her father as her mother had been killed.

Addie's greed for things was insatiable, as was her intense taking in with her eyes without ever remembering what she was taking in. This was interpreted as her hunger for people and her longing for her mother and father and the analyst in the transference. Addie frequently pretended to make "magic tricks" with her eyes. She would cross her eyes or move them in different directions. She stated that in this way she could make the analyst appear twice or move him to different places. We understood that this was partly an attempt to make her past history nicer and easier to think about, as her grandmother recalled it, rather than the truth which was painful to think about. Her magic eye tricks also represented her wish to make one person into another, to change the analyst into her mother. Work on these aspects of the material brought instances of acute longing for her mother—for example at a kindergarten party where the other children had their mothers and she only had her grandmother, and at home, where she was jealous of her uncles and her grandmother's appreciation of their achievements. She also began to recall somber memories of her father hitting her mother, of his not bringing food or money home. She had to relive the truth in all details. In one poignant session Addie said that she wanted to tell me a secret about her father. "Did my daddy get drunk? Did he hit my mommy? Did he feed himself but not us? Did my mommy have to call the police? Did my grandma and grandpa have to feed us because he wouldn't?" She answered all her own questions with a sad, "Yes."

Addie was very provocative and agressive with me. This softened somewhat when I limited her in her acting out, with the explanation that this would help her to feel less guilty and less needful of punishment. She then brought in her own guilt regarding her mother's death by telling first of a friend whose mother had died in a fire and whom the friend failed to rescue. Later she recalled persuading her mother to let her father into the house, at which time the father beat the mother. Usually Addie had asked her mother not to let him in. For a considerable period Addie identified with the hurt and damaged mother, asking to be punished and beaten, wanting to bleed and be run over by a car, asking the therapist to stick pins into her. This led to Addie's memories of witnessing the primal scene while hiding under the bed and her confusion between fights, illness, medical care, and sexuality. From all of this Addie had to extricate her concept of sexuality and death. The confusions made it both fearsome and desirable to be like the mother. But loving and hurting also represented an aspect of her relationship with her mother, reconstructed from an incident in which Addie rebelled at a volunteer lady who combed the children's hair. In the following session Addie loved and mistreated the doll's hair, which led to her missing of this kind of loving-hurting care by her own mother.

Addie could not tolerate sleeping alone. She shared a bedroom with her two sisters because it was not possible for her to have her own room. She not only did not want her own room but insisted on sharing a bed with one of her sisters despite efforts of the grandparents to keep her in her own bed. This problem appeared to have several meanings. One aspect we came to understand as being a protection against the wish to masturbate. As long as another child shared her bed, Addie could ward off her urge to masturbate. Another aspect was a link to Addie's earlier life with her mother. Addie's mother was lonely with her husband away from her most of the time. It was the mother's custom to watch television late at night with Addie sharing the bed with her. The analysis of these factors led to a resolution of the sleep problem.

About two years after the start of analysis an aunt, who closely resembled Addie's mother, suddenly appeared on the doorstep in the midst of a snowstorm. Addie became extremely attached to this aunt during her two months' stay, believing at first that her own mother had reappeared. When the aunt left, everyone in the family missed her except Addie who instead reacted with a recurrence of her stiff neck, and with a period of leaving analytic sessions early, turning passive into active. The interpretation of this defense led to a recollection of her mother's many visits to the doctor. Addie was confused about why her mother had gone to see the doctor so often. She herself had had little experience with doctors prior to her treatment. She recalled that her mother was exhausted upon return from appointments with doctors. The mother also went to doctors to get new babies. It seemed to Addie that everyone who left her became excited or died. We could understand the symptom of the stiff neck as an identification with those who leave to get excited and killed. One aspect of the stiffness represented the father's personal and sexual attributes. Another aspect was to be stiff and dead like her mother in the funeral home, as the neighbor child had described her.

After working on the feelings about her own true life history, her confusion about sexuality and death, and her identification with the hurt mother, Addie could deal with the concept of death. She came to it by becoming interested in seeing dead people in a funeral home and, later, by visiting her mother's grave for the first time. This period was ushered in by work on Addie's hyperactivity. It was understood to represent a way of warding off the dreaded stiffness of death. The visit to the cemetery helped Addie to formulate her own concept of death and to differentiate herself from her grandmother in this respect. The visit to the grave was a turning point in Addie's ability to come to terms with the concept of death with which she had grappled for some time and which she had to work out without the grandmother's support. The grandmother feared going to the cemetery; she sometimes threatened Addie when she was naughty that the mother would turn up in Addie's dreams, all signs that the grandmother could not quite face the reality of death. She had resisted Addie's request for a visit to the cemetery with, "What do you want to go there for? There is nothing but bones."

However, the corresponding affect of sadness was much more difficult to reach. Addie always wondered how people feel after a family death, wanting to hear of how sad others were, for example, after President Kennedy's death, but always reacting angrily herself with, "I never feel sad." This was again very prominent after Martin Luther King's death, when she viciously attacked me. Interpretations of anger being used to ward off sadness were given often but did not basically affect her defense. Her grandmother had similar difficulty with sadness. She was unable to mourn her daughter's death, and, on being reminded of sad feelings, burst out with anger.

One day Addie was very upset by a picture in a magazine showing a sad-looking Korean child who had lost his parents and needed adoption. I suggested that it was hard for her to see the sad look of the Korean child because it reminded her of how she felt about losing her parents. At the same time, Addie often looked for sadness in my face, imputing this feeling to me or anticipating it in me. Interpretations of projection of her own sadness were met with much resistance.

On a few occasions Addie's sadness burst out suddenly in an overwhelming way. Once on a visit to her aunt out of town, when the aunt promised to take her own child somewhere but not Addie or her sisters, Addie cried and sobbed for hours. That night she wet her bed, which could be linked to her crying. Another time, when she felt the teacher had been unfair and had withdrawn her love, Addie came home and cried for six hours inconsolably. In the transference she developed a symptom of slight wetting after analytic hours, which was again seen as displaced tears relating to leaving and being left. But these signs of sadness and softness were strongly warded off at other times by a hard, brittle attitude. In part this stemmed from her feelings of being rejected by her father and defensively identifying with him as she saw him: seductive, cruel, heedless of the feelings of others, and immune to hurt himself. If you show warmth you expose yourself to being hurt, was her conviction, based on her memories of father with mother and her own experiences with her father.

Addie's sadness could be reached in a truly meaningful way only when I dealt with her continued scrutinizing of my face and her expectation of my being sad. I interpreted this as a transference manifestation and suggested she was recalling her mother's sadness. I told her that she must have looked at her mother's face very closely and have been very concerned about her mother's feeling of sadness. When I discussed this reconstruction with the grandmother, she reluctantly and painfully confirmed that the mother had suffered from a chronic depression during Addie's early years. We could then see that Addie's repeated fantasies about the therapist's "perfectly happy family" were a defense against recalling the sad memories about her own early life with her depressed mother. When Addie insisted that her not getting over her problems made my life miserable, I interpreted it to mean that she must have felt she was responsible for her mother's sadness, that her misbehavior and naughtiness had caused it. The analytic work with Addie enabled her to be sad at appropriate times, for instance during a serious illness of her grandmother, when she missed friends who were separated from her, and in accepting the limitations of her father's personality and his inability to maintain a relationship with her.

From the beginning, Addie expressed unusual fear that she would not be able to remember people during their absence. This was repeatedly worked on in the transference but the problem was not resolved. When the grandmother was hospitalized Addie again feared she would not remember her and was greatly relieved on a visit to the hospital to find that she had remembered. After we worked on the material concerning the sad face of her depressed mother, Addie no longer feared that she would forget how absent people looked.

At the start of her analysis Addie maintained close relationships with her grandparents, but her dead mother and absent father were still her oedipal love objects. As she gradually decathected these object representations she transferred her oedipal attachment to the analyst. Addie brought a great deal of material about wanting me exclusively. She worried about what my wife would think of my association with her. She had thoughts about marrying me and taking me away from my family. She was jealous of my speaking to anyone else at the nursery school where I saw her. She feared my wife would take revenge on her. Each time she saw a white lady near the nursery school Addie hid, fearing it was my wife coming to hurt her. I pointed out how she avoided conflict with her grandparents by displacing her oedipal feelings to me and my wife. How come she worried so much about how my wife, a stranger, would feel about her, when she didn't seem to care how her grandmother felt? I suggested it was safer to think about marrying me than her grandfather because that would make her angry at grandmother and might make grandmother jealous. She brought fantasies about my sexual life with my wife. When I asked her why she never thought about her grandparents' sexual activities, she protested that they were too old for that. I suggested that she couldn't think of her grandparents having a sexual life because it made her angry about being left out and put her in danger of repeating the feelings she experienced when she was a young child with her parents.

The oedipal phase with her grandparents was a slow and difficult process for Addie to work through. For a long time she had a need to deny that her grandmother was a person who possessed feelings of anger or sexuality. On a visit out of town Addie could for the first time let herself hear her grandmother get angry and swear. A few weeks later she reported that the grandmother had sworn at and threatened some boys when they had approached Addie and her sisters to steal the girls' Halloween candy. Eventually Addie resumed her oedipal development with the grandparents. She was greatly helped by the wholesome relationship between the grandparents and by the fact that the grandfather was a very nice father, both to his own sons and to Addie and her sisters. She was able to resolve her oedipal conflicts and entered latency with an appropriate development of super ego and ego ideal. Addie could identify with the best of what she remembered from her mother as well as with the grandparents' attitudes. She was able to make an adequate school adjustment despite a weakness in mastering mathematics. Relationships with her siblings and peers improved as she became less bossy.

Addie dealt very differently with the death of her mother and the loss of her father. Initially, Addie identified with father by becoming harsh to ward off being soft, feminine, hurt, and killed. However, she also clung to him with hopes of oedipal gratification. When she received news about her father or when he made an occasional appearance, her hopes would be aroused, only to be followed by a great feeling of rejection. After Addie worked out her confusion between death and sexuality, the mother's death no longer represented a rejection to her. In regard to father, however, she continued to feel that he was away because he did not want her. This showed itself in the transference relationship too. When I went away on vacation or on weekends Addie felt humiliated. It was a hurtful rejection. She was able to accept her mother's death long before she could stop feeling her father's absence as a terrible narcissistic hurt. She eventually could see that he was disturbed, rather than interpreting his behavior as a personal insult. Addie could achieve her final "distance" from the father only after he was actually living in her home town again, when she was already in prepuberty. At that time he complicated Addie's pubertal feelings with his increased seductiveness, which alternated with withdrawals. In contrast to her younger sisters, however, Addie was much more realistic about her father's return and used his presence to further work out achieving her emotional independence from him, while her sisters were swamped by unrealistic expectations and excitements.

During prepuberty, Addie's missing of her mother and fear of

becoming like her were revived around discussions of menses. She
was concerned about the possibility of bleeding like her mother, an
early confusion of menstrual bleeding with the mother's symptomatic
bleeding during the terminal phase of her illness. She particularly
missed her mother when she reached the point when a girl would or-
dinarily talk to her mother about menstruation and related matters.
There was some resentment that I had to tell her things which her
grandmother could not talk about. She developed a respect for her
own body, which she associated with coming to terms with her own
sexuality. Several years later during adolescence she told me about
her ability to understand her body and protect herself from the sexually stimulating activities of her peers. Having achieved an integrated image of herself as a woman allowed Addie to make selective identifications with the healthy aspects of people.

Seth was a slight, handsome boy of almost seven years when he entered analysis. His mother had been dead for about three years and he had acquired a stepmother. When not unduly anxious he was friendly and outgoing with almost everyone and, especially with policemen, whom he seemed to revere.

Policemen had been important in Seth's life. When he was one year old he fell down a flight of stairs and was rushed by squad car to a nearby hospital for X rays. Fortunately he was not seriously injured. Three years later, when his mother fell out of bed and lay helpless on the floor, policemen were called to pick her up.

Seth's mother had suffered from lassitude throughout his babyhood. Perhaps it was her relative immobility which he reflected in not walking until he was around eighteen months old.

When he was three and a half, his sister Sally was born. Mother began to toilet train him at that time, but it was difficult for both of them. He resisted and never quite accomplished it, and she became more tired and weak until, in less than a year, she was unable to do housework or care for the children.

Her death came as a complete surprise to everyone, even though her condition had seriously deteriorated, because her illness was undiagnosed and suspected to be psychosomatic. Only when she fell out of bed and was unable to get up did the doctor feel she needed hospitalization in order to undergo a thorough diagnostic workup. Two weeks after her fall she packed her bag, said goodbye to the children, walked with her husband to the car, and rode to the hospital. Seth watched her from the window as she got into the car and rode away.

It was the last time Seth saw her. She died in the hospital on the following day. While the cause of her death was not immediately known, his father, a kind and gentle man, explained her death to him right away. He was completely realistic in his explanation. Mother had died: she had stopped eating, breathing, moving, and feeling; and her body would be buried in the ground. Seth was sad and cried briefly but did not ask questions or make comments. Therefore, when the father later learned the cause of the mother's death, he found no opening to explain the obscure illness that had claimed her life. For Seth, the cause of her death was unknown.

Seth did not go to his mother's funeral and did not see her grave until a year had passed. When taken to see it, he again cried softly but said nothing.

After the mother's death, the father and his two children moved into his parents' home. The grandparents were warm, loving people who tried very hard to do everything they could for the children in order to relieve their unhappiness. They even sought professional help in order to help Seth talk about his feelings and memories of his mother, but it seemed of little practical use. The father, for his part, became very despondent when reminded of his dead wife and could not bear to talk about her or to recall the past. Seth started nursery school several months after his mother's death. He was reported to be a "good" and nice boy, but with difficulty in all areas of spontaneous expression—talking, dancing, singing, art. During his kindergarten year he sometimes asked where his mother was, but that was all he said about her.

When his father told him of his plans to remarry, Seth's behavior regressed and symptoms developed. The father remarried when Seth was six years two months old. The couple had a short honeymoon alone and then lived with the two children in a single room for several weeks before moving into their own home. Contact with the grandparents was interrupted, with the aim of strengthening Seth's ties to the stepmother.

Seth's neurosis and attendant symptoms reached a peak after his father remarried. Uppermost was his complete disregard of bodily safety, shown in running into the street without looking and jumping from high places. He was hyperactive, preoccupied, confused, and unable to concentrate on schoolwork. With his stepmother he maintained a sado-masochistic relationship, toward his sister he was alternately excited and aggressive. Seth was destructive of his clothes and toys, messy in eating and appearance, given to temper tantrums, enuretic and encopretic. He complained of many bodily aches, could not easily fall asleep, and was phobic about leaving home.

Nine months after his father remarried, Seth entered analysis. His defenses were manifold and generally typical of a child two or two and a half years old: denial, avoidance, passive into active, reversal, bodily discharge (especially hyperactivity) in lieu of feelings, magical omnipotent thinking, and primitive identification. Instinctually his anal-sadistic impulses prevailed, to some extent at least, in the form of regression. His relationships were plagued by severe ambivalence.

During the first few weeks Seth introduced three major themes: his problem over his loyalty conflict and difficulty in fusing love and anger within one relationship ("I love my old mommy and I love my new mommy"); his wish for real knowledge about his mother's death and his fear that he had caused it ("What did my mommy die of?"); his fear that he had been brought to the clinic as a deadly punishment for his badness. He told stories about a boy who was left, ran away, and ended up in a hospital to die.

Seth's difficulty with his loyalty conflict showed, at first, in ambivalence to the therapist and fearful claims that all was well at home with his love for the new mother. But soon the therapist became the "good mother" in the transference, and he allowed himself to bring forth his dislike and fear of the stepmother.

From the beginning, the home reality presented a serious problem, namely the stepmother's overt aggression which was so severe that she represented a true bodily threat to him. This made it necessary for him to deny or distort real events at home and made it impossible in the analysis to explore castration anxiety in psychic terms. In addition, although the stepmother had urged the referral to analysis and needed the therapist's support, she also found it hard to tolerate Seth's relationship with the therapist. Within several months of the start of treatment, the stepmother developed an acute neurotic depression and was hospitalized for about a month. She gradually returned home and, with the help of psychotherapy, achieved a more controlled adjustment. Housekeepers and the paternal grandmother provided the daily care of house and children.

When the stepmother was hospitalized, Seth's fear that he had made her sick was discussed, and much time was spent on clarifying the differences among his real mother's bodily illness, his stepmother's mind sickness, and his own "feeling troubles."

Seth's concern about the cause of his mother's death led to his father's explaining the facts to him. Later he asked to visit her grave with father, and he managed it with appropriate sadness and thoughtfulness.

Knowing the reality about his mother's death helped Seth to explore his psychic reality about it. He feared he had killed her with "sick power," a magical power from which he needed to protect people—a theme enacted many times in the transference. "Sick power" was rooted in his anal-sadistic anger and, in part, was expressed by his bowel-movement pellets which he threw about the room as if they were bombs of destruction. At the same time his BM represented a union with his mother, babies, and mother herself. His withholding of BM until he soiled and his extreme reluctance to flush the toilet were due to his fear of losing these part objects. He felt weak and limp after evacuating, and spoke in what he called a "cold voice." His identification with his dead mother was seen both as a fear of illness and hospitals and as a wish to join her in death. His repeated jumping and falling attested to his identification with her. He could recall the tragic time when mother fell, and he was powerless to help himself and her. A reconstruction was made to the effect that at that time of overwhelming, he had soiled himself, losing inner control as well.

With this work on Seth's anal and sadistic fantasies about his mother's death, Seth regained a phallic position, albeit with many ups and downs. His extreme castration anxiety manifested itself in bodily exhibitionism: open masturbation, bodily risk, and clowning and silliness which reflected his lack of self-esteem. His extreme guilt was closely linked to his masturbation and feeling of inadequacy. He constantly acted in such a way as to make people think he was a bad boy.

This attitude particularly interfered with his schoolwork, and eventually he had to be enrolled in a special class. Interpretations of his guilt and castration anxiety helped sufficiently to enable him to adjust in the new class and eventually to catch up to his grade level.

Along with the phallic position, Seth evolved new fantasies about the death of his mother. He pretended to stab her to death, played hair-raising games of cars crashing, and listened excitedly to noises from other rooms. It was hypothesized that he had observed parental intercourse, but this was never analyzed.

Toward the end of the first year of analysis Seth's behavior had considerably improved, mainly because he had worked through some of the infantile anxieties about his mother's illness and death, which had terrorized him earlier. As he put it, "I now understand better about my first mommy." The stepmother was improving sufficiently to be in the home again, and the father was doing all he could to support her.

With a measure of stability at home, it became apparent that the stepmother could not build a relationship with Seth as long as he was in treatment. The situation was discussed with parents and child, the ending of the analysis was set for several months ahead, and the assurance of follow-up contact was given. It was clearly understood that Seth's analysis was unfinished, and it was hoped he would be able to have more treatment when older.

Seth reacted to the pending separation from the analyst by becoming bodily unsafe and, at the same time, expressing an earnest wish to get in touch with his dead mother. His unsafety was related to his upset about feeling unprotected by the therapist, much as he had felt unprotected when his mother died. It was also related to his fear that his excitement, anger, and masturbation would get out of control and cause him bodily harm. But Seth also wanted to get hurt so that he would be hospitalized and die. He had long "conversations" with his dead mother and strung tape "wires" in the treatment room in order to call her up. Often the therapist had to restrict his climbing to keep him safe. One day he climbed onto a windowsill, fell, and broke his elbow. He was taken to the hospital where his arm was casted. In time the fracture healed without residual damage. To a large extent the accident related to Seth's anger and sadness at the therapist's leaving him and his defense of turning aggression against himself. Early feelings about his mother were revived in this way in the transference and could be worked on.

Although some difficulties remained, later contact with Seth showed that he could progress in his personality development and attain a fairly good adjustment.

Seth's inability to care adequately for his body contained meanings from every phase of his development, including the initial early period with his mother. It seems she could not properly protect him when his gross motor activities began.

At the time of his mother's death, after years of increasing weakness and incapacity on her part, Seth either had not outgrown the anal-sadistic phase or had, in great part, regressed to it. His ambivalence, anger, and guilt, as well as inadequately expressed sadness, caused an inability to mourn the lost object and became a serious interference in his further maturation. The second loss of love object, the paternal grandmother, although not a loss through death, upset his precarious defensive balance. These losses, compounded by the stepmother's difficulties and, perhaps, the experience of the primal scene, caused acute regression and exacerbated earlier difficulties as well as creating new ones.

by Marion J. Barnes

The family's first contact with the therapist long predated the tragic event of Kathy's father's death. The mother and father were a happy young couple, devoted to each other and to their children, Ted, aged four, and Kathy, a young toddler. Danny, their third child, was not yet born. The mother sought help for Ted's hyperactive uncontrolled behavior. A few sessions with the parents dealt primarily with the father's roughhousing with Ted and were successful in bringing about some changes in handling after which Ted's behavior improved. At that point the family moved to another state because of father's change of job.

The mother again enlisted the therapist's help some two years later because Ted, then in his sixth year, had developed some very troubling symptoms after the father's death, which had occurred four weeks previously. Ted's problems related to his feeling of responsibility for his father's death. In addition to the oedipal aspects there were the real circumstances. Ted had disobeyed his parents by walking through a swampy area. The father, in looking for Ted, had walked through the same swamp and gotten wet. The following day, Ted was ill with a cold. Quite shortly, the father also developed a virus infection, became seriously ill, was hospitalized and died forty-eight hours after admission to the hospital. All members of the family were ill at this time and Danny, the eleven-month-old youngest child, was hospitalized at the same time as the father (see the analyst's report on p. 198).

On hearing of the father's sudden death, the mother, shocked and distraught, immediately shared the news with Kathy and Ted and left town with them to arrange the father's funeral. Kathy and Ted did not attend the funeral but stayed with their grandparents during that time. Within the week the mother returned with her older children and brought Danny home from the hospital. She sold their home in a few days and moved with all three children to their former state of residence. They lived there from then on in the maternal grandparents' home. The mother remained at home to care for the children.

During the initial work with the mother, Kathy was discussed least of the children because her difficulties were the least dramatic. Kathy was a "perfect" baby, a good eater, alert and beautiful. When she was a little over one year old the family moved to another state. It was learned later that she had a period of loss of appetite following this move. At fourteen months Kathy had a great fear of being bitten. The pediatrician advised the family to get a kitten. This cat was quite aggressive, scratched and bit everyone except Kathy, who was very fond of the cat and indeed lost her fear of being bitten. Having watched her older brother, Kathy toilet-trained herself at eighteen months. She was already very verbal at that time but had some difficulty in expressing negative feelings. She was very clumsy as a toddler. There were many falls which resulted in damage to two of Kathy's teeth. At about age three, orthopedic shoes greatly helped her coordination and there were no more falls after that. Other aspects of motor development proceeded more smoothly and provided much pleasure for Kathy. She dressed herself by two years with great pride, mastered many activities and was a keen helper to her mother in the house. As a baby and toddler, Kathy sucked her forefinger for comfort and was attached to a blanket. Both these habits subsided by the time she was about two and a half years. Her only younger sibling, Danny, was born when Kathy was nearly three years old. Beginning at that time, and increasingly during her fourth year, Kathy entered the oedipal phase. She had always been the father's openly acknowledged favorite and was even more so now. He loved her curly long hair and always hugged and picked her up first when he returned from work. Kathy was equally fond of him. With the mother she showed beginnings of identification; she liked to cook with her and helped make the beds. She also had a keen interest in all kinds of age-appropriate neutral activities and was very handy with paste and scissors. She could concentrate for long periods of time and took great pleasure in achievement.

The father's sudden death occurred when Kathy was three years ten months old. The major stresses of the first two weeks included the funeral in another town, the week's hospitalization of little Danny and the sale of their home. After that Kathy was faced with the task of adjusting to a new home without daddy, with both brothers severely upset, with her mother still preoccupied and affectively changed. She had known her grandparents from occasional visits but Kathy's attempts to build closer relationships with them encountered many obstacles. The grandfather preferred the boys and the grandmother's high standards of cleanliness were not suited to young children's ways of life and play.

During the first days and weeks following the father's death, Kathy cried and showed overt sadness on many occasions. She suffered loss of appetite and resumed sucking her forefinger and using her old blanket which had been given up for one and a half years. Soon, however, she also said, "I don't want to be sad." At times she even showed a euphoric mood, suggesting reversal of affect. The mother mourned deeply but had considerable difficulty in expressing sadness and grief. Her containment of feelings appeared to interact with Kathy's. With help, the mother could share a little more of her own sadness with the children, talked with them about the father and reassured Kathy that it was all right to be sad about some things, like the death of their daddy. Kathy's euphoria subsided after these discussions but an unusual degree of affective control persisted. This led the therapist to refer Kathy to the Hanna Perkins Nursery School, mainly for preventive reasons. Kathy entered the school five months after her father's death, at the age of four years and three months. She attended for over two years, completing the kindergarten year. Weekly appointments with the mother continued throughout this period and extended into Kathy's first year of public school. Less intensive contact with the mother was maintained for some time later.

When Kathy entered the Hanna Perkins Nursery School her separation from the mother was marked by great affective control and a speedy adjustment. After one week she was ready to stay at school for lunch and even wanted to stay longer. She expressed few feelings of missing her mother and quickly adapted herself to all the new routines and expectations. Kathy's control of feelings took its toll. She did not make close relationships with the teachers or children. She was not sure when to show anger appropriately. She could not defend her property but would call to a teacher for help. Later, she would tell a child herself, "Don't push me," but only when a teacher was nearby.

Kathy talked about her father at once, "My mommy taught me to paint and my daddy teaches me to swim," adding, "My daddy died." This was characteristic of Kathy. She immediately informed everyone she met of her father's death. This was understood as an attempt to prevent others from bringing up the topic and to cut short all discussion of it by stating the facts. On the third day of Kathy's nursery school attendance, a turtle died at school. She wondered whether she had fed the turtle too much. When another child put the dead turtle back into the tank, Kathy insisted on removing it. She stated that the dead turtle did not belong there. It should be buried. It might make the live turtle dead. In general, Kathy showed a good understanding of the concrete aspects of death.

Three months after entering school, Kathy visited her father's grave for the first time. She wanted to go but was also reluctant and cried bitterly. She brought flowers and placed them on his grave, and asked many questions that were too painful for the mother to answer. ''Are there snakes in the ground?'' ''Has the box come apart?'' Most of the time, and in spite of her own difficulties in these areas, the mother struggled bravely to help Kathy understand the reality and to express feelings. At moments of extreme stress the burden was too great.

During the following few months, Kathy, now aged four and a half years, experienced several partial withdrawals by those she loved and depended on. Danny began to walk again. It was his first resumption of motility since the father's death and his own hospitalization. As Danny's new activity was very intense and heedless, the mother's attention had to focus on him in a new way and he absorbed much of her time. Ted had, until this time, chosen Kathy as his main companion in games which she dominated and controlled. Now he became more independent, joined his peers and refused to continue his earlier exclusive play relationship with her. The grandfather's preference for the boys resulted in an ever closer tie with them. Kathy was excluded from these relationships and from some of the treats and gifts the boys received. To make matters worse, the development of an orthopedic problem required that Kathy wear a cast on one leg for six weeks. Intensive and good preparation for this procedure by the mother and teachers could not fully avert the blow this represented to Kathy.

These experiences complicated and enhanced Kathy's phallic-oedipal development. Her penis envy became very pronounced. Initially she warded it off in a variety of ways, for example by constantly wanting to wear fancy clothes and jewelry. Her masturbation increased, partly as a consequence of having again given up finger-sucking and her blanket, partly in response to the enforced immobility. It appeared to be particularly trying for Kathy to have her motility restricted so severely at the time when her younger brother became so very hyperactive and had to have mother follow him everywhere. It was learned also that masturbation had been a long-standing difficulty for Kathy. She had many questions about conception during this time and repeatedly asked whether the father used his hands to make the baby. The mother sensitively discussed with Kathy her developmental concerns and questions and helped her to differentiate the current changes and events from their instinctual meanings. This relieved Kathy's troubles only to an extent.

Kathy's appetite became quite poor again as it had after the father's death, and before that, after the family's move when she was just over a year old. Now she also became quite messy with her food. This further strained her relationship with her grandmother who, until this time, had at least viewed Kathy as less disorderly than the boys. Kathy lost interest in neutral activities. Her good work deteriorated and she tended to be more messy with art and play materials. She turned to competing and playing with the boys. She became demanding with the teachers, irritable and petulant with her mother. In conflict over her ambivalence, she insisted on being kissed at night and reassured of mother's love. Her lovely hair, so treasured by the father in the past, was terribly unkempt. When the mother had it cut in the hope that it would be easier to make it look pretty, it became even less neat, and Kathy bemoaned the loss of her hair. She was further distressed when her cast had to be replaced and the period extended for another two weeks. Yet when the cast was finally removed, Kathy's mood did not improve. She missed the attention and special favors she had received as a patient. Throughout this time she felt left out, deprived, and not well provided for. She showed deep sadness, crankiness, withdrew at times, had trouble sharing her possessions, and felt a great need for help from teachers and mother. At nap time she needed many toys. Watching a Charlie Brown program, in which Linus comforted himself with his blanket, revived Kathy's wish for her own blanket and the mother returned it to Kathy for a time.

During these months Kathy's longing for her father was particularly intense and accompanied by strong feelings. Both at home and at school she often commented about her daddy and all the activities he used to engage in with her. She now often talked of father as a hero and rescuer in the past and in fantasies. In her stories, father usually rescued her when she was scared and alone. The Christmas visit to her father's grave was marked by deep sadness in Kathy. She placed a wreath on the grave and wished for his return. She had no wish whatsoever for Christmas or birthday gifts. When asked for suggestions by mother and relatives, she just dejectedly said, "Nothing."

Oedipal conflicts and mourning for the dead father were closely linked. Even minor disappointments could no longer be handled by Kathy with her earlier striking self-control. Instead she showed open despair and was sad, angry, and unreasonable with her mother. For example, on one occasion the mother had promised sledding after nursery school but had to cancel the plan because the snow had melted by the afternoon. Kathy was inconsolable and her reproach then, as in similar situations, was, "I can't stand people breaking their promises." When mother took this up with Kathy, the latter reminded mother that, on the day prior to father's hospitalization, he had promised her a trip to the candy store for the next day. He could not keep this promise. Discussion of this helped Kathy to come to better terms with her anger at father's death and at the frustrations it had brought for her. She was openly sad about not having a father any longer and expressed how much she missed him, at home and at school. She had lost a balloon at that time and said, "There are only two things I want, my daddy and another balloon." Kathy's painful mourning, especially around the age of five, appeared to be a combination of mourning the real father and giving up the oedipal father. After accomplishing these tasks, her sadness and longing lessened considerably. In the latter part of her sixth year there were increased identifications and appropriate super ego development.

Other aspects of Kathy's difficulty with sad feelings were understood during the main mourning period. In the past she had not only warded off her own sadness but had also been very thoughtful and comforting of others when they were sad. In particular she used to concern herself with another nursery school child, a boy whose father had died. Kathy tried to distract him from his sadness by comforting and amusing him. She now recalled how very poorly her father looked on the day before his hospitalization. She said he had looked "sad" to her and she had connected this later with his dying, "I always felt if you're very happy you won't die." For this reason Kathy had tried to be happy following father's death. Her fear of dying had been observed on many occasions, especially when there was illness. When she herself was not well, she questioned whether all daddies died, would mother die, would she herself die, adding with much feeling, "I don't want to die because I don't want to be without you." The mother many times discussed these thoughts and feelings with Kathy and helped her to differentiate herself from the father's fate. Another aspect of Kathy's fear of death could be seen in connection with early super ego development. She was afraid of puppets ("the man who spoke but was not seen"). This caused her great anxiety at birthday parties and on other occasions. In spite of much work and discussion around this, she persisted for a long time in wanting mother or teacher close during puppet shows.

At this time the home situation became very difficult for Kathy. An uncle, of whom all the children were fond, left town. The grandfather was interested only in the grandsons. The grandmother became increasingly restrictive and critical of Kathy, especially when she expressed anger at her mother or longing and sadness about her dead father. Kathy had to show her feelings mainly at school. This concerned the mother and she decided to have a long talk with the grandfather; she pointed out his relative neglect of Kathy and helped him to understand how much the little girl needed his love. The mother also decided to move with the children into a house of their own. These changes helped Kathy somewhat, and regular visits with the grandfather served to maintain his improved attitude.

There were, however, new libidinal losses. Younger brother Danny entered Hanna Perkins Nursery School, which absorbed much of the mother's time and thought. At the grandparents', Kathy had shared a room with mother; now she slept alone. The move also coincided with the mother's beginning to date men, which Kathy at first experienced as a loss. At the beginning of kindergarten, orthopedic shoes were recommended for her. Whereas in early childhood these had helped Kathy's coordination and been appreciated by her, now she felt ashamed of them. She often changed to tennis shoes and some incidents of falling and undue clumsiness were repeated. The topic of the shoes served the mother as a starting point for much renewed work with Kathy on her feelings of inadequacy as a girl and her wish to be a boy. Kathy was helped by this. Her sublimations increased and she was a good learner. She developed an interest in horses, which assumed different forms over a period of time. Initially her clumsiness was supplanted by very active play at being a horse; this changed gradually to a preoccupation with drawing horses and a special liking for stories about horses. This play and interest represented the main identification with masculinity. Most of Kathy's identifications were feminine, modeled on the mother. Kathy's difficulty with phallic inadequacy was partly revived again in first grade when she had a particularly critical teacher. This teacher thought Kathy had poor eye coordination. The child underwent several tests, had to do optometric exercises, and glasses were prescribed. It turned out that the eye difficulty was very minor. Mother and Kathy discussed these events and related them to earlier concerns.

By the summer of her first grade Kathy had regained her equilibrium and showed good adjustment. From then on she was a well-structured latency girl enjoying success at school, in relationships, and in varied interests. Kathy was fond of the mother's serious suitors and accepted well her new stepfather when she was about ten years old. Her oedipal feelings, however, did not revive in latency to focus on these men.

Of the children in her family, Kathy appeared to have least difficulty in mourning her father. She did not experience guilt over the father's death and there seemed to have been little ambivalence in her relationship with him. She had begun her oedipal phase with her father and he remained her main oedipal object even after his death. Only later on, and to a certain extent, did Kathy extend some of these feelings to her grandfather. She did not use identification as a means of dealing with the loss of the father. Perhaps this added greatly to her prolonged sadness and longing. At the same time her continued active longing appeared to play an important part in helping her to experience oedipal feelings and to grapple successfully with her phase-appropriate conflicts. Although a residual cathexis of the father was still evident during Kathy's latency, the major decathexis of his object representation occurred at the time of the resolution of the Oedipus complex.

Kathy's initial difficulties with excessive control of feelings and in expressing anger and sadness predated the father's death but were augmented by it. She brought out some of her own reasons for not wanting to be sad, but her mother's attitude to expressing and accepting feelings appeared to play a more prominent role. The mother's recognition of this and her attempts to work with Kathy in this area were very helpful to her, as was the support of the teachers.

Kathy's difficulty with penis envy also appears to have predated the father's death. Had the father lived, however, there seems to have been a good chance that his appreciation of Kathy and his relationship with her could have sufficiently counterbalanced this conflict. Apart from the loss of the father at that crucial stage in development, Kathy also suffered many other losses, such as withdrawals of loved ones, loss of motility, diagnosis of a bodily "defect." At the phallic level these experiences alone would assume the proportions of a cumulative trauma which could have been too much for any child to cope with. Kathy, at the same time, had to contend with the death of her father. The mother was able to help her with these phallic conflicts each time they occurred. This working through enabled Kathy to master her feelings about being a girl.

7. Some Effects of the Parent's Death on the Child's Personality Development

Short and Long-Term Effects of a Parent's Death

When a loved person dies, the bereaved has a threefold task—to cope with the immediate impact of the circumstances, to mourn, and to resume and continue his emotional life in harmony with his level of maturity. None of these tasks is completed within a circumscribed period of time. Depending on internal and external factors, each task may present ongoing difficulties for the bereaved or it may be resolved in such a way as to impede functioning in later years. Within the personality, these psychic processes are interrelated and mutually influential, but there is merit also in recognizing the differences between them. Our clinical and theoretical understanding profited from examining them separately and in their interaction. Our understanding of these processes was gained through work with patients at the time of the parent's death or from treatment at a later period in their development.

We found that in some instances a child's difficulties stemmed primarily from his inability to cope with the impact of the circumstances of the parent's death. We include here the stresses connected with the form of death or those arising from major interference with the bodily and psychological need fulfillment following the death. In other cases the child's problem related especially to some aspect of the mourning process, for example failure to understand death, inability to tolerate sadness or anger, or pathological identifications. With a number of children the trouble lay predominantly in the establishment of new relationships and continuation of emotional development. In this phase the problem sometimes focused on conflicts with the stepparent. Inevitably, difficulties in one area overlapped with and affected those in another area. It proved clinically important to trace the patient's conflicts to their specific causes, and it helped our theoretical understanding to distinguish difficulties with mourning from other problems related to the parent's death.

The immediate stressful impact of the parent's death has been discussed—fear of death, difficulty in appropriate differentiation from the dead, anxieties related to the way in which the death occurred, concern with bodily and psychological need fulfillment. Some developmental differences in experiencing these concerns were emphasized, as well as the fact that the bereaved person's capacity to master them depends on internal and external factors—personality makeup, nature of actual experiences, extent of support from surviving loved ones. The individual variations and interrelations of these factors are infinite in number. Intensive psychoanalytic observation and exploration enabled us to come close to the necessary understanding in individual cases. Even using this approach, at the time of bereavement or through later reconstruction, there were inevitable limitations.

By comparing our data from many cases we come to feel certain that the circumstances of the loved one's death and the life situation in which it places the bereaved constitute an important set of events. Their impact on the individual and his means of dealing with them are a mental task separate from mourning. We found that some persons began their mourning while they still coped with their reactions to the immediate situation. With others the mourning process was delayed until they had come to terms with these anxieties. There were some whose mourning was jeopardized altogether because they could not master the stressful circumstances. No instance was observed in which mourning could appropriately proceed and be completed unless a person had first dealt adequately with immediate concerns and anxieties. It sometimes appeared that a patient had difficulty in mourning; closer study revealed that the patient's difficulty lay primarily in coping with his anxieties about the circumstances surrounding the death, which his mind could not master and his environment failed to allay.

The stress of the circumstances is usually greater for the younger child. This is due to his limited ability to test reality and to master anxiety, as well as to his bodily and psychological dependence on the adult. In some cases, however, the circumstances are so upsetting that even latency-aged and older children cannot cope with them adequately. Unmastered conflicts and anxieties may result in behavior difficulties and symptoms at the time of the initial stress or at a later date when additional hardships have produced a cumulative effect on the personality. They may also affect a child "silently"; that is, he may adopt defense measures or characterological solutions which at first appear adaptive but which later impede growth and adjustment because they are too rigid or extensive. The unmastered stress of the circumstances surrounding the parent's death also interferes with the child's ability to mourn, which further jeopardizes his chances of healthy development.

Geraldine was almost eight years old at the time of her mother's death (see the analyst's report on p. 69). She had experienced years of her mother's hospitalizations, operations and bodily disintegration. In the absence of realistic explanations, she linked her mother's illness with the parents' violence and sexuality, which she had repeatedly witnessed. After the mother's death Geraldine lived for one and a half years in the homes of relative strangers who barely met her bodily needs and did not intend to keep her. She used a number of defenses in order to maintain herself in the face of these stresses. She denied and repressed what she had seen, repudiated all aspects of sexuality and aggression in herself and others, and functioned like a "good" schoolgirl who made diligent intellectual efforts. In spite of lapses this adaptation served her well for some years. It ingratiated her well enough with her wardens so that they continued to care for her and it staved off her conflicts around her earlier experiences. Her strong defenses, however, contributed to her inability to mourn, prevented her from forming appropriate new relationships later, and jeopardized her adolescent development. At a later time of additional stress, her defenses proved inadequate and she developed severe hysterical symptoms.

After mastering the stressful circumstances surrounding the death, the bereaved person's next task is to adapt psycologically to the loss of the loved one. Mourning, as defined earlier, is the best means of accomplishing this adaptation because it paves the way for a continued healthy mental life. Through mourning, a bereaved person frees himself for establishing new relationships and enriches his personality with selected new identifications. Failure in mourning may present an obstacle to the individual's future growth and adjustment. This is particularly important with children at all stages of development when their parent dies. The child's maturation is not complete and, at least before late adolescence, he must invest his love in a parent figure in order to progress. Therefore the child is especially handicapped in his mourning for a parent, since he needs a parent's help with this task. Under favorable circumstances the surviving love objects can fill these gaps sufficiently to create a milieu in which a child can utilize his capacity for mourning and in which his efforts receive the necessary support.

For the purpose of the present discussion, the child's internal difficulties in mourning his parent are not separated from those that stem from external sources, such as the failure of his environment to extend sufficient help. In clinical work such a differentiation is important to understand the child's problems and to assist him in resolving them. In the following assessment of the effect on the child of an incomplete or pathological mourning, only the outcome of the combined internal and external factors will be considered.

At the stage of achieving object constancy and during the toddler period, the death of the parent, especially the mother, may deplete the infant's personality to the extent that the functions necessary for the mourning process may not be maintained. This not only prevents mourning but also seriously affects the child's functioning in some or all areas and manifests itself in immediately discernible pathology. Among some of our patients in this age group we observed loss of such recently acquired ego functions as walking and talking, failure of affective response, regression in object relationships, and impoverishment of the libidinal cathexis of the self-representation. Recovery of these aspects of the personality was a painfully slow and laborious effort. Even when educational and therapeutic help was available at once it had to extend over many years.[1] Many studies by others show that such damage cannot be repaired fully at a later period in the person's life (Bowlby 1951; Gyomroi 1963).

In other toddlers, in older preschoolers and latency children, the death of the parent did not interfere with the child's functioning. The continued absence of the parent, however, led to the child's inadequate investment of new functions and activities in some instances. With many of our patients, even those at the toddler level, basic personality functioning was not affected by the death of the parent. Al-

---

1. The case of Danny illustrates this work.

though they had reached different developmental stages at the time of their bereavement, the mental functions necessary for the mourning process were sufficiently developed and maintained. They encountered numerous difficulties, however, with different aspects of the mourning process so that they either could not complete it or did so in a pathological manner. Some of their symptoms and maladjustments resulted directly from their impeded mourning; others were caused by their inability to progress in their emotional development, an indirect outcome of the same difficulty.

Some could not master the initial steps in mourning, that is, understanding and accepting death and differentiating themselves from the dead parent. The children's difficulty in understanding and accepting death was intensified by inaccurate information conveyed by the adults. In time the children usually acquired some realistic knowledge through their own efforts at observation and exploration, but this sometimes brought them into conflict with the expectations and views of those on whom they depended. They then either rejected their own evidence and interrupted their quest for knowledge so that they never attained a coherent concept, or they guiltily maintained their ideas side by side with the adults' story. Death became linked to instinctual conflicts instead of being mastered intellectually and emotionally. Since these solutions were for the most part not arrived at consciously, the children's defensive struggles tended to lead to symptom formation.

Addie, aged four years, lived with her grandparents during her mother's terminal hospitalization (see the analyst's report on p. 140). She was not told of her mother's death and was expected not to know about it. She later learned the sad reality from a peer who had visited the funeral home and who initiated Addie into the forbidden knowledge of the concrete aspects of death. At first Addie managed to ward off her anxious thoughts and feelings, but a year later she developed a hysterical stiffness of the neck. She also became very hyperactive. In her analysis the stiffness of the neck was found to be related to the stiffness of the dead body, and the hyperactivity was seen to ward off the motionlessness of death.

The need to differentiate themselves from the dead was a special developmental difficulty for the youngest children, who were still in the process of delineating and stablizing their object and self-representations, especially in relation to the parent. The experience of death overtaking a beloved person sometimes constituted a great threat to themselves, endangered their feeling of personal safety and colored their later developmental concerns, for example castration anxiety at the phallic level.

Danny was only eleven months old when his father died of a viral infection (see the analyst's report on p. 198). Danny himself was hospitalized at the time and survived an infection of the type that took his father's life. Danny learned about death and the circumstances of his father's death from his mother and older sibling. His ideas about his father were closely linked to his feelings about himself because he had not only barely escaped his father's fate but bore his name and resembled him physically. During his phallic phase Danny was terrified of illness both in himself and in others. He always expected illness to be followed by death. Sometimes he warded off his anxiety by scaring others, at other times he denied injury to himself.

Many children of all ages encountered difficulties with aspects of the mourning proper. Among the causes were inappropriate defenses against affects, conflicts over ambivalence, inability to detach love from the deceased parent, undue proportion of identification, or identifications which were too primitive or pathological. The resulting symptoms and behavior problems encompassed a wide range. On the surface they did not appear to be related to the parent's death. There were hysterical symptoms such as amnesia; phobias, fears, and bad dreams; disturbances of ego functions such as restriction of motility or hyperactivity; difficulties in relationships with adults and peers, in learning, in frustration tolerance and self-control; apathy, truancy, stealing, accident proneness, and self-injury. For the most part these problems did not arise at once but tended to follow a long period of relatively appropriate functioning, marked by controlled behavior, subdued affective response, and little reference to the parent's death. The adults in the child's environment tended to regard this quiescent period as a sign of good adjustment, and even those who were concerned or puzzled at the child's apparent lack of reaction often welcomed it and hesitated to interfere by bringing up the subject of the dead parent. It was therefore striking that with the children who were referred for help some time after the parent's death the family usually did not relate their presenting problems to the bereavement.

Most frequently the child's maladjustment became manifest when his mourning difficulty interfered in his progressive development. In some instances the child remained arrested at the level he had reached at the time of the parent's death, in others he could not cope with the conflicts of the next maturational phase. This led to a pathological exaggeration of phase-adequate conflicts or to regression in some areas. In a number of cases such problems arose around the adjustment to a new parent, which highlighted the developmental failure and made it impossible for the child to resume his place in a normally constituted family.

A different problem arose for those children who were consciously grappling with their mourning but whose struggles were prolonged, intensified, and distorted because no new parent figure of the same sex as the deceased was available to them at the appropriate time. The further structuralization of their personality depended on two parents being available. In some cases this real lack led to a prolonged hypercathexis of the deceased. These children utilized every resource to maintain their image of the dead parent—such concrete reminders as photographs and belongings; and stories told them about the parent, describing his appearance, qualities, interests, and incidents in his life. They also modeled their ideas on observations of other children's parents and on their own fantasies, wishes, conflicts, and anxieties.

For the prelatency children this hypercathexis was particularly important and contributed to their chances of maintaining emotional health. It exposed them, however, to constant frustrations, anger, pain, and disappointment, as in many daily situations they were faced with the contrast between inner and outer reality and had to compare their hardship to the good fortune of peers. At the same time their relationship with the surviving parent was burdened. The libidinal attachment was intensified and insufficiently limited or frustrated by reality. Aggressive feelings against the surviving parent were also complicated. The children tended to direct their anger at the dead parent against the living one so that the latter would receive more than double the amount of anger. Yet the children's intense dependency on the only living parent made it particularly difficult for them to tolerate any anger against this parent. These complications placed a special burden on the child and on the parent–child relationship. They sometimes impeded the child's ability to resolve phase-appropriate conflicts and left their mark on the development of his character. Our experience suggests that the danger is especially great for the prelatency child whose oedipal experiences are affected and consequently imperil the formation of the super ego. Some children in that age group could nevertheless be helped to mature adequately.[2]

The child's ability to continue a healthy emotional life depends on his mastery of the previous tasks—coping with the stress of the circumstances surrounding the parent's death and mourning. It also depends on whether a new parent or parent figure is available at the appropriate time to provide, in Winnicott's words (1949), a "good enough" relationship.

When an adult is ready to reinvest his love he can actively seek a new person. The child cannot do that, particularly when he wants a new parent. The decision rests with the adults in his environment. The child under five years of age is quite helpless in this respect. Latency children can more easily procure for themselves helpful relationships with adults who fulfill a partial parental role. This differs from a defensive search for a parent substitute. Children in analysis, or those who were treated via the parent, usually assigned this role first to the therapist if he was the sex of the dead parent. Work with the patient showed to what extent healthy or defensive reasons predominated. It showed too whether the defenses helped or impeded the treatment process and the child's development at any given time.

Hank was four and a half years old when his father died suddenly (analyst's report on p. 129). Hank coped with his mourning with the help of treatment-via-the parent and progressed into latency. At six and a half years of age he left kindergarten but independently maintained contact with the male analyst who had worked with his mother and whom Hank had gotten to know well. Hank wrote him many letters and the analyst replied to them briefly, feeling that this contact was important and meaningful to the boy. Hank also became interested in woodwork, found a neighbor who shared his interest, and enrolled this neighbor as an advisor and older friend in regard to this hobby.

Jerry, Hank's older brother by one year, was close to six years at the time of the father's death. Jerry's more advanced personality structure and his set defensive patterns made it impossible for his

2. Danny and Kathy illustrate such a development.

mother to work with him at the time when she could still be helped to assist Hank. Jerry could not mourn, but repeatedly sought out father substitutes in order to ward off his longing and sadness. Invariably his contacts with these people proved disappointing and were interrupted by Jerry. For example, Jerry insisted on joining a father–son social group and enrolled a neighbor to accompany him. Jerry behaved very poorly in the group. It did not work out and he soon gave it up.

The adolescent is at a greater advantage. His need for a parent is less and he is more able to find new love objects. He is helped by his tendency toward object removal and by living more independently in the wider community with its opportunity for meeting a variety of people.

In some cases the main difficulty for the child arose from the unsuitability of a new parent and from the circumstances associated with such a change in the family's way of life.

Bobby's mother had died when he was two and a half years old. His grandparents had cared for him in their home following the mother's death and he had been close to them in spite of some difficulties. The father remarried after a brief courtship when Bobby was six years old. The family moved into a small apartment where Bobby shared the parental bedroom. The stepmother insisted on breaking off all contact with the grandparents and demanded Bobby's exclusive love. When he developed behavior problems she was appalled and alternately attacked Bobby and withdrew from him. Her mental condition deteriorated to the point where she was unable to care for Bobby.

Not all situations were so extreme, but several were serious enough to jeopardize the chances of a normal parent–child relationship, to cause new maladjustments in the children, and to reinforce their previous problems.

For some children the difficulty in continuing their emotional lives lay neither with their current environment nor with their pathological resolution of the tie to the dead parent. Rather it stemmed from personality difficulties which had preceded the loss of the parent and had not interfered with the child's mourning but handicapped his maturation.

Ken, aged thirteen, had been in analysis for some time when his father died suddenly. Thanks in part to analytic work he had already accomplished in relation to other losses, Ken could cope well with the circumstances of the father's death and mourned for about eighteen months. Ken's bisexual conflicts had mainly caused the symptoms for which he had come to treatment. These conflicts were not signficantly affected by the father's death and did not interfere with Ken's reaction to it, but they continued to affect his personality in the later phase of adolescence.

This does not imply that the death of a parent is ever a negligible event in the child's life. In some instances a child can be helped to cope with the tragedy of his loss and to mourn adequately. In others he may be so young that the parent was not yet a major love object for him and he was not affected by the stress of the immediate circumstances. In either case the child's life is from then on shadowed by the death of the parent. A parent who was well known and loved will forever be missed to some extent with each new developmental step, be it a new emotional phase or an important event, a period of personal distress or a time of special pleasure to be shared. A parent who was hardly known accompanies the child through life differently but remains as meaningful. What was my parent like and would he have liked me? Shall I be like him and would I have liked him? Am I glad that he died or am I angry that he is not with me? Above all the death of a parent faces the child with an early excess of helplessness at the hands of fate, a need to accept the utterly unacceptable at a time when his mental resources are not yet equipped for doing so. Some may be better able to cope with this tragedy than others; for all it becomes a lifelong burden.

Psychoanalytic studies of adults who lost a parent through death in childhood show various serious effects on the adult's mental health (Deutsch 1937; Jacobson 1965). Some of our colleagues had treated such adults but noted different pathological resolutions and interferences in later functioning. In our contacts with parents of child patients we repeatedly encountered interferences in parental functioning, which appeared to stem from the parent's experience of bereavement in childhood.

Effects of the Parent's Death on Developing Ego Functions

In patients who experienced the death of a parent as babies or toddlers, the stress appeared to affect basic aspects of their personality development. Our observations of them at the time of the parent's death, and analytic work with them at a later point in their development, showed that, in some, the impact resulted predominantly in instinctual fixation points. In others it caused deficiencies in the narcissistic investment of the self-representation. Sometimes it appeared to affect especially the ego's ability to deal with anxiety as, at each level, they dreaded being overwhelmed.[3] Our interest focused on several patients whose difficulties centered especially on interferences with developing ego functions.

Lisa was seen at eighteen months. She was a well-developed toddler with markedly good early speech development and comprehension and with even more advanced large- and small-muscle control. She used her motility safely and carefully with much pleasure and self-assurance and with justified trust and special enjoyment by her parents. During succeeding months her father's illness worsened rapidly. It was a period of turmoil and upset resulting in the parents' emotional withdrawal. They did not explain to Lisa anything about the father's illness or the reasons for their preoccupation. When Lisa was two years old her father died suddenly but Lisa was not told for several days. Already before the father's death Lisa's speech development had lost its impetus, apparently in response to the diminished parental investment and to the barrier in verbal communication about the parental illness and upset. Lisa's immediate reaction to the father's disappearance was that she abruptly stopped asking for him and about him but at once resumed this when her mother informed her that dad had died and would not come back. The mother subsequently maintained excellent verbal communication with Lisa in many areas, but a partial barrier persisted. The mother could not mourn and she discouraged Lisa's expression of sad and angry feelings about and memories of the father. Although she showed unmistakable interest, Lisa was never told the cause and circumstances of her father's death. Lisa's speech development began to lag and its infantile features were the

3. The case of Seth illustrates these aspects.

more striking the older she got. By age five she spoke in an unclear babyish manner, often lisping and becoming almost inaudible. She evidently did not enjoy talking and tended to express herself in action rather than words. During her analysis her speech improved when its infantilisms and restriction could be linked to Lisa's fear of expressing her feelings, particularly anger, and to her need to hide her thoughts and fantasies, particularly in relation to her father.

With the father's death Lisa lost not only his admiration of her motor skills but her mother too changed her attitude to Lisa's motility. She became much more fearful for Lisa's safety and restrictive of her exploits, especially as Lisa age-appropriately ventured into outdoor play. Some of Lisa's activities in play suggested that she linked bodily harm to her vague knowledge of her father's illness. Increasingly, Lisa's motility became distorted. She remained very active bodily but derived little pleasure from it and became clumsy and often unaware of what her body was doing. In her analysis this difficulty too was related to inhibition of aggression and to aggression turned against the self. Aspects that appeared to be related to Lisa's ideas about her father's death could not be explored before the end of her analysis.

Some of Lisa's lack of motivation and difficulty in learning stemmed from her disinterest in perceiving what went on around her and from her not gaining gratification in making observations of her own. She had been an intensely aware toddler, ready to explore everything and to ask questions about it. It appeared that she had also observed more of her father's illness and death than she could understand or get answers to. Her mother welcomed Lisa's observations in some areas but not in others. Before the onset of the phallic-oedipal phase, Lisa's cathexis of perception appeared only somewhat diminished. Following her conflicts of that phase, her difficulty in this area increased greatly, although the mother had been able to answer Lisa's sexual questions. The function of perception now suffered secondary interference by defenses. The analyst supported Lisa's capacity to observe and explore her outer and inner reality and helped her to gain a partial analytic understanding of her defenses against conflicts about her father's death. This helped her to make the developmental step into latency and to regain her interest in learning sufficiently for adequate academic progress.

It seemed to us that the development of Lisa's functions of perception, motility, and speech had suffered interference through the father's illness and death as well as through their aftermath. Lisa lost her father's intense positive investment in these functions. The mother's earlier equally great pleasure and encouragement underwent a considerable change. In some respects she continued to support Lisa's skills, in others she discouraged and restricted them as a result of her own unresolved concerns about the father's death and its repercussions on her relationship with her daughter.

Danny's functions of perception, motility, and speech also regressed under the stress of the circumstances associated with the father's death (see analyst's report on p. 198). During his hospitalization he lost the father's and mother's libidinal investment and through the experience of medical procedures he apparently suffered damage to the narcissistic investment of his body image and early self-representation. These libidinal depletions were followed by a life in which his mother's affective attitude changed to some extent. Although her love for and devotion to Danny were undiminished, her preoccupation with practical demands caused a partial withdrawal. Her own mourning, with its restrained sadness and lack of joy, affected her emotional expression. Her relative difficulty in expressing and accepting anger influenced her interaction with Danny, as well as her tendency to take over her children's self-protective functions. The subject of the father's death however did not represent a direct interference. The mother could be helped to discuss the father's illness and death with her older children quite soon. She gauged sensitively Danny's ability to understand and integrate these facts, assisted him with his concerns and answered his questions. Perception, speech, and motility were always encouraged by her. No aspect of these functions was forbidden or linked to the father's death. In spite of these helpful factors, recovery of development was very slow with each of the affected ego functions. They showed some distortions and were subject to secondary interference by defenses.

Lucy was ten weeks old when her mother died suddenly (see analyst's report, p. 219). In contrast to Lisa and Danny, whose development could be observed through treatment-via-the parent from the time of the parent's death and whose reactions could be studied later in analytic treatment during the phallic–oedipal phase, Lucy began her analysis in her eleventh year. The therapist had no previous knowledge of her development, and the family situation made it particularly difficult to obtain a consistent history. Lucy had attained a structured personality and was capable of establishing relationships in spite of many difficulties. Her entire personality, however, as well as her analytic work, was affected by her impaired synthetic function. Although many of Lucy's experiences throughout her childhood contributed to this problem, the analysis showed that the earliest damage to the developing integrative function was sustained during the first year of life. It affected the cohesion and stability of her body image and basic self-representation.

It appeared that the death of the mother when Lucy was ten weeks old constituted a serious interference and ushered in a period of changes during the next few months which augmented the harmful effects, including damage to the developing synthetic function. The family's later handling of the topic of the mother and her death further interfered with the development and use of Lucy's capacity for integration. Subsequent secondary interference by the defenses of denial, isolation, and repression played an important part.

The maturation of certain ego functions proceeds autonomously. However, the apparatus must be activated by instinctual energy and only gradually comes under the control of the ego (Hartmann 1950). The effect of a positive object relationship on these processes was discussed by A. Freud (1952). A number of authors studied the influence of the parent–child relationship on ego functions and compared the relative importance of this factor for the development of specific functions. A. Freud and Burlingham (1944) found that toddlers raised in a group setting lagged in speech but excelled in motility compared with toddlers raised in families. Provence and Lipton (1962) also found that, in the institution children they studied, the development of motor activity was least affected by the absence of a mother–child relationship. They noted, however, that the motility of these children gained in grace, purposefulness, and pleasure after a period of foster home placement. The authors suggest that the close, consistent relationship with a parent figure helps to bring motility more under ego control. Pine and Furer (1963) studied the effects of varying maternal attitudes on some of the toddlers' developing ego functions. In regard to their observations of motility they stated (p. 340), "In the normal toddlers, for example, the children not only worsen but also improve in certain kinds of functioning in the mother's absence, and also change in the quality of their functioning. In any of these cases there is a suggestion that the child's functioning is not yet autonomous but draws in some way upon the mother for its enhancement or impairment.''

We compared our data from the study of bereaved youngsters with material gained in our clinical work with other young children (R. A. Furman and A. Katan, 1969). Our experience suggests the following tentative formulation: each developing ego function requires a certain amount of instinctual investment, both from the child and from his main love object, in order to follow its maturational course and to establish itself as an autonomous function integrated in the service of the ego. A "good enough" emotional milieu is essential to these aspects of ego development. There is a critical period, from the beginning of the development of a function until it achieves autonomy and comes under ego control. During this period, withdrawal, imbalances, and changes in the instinctual investment may lead to interferences with the function. Although not altogether satisfied with the term, we called this a primary emotional interference with an ego function. This enabled us to differentiate it from a primary organic interference due to physical defects in the apparatus, and from a secondary interference caused by defensive measures. A primary emotional interference can have a variety of outcomes. It may lead to total arrest of the development of the function, to regression, to impairment or distortion. When arrest occurs, the function does not progress beyond the achieved level, as happened with Lisa's speech. Regression results in loss of the function, as was observed in Danny's speech and motility. This phenomenon was described by A. Freud (1965) as ego regression under stress. We noted impaired or distorted development in Danny's motility and Lucy's synthetic function.

We discussed the possible relationship between primary emotional interference in a developing ego function and later forms of ego regression. A. Freud distinguishes several types of functional regression (1965). In developmental regression, due to fatigue or illness and regression under stress, it is always the last-acquired function which is first lost. "In contrast to drive regression, the retrograde moves on the ego scale do not lead back to previously established positions, since no fixation points exist" (p. 104). As far as we know, Blos alone (1967) speaks of developmental ego regression harking back to specific points in early life. In his discussion of adolescent processes he writes, "Ego regression connotes the re-experiencing of abandoned or partly abandoned ego states which had been either citadels of safety and security, or which once had constituted special ways of coping with stress"; and, "Ego regression is, for example, to be found in the re-experiencing of traumatic states of which no childhood was ever wanting" (p. 173).

Our case material showed that functions which had suffered a primary emotional interference were frequently subject to later interferences. This appeared to be in part due to the function's delay in coming under ego control, in part due to secondary defensive interference. Could it be that a function which suffered primary emotional interference becomes the matrix in which later secondary interferences take place? Does this function remain more vulnerable to defensive interference when there is an early interference of this nature and full ego control is not achieved or is labile? Our clinical findings are insufficient to provide answers to these questions.

We agreed on a hypothesis yet to be tested: While instinctual fixation points are caused by excessive amounts of energy remaining at earlier levels of development, ego functions may have "weak points" in their early development owing to a deficiency in instinctual investment. These weak points may cause delays or distortions of ego function development and may in some instances contribute to later secondary defensive interference with ego functions.

Parental Bereavement Related to Earlier and Later Losses

In initial discussions of bereavement we noticed how frequently an object loss in adulthood revived earlier, particularly infantile, losses, and intensified the mourning. Many examples were given in which adult mourning was facilitated or handicapped by the manner in which object losses and developmental losses had been dealt with in childhood. In our child patients we also noted some instances where the child's reaction to his bereavement was affected by earlier experiences of loss. In others the bereavement in turn influenced the child's handling of subsequent losses. It seemed logical that such connections should exist, but their exact nature and extent were unclear. Does each bereavement revive all previous losses by association, so that mourning becomes a cumulative task, intensified with each additional loss? Are there only certain losses or forms of dealing with them that affect the later attitudes to bereavement? Does an appropriate mourning for a parent in childhood facilitate an individual's ability to cope with some or all later losses? In reviewing case material we focused on this topic and on finding some answers to our queries.

Does a bereavement revive all previous losses and intensify the current mourning?

The following examples illustrate the complex nature of the clinical data.

Ken was thirteen years old when his father died suddenly (see analyst's report, p. 27). During the preceding three years Ken had experienced the deaths of a grandmother, uncle, and grandfather. Each of these deaths occurred after a prolonged illness which required his mother's involvement and resulted in her partial withdrawal from Ken. The relatives' deaths were handled realistically and with feelings by the parents as well as by Ken. His reaction was, however, affected by his difficulty in coping with the mother's partial withdrawal. Since the death of the father had been very sudden it was not preceded by a maternal withdrawal. This death did not revive Ken's mourning for his relatives nor his memories of earlier losses. In his mourning for his father Ken utilized those strengths which his family had helped him develop in connection with the previous deaths. He understood and accepted death in its concrete form. He could tolerate strong feelings of sadness. He could count on his mother's understanding of the need to mourn and on her support of his individual manner of mourning. Ken also drew on many other strengths derived from his advanced developmental position and from his particular personality makeup; for example, his aggression was sufficiently fused, his memory was intact.

Seth's mother died when he was three years old (see analyst's report on p. 149). She had been ill for a long time, increasingly unable to care for him. He had spent much of his time with an elderly aunt who lived with the family. The care she provided for him was also limited by her poor health. Internal and external factors combined to foil Seth's mourning. Following his mother's death he lived with his grandparents. He liked them and his wide-spread restrictions of affect and ego functioning enabled him to make a superficially adequate adaptation. During Seth's sixth year the father remarried and Seth joined the new family. In contrast to the defenses used after the mother's death, Seth reacted to the separation from the grandmother with instinctual and ego regression as well as symptom formation. The analysis showed that the loss of the grandmother reactivated the anal-sadistic conflicts which prevailed at the time of the mother's death and that the mother's death cast its shadow on the conflicts of the later phase: in the context of his recent phallic–oedipal relationships with father and stepmother, Seth reinterpreted his mother's death in phallic-sadistic terms and linked it to his ideas of sexual intercourse.

During this period Seth experienced another loss. His aunt, who had helped care for him during his mother's lifetime, died. He had continued to maintain his relationship with her through visits but had grown less close to her. Seth had no difficulty in understanding and accepting her death and in reacting to it appropriately. The aunt's death did not revive his memories of his mother's death, nor the separation from the grandmother, nor his experience of the parent's withdrawal in connection with their adult relationship.

These and similar clinical experiences suggested that a current object loss through death revives earlier losses in a selective manner. It is impossible to know all the losses a person has experienced if one thinks of losses in the wider sense, including partial and developmental ones. The revival of a specific past loss may, however, represent the telescoped experience of several losses.

We agreed that a current object loss and mourning does not necessarily revive previous experiences of loss. The circumstances and nature of the current loss and the framework of the individual's personality at the time appear to determine whether, which, and how many earlier losses are revived and how much they contribute to intensifying the present reaction.

Are there certain earlier losses or certain earlier forms of handling them that adversely affect the individual's capacity to mourn a later object loss?

Geraldine was almost eight years old when her mother died after years of illness and several hospitalizations (see report, p. 69).

She entered treatment in her twelfth year after she had developed a hysterical amnesia which extended back to just before her mother's death. Although Geraldine had a fully structured personality, it was noted during her analysis that she sometimes dealt with the conflictual feelings about her mother's death with primitive mechanisms of introjection and of merging. In some instances she employed the same mechanisms when her current love objects became ill and required hospitalization. Geraldine's use of these early forms of handling loss subsided when, through reconstruction, they could be traced to repeated short-term separations from her mother during her first two years of life. These early experiences with loss determined some, though not all, of her current reactions. Subsequent stressful factors appeared also to play an important part in reactivating these mechanisms.

From birth Sally had lived with a foster mother until, at twenty-two months of age, she was adopted into her present family (see report, p. 129). Sally was just over four years old when her adoptive father died suddenly. Sally could accept the father's death intellectually and realistically and, in contrast to her mother and siblings, could experience and contain her strong feelings about it. She talked about him and remembered him appropriately both in the family and with outsiders. In time the mother recognized Sally's mourning and began to share and support it. An important aspect of the work centered on helping the mother to understand Sally's feelings about the loss of her foster mother. Since her adoption Sally had played games with cosmetics and made requests for certain foods which led to some friction between mother and child. When the mother began to encourage her to express feelings in words, she learned of Sally's continued longing for the foster mother. It was now understood that Sally's special games and food requests represented memories of affectionate interactions with the foster mother.

Sally's appropriate reaction to her father's death appeared to stem in part from the personality strengths she had earlier developed in her relationship with her foster mother. Among these strengths were ability to tolerate feelings, inner and outer reality testing, and adequate drive fusion. Without help from her love objects, however, she could not come to terms with the loss of the foster mother. This resulted in some behavior difficulties and some interferences in her relationship with her adoptive mother. One does not know whether, without help, Sally's mourning for her father could have been completed. Her manner of mourning her father was, however, age-appropriate and did not repeat her earlier ways of coping with the loss of the foster mother.

In reviewing these and other clinical data it appeared to us that there are no specific previous losses or forms of handling them which directly impede the individual's capacity to mourn a later object loss. The effect of the experiences of earlier losses lies in the manner in which they contribute to the shaping of the total personality. The circumstances of the later object loss and the framework of the personality at that time are deciding factors in the individual's reaction. They determine which strengths can be utilized or which weaknesses are exposed.

Does the appropriate mourning of a love object increase the ability to mourn another loss at a later time?

Billy's mother died in his sixth year. He was in analysis at the time and mourned her loss appropriately. In his prepuberty a young relative of Billy's died from an illness similar to the mother's. The relative's death reminded Billy of his mother's death. He mourned his relative appropriately.

Jim was seven years old at the time of his mother's sudden death (see report, p. 88). In his later treatment he worked on his bereavement for years, gradually allowing himself to experience the full extent of his feelings. During this period the death of an elderly relative affected him strongly. This loss appeared to revive the loss of the mother. His feelings intensified and extended from one death to the other. Some years later, at the time of finishing his analysis and coping with the impending separation from the analyst, Jim suffered another loss. A close friend died. Although this death revived memories of his mourning for his mother and relative, the losses did not become confused. There was no intensification of feelings and Jim dealt with the death of his friend appropriately.

These examples suggested that a completed mourning has a beneficial effect on the person's ability to mourn a subsequent death.

It seemed inaccurate, however, to view the earlier and later loss reaction as directly connected. The death of a love object other than the parent cannot be compared to the death of a parent. Our patients' later experiences of deaths fortunately never concerned the only surviving parent. Even if that had been the case, the death of the second parent would place the child in a very different psychological situation. Moreover, the actual circumstances surrounding a death differ in each instance, as does the personality development and equilibrium of the bereaved.

In the cases studied we found many indications of indirect, rather than direct, favorable effects of a completed mourning on the reaction to later losses. We noticed that in the process of assisting a child in his mourning he was sometimes helped to mature in some areas. Among these were the ability to tolerate and verbalize affects, improvement in reality testing, fusion of ambivalence in relationships. With such gains a child stood a better chance of handling a number of later stressful experiences, including those of object loss.

All experiences, positive and negative, leave their mark on the personality and contribute to its individual makeup. At a time of severe stress, such as the death of a parent, developmental and individual strengths are helpful, and weaknesses tend to be exposed. If a child has developed adequately and learned to master stresses age-appropriately, he is better able to deal with a bereavement. If he has not been exposed to age-appropriate stresses or is burdened by unmastered ones, including earlier object losses, he tends to experience difficulty. The experience and handling of losses has a general effect on the personality rather than a specific effect on the ability to mourn. The extent to which earlier losses affect the reaction to later object losses in a specific manner depends mainly on the nature and circumstances of the later bereavement and on the framework of the bereaved individual's personality at the time. Appropriate mourning for a parent does not specifically strengthen a child's personality. At best it enables him to cope with the future without carrying a burden greater than it need be.

8. Observations on Depression and Apathy

Two considerations prompted us to attempt to understand the phenomena of depression and apathy. The first was our case material, which included these symptoms prominently in some instances. The second was our knowledge that, starting with the studies of Abraham (1911) and S. Freud (1915), many analysts associated depression with object loss.[1] In our own minds, too, there was a definite idea that loss and depression were related. We felt it important to understand whether or not our cases showed this link, and when and why.

We were surprised at our great difficulty in achieving clear and meaningful definitions of depression and apathy. We found, however, that we were not alone in our quandary. Sandler and Joffe (1965) start their discussion of this topic by stating, "The research worker who aims to investigate the subject of depression in childhood must inevitably find his task extraordinarily difficult" (p. 88).

After some preliminary discussion we agreed to exclude considerations of depressive psychosis and limit ourselves to "depressed," "depressive reaction or response," "neurotic depression." We, like others, had not encountered depressive psychoses in childhood.[2] In addition, we considered psychoses to be other than an extension of normal or neurotic states.

Having narrowed our topic, we next accepted a working definition based on descriptive clinical manifestations of the depressive reaction: "A dejected, helpless mood; a restriction of motility; a restriction of interest in the world and in objects; a loss of self-esteem." This description compares closely to the one given by Bibring: "Basic depression represents a state of the ego whose main characteristics are a decrease of self-esteem, a more or less intense state of

1. Some psychoanalytic investigators consider object loss only one among many events that can precipitate a depression (e.g. Bibring 1953; Zetztel 1960; Sandler and Joffe 1965). Others claim that certain forms of object loss always lead to a depressive reaction (e.g. Klein 1935, 1940).
2. In this respect our findings coincided with those of Anthony and Scott (1960) and Sandler and Joffe (1965).

helplessness, a more or less intensive and extensive inhibition of functions, and a more or less intensely felt particular emotion'' (1953, p. 27).

Even this descriptive approach at once raised thorny questions. How could we apply "loss of self-esteem" to a one-year-old? We were aware that in the literature babies not only were described as depressed in appearance (Klein 1935; Spitz 1945, 1946; Winnicott 1954), but that we ourselves had also loosely used this term to characterize some of our own patients in that age group. Should we modify "loss of self-esteem" to "loss of the libidinal cathexis of the body image or earliest ego functions" or to "narcissistic depletion" for the children at the stage of beginning object constancy?

We also thought there might be substantial differences in depressive symptomatology between children and adults, and between children at different levels of personality development. The clinical picture of depression could be the same but could be caused by different psychic conditions. Conversely, the same underlying factors could produce different manifestations at the various developmental levels.

It was pointed out that in adult depression one or another clinical characteristic may be lacking in the manifest picture of individual cases or may be represented by its opposite; for example, hyperactivity may take the place of restriction of motility. On the basis of some of our material it seemed likely that such variations in symptomatology would be seen in children. Eight-year-old Jim had frequent "depressed" periods which concerned his family. At other times he was unmanageably hyperactive. Also, there was the difficulty in clinically distinguishing depression from apathy, particularly in very young children.

Yet another problem was raised by the question of "underlying depression"; that is, instances where none of the manifest symptomatology was in evidence, but the analyst either surmised that certain defenses warded off a depression or depressive reactions became manifest in response to the interpretation of these defenses. We decided to include manifestations of "underlying depression" or "depressive equivalents" (Toolan 1962) only in instances where the relationship between such symptoms and an overt depressive reaction could be understood in the course of the child's analysis.

For these reasons we were dissatisfied with the description of the clinical manifestations as an approach to a psychoanalytic definition of depression or depressive reaction. We reminded ourselves that the term depression derived from adult psychiatry, where it denoted a particular disease syndrome, unrelated to metapsychological factors. The term depression, like psychosis, never lost the meaning it had in its earlier context of adult psychiatry. It appeared to us that this handicapped analytic studies and their application to the understanding of childhood pathology and development. It seemed necessary to us to have a metapsychological understanding of depression as well as an understanding of it at all the developmental levels.

In our search for a metapsychological definition of depression we turned to some of those authors who had considered the developmental point of view in their theoretical formulations. Even a cursory survey showed that their views differed widely in many respects. Was depression an affect appropriate to situations in which there was an unbridgeable discrepancy between the actual state of the ego and its narcissistic aspirations (Bibring 1953)? Was it a selective affective response to such situations by certain individuals (Joffe and Sandler 1965)? Was depression caused by the guilt resulting from ambivalence to the love object? And, if so, was it a necessary developmental step in the first year of life (Winnicott 1954)? Was it a prototype model determining the reaction to all later experiences of loss (Klein 1935)? Or was it impossible for depression to occur in young children (Rochlin 1953, 1959, 1961; Beres 1965)? Did restricted motility and interests in the depressive syndrome represent inhibitions of aggression or turning of aggression against the self, or did it represent a state of "suspended animation" and imply a protective quality?

Some of us favored aspects of one theory, some aspects of another. All of us searched for a possibility of combining the different views and of including wider aspects of personality development in a developmental understanding of depression. These theoretical exercises, however, led us nowhere. In some instances our case experience did not appear to fit any of the theoretical models; in other instances, one or the other theoretical concept did apply but we did not see the accompanying clinical manifestations.

A closer examination of available clinical studies showed a marked lack of material derived from analyses of depressed children. The widest range of studies is based on analytic observations of infants and toddlers in relation to separation from the mother (Spitz 1946;

Rochlin 1953, 1959, 1961; Bowlby 1960a, 1961, 1963; Mahler 1961) and in relation to developmental processes (Klein 1935, 1940; Winnicott 1954). Some authors describe clinical manifestations of depression but do not equate or correlate them with the depressive phenomena of adulthood (Rochlin, Mahler). Others do not describe an overt clinical depressive response in infancy but claim that the content of the infants' unconscious mental struggles underlies and repeats itself in adult depressive responses (Klein, Winnicott). Spitz suggests a possible relationship between "anaclitic depression" and adult depression both in clinical manifestations and mental conditions. Bowlby is more explicit by stating that some phases of the infant's-reaction to separation from the mother resemble later reactions to object loss both in appearance and underlying mental processes and, under certain circumstances, create a predispostion to adult depressive illness.

Many analysts working with adults focus on the genetic aspects of their depressed patients' illness. On the basis of material gained through reconstruction, they stress the importance of certain early childhood experiences, though not specifically object loss, for the development of adult depression (e.g. Abraham 1911, 1924; Rado 1928; Klein 1935, 1940; Jacobson 1946, 1953, 1957, 1967). In the context of our study of bereaved children the views of Deutsch are of special interest in this connection. She comments, "Probably the inner rejection of painful experience is always active, especially in childhood. One might assume that the very general tendency to 'unmotivated' depressions is the subsequent expression of emotional reactions which were once withheld and have since remained in latent readiness of discharge" (1937, p. 22).

Relatively few studies deal with depression in preschoolers and latency children, and there is a great dearth of detailed clinical material from the analyses of such children. Toolan's (1962) contribution is based on psychotherapeutic work with latency children and adolescents. He was impressed with the frequency of depression in children of these age groups, but it occurred primarily in the form of "depressive equivalents" (e.g. psychosomatic symptoms, eating and sleeping disturbances, boredom, restlessness), which were viewed as defenses against dejection, worthlessness, and sadness. The children lacked overt manifestations of a depressive response. Sandler and Joffe (1965) comment on some reasons for the lack of referral of depressed children, such as the parents' unwillingness to recognize and acknowledge such a symptom in their child. With the help of the Hampstead Index they examined some one hundred cases of children of all age groups treated psychoanalytically at the Hampstead Child Therapy Clinic. They searched for "the existence of a manifest constellation which would comprise depressive mood in one form or another and which would bear some resemblance to one or another of the depressive states met with in adult psychiatric practice" (p. 89). They found that "a number of children of all ages showed what could be termed a depressive reaction to a wide range of internal or external precipitating circumstances" (p. 89). Unfortunately, clinical analytic material is not included in this paper or in their subsequent one (Joffe and Sandler 1965).

As far as could be ascertained, Putnam, Rank, and Kaplan (1951) are the only ones to report specifically on a prelatency child, an "atypical" boy three and a half years old. Evaluating their data, gained during two weeks of observation, they state, "We have considered his state of mind prior to the onset of his illness [18 months] to be one of 'chronic mild depression' and his reaction to the two subsequent events already described [two weeks' separation from the parents, followed by the mother's pregnancy and birth of a sibling] as an 'acute exacerbation of grief,' a kind of 'primal agitated depression,' in which even more extensive regressive withdrawal of the libido from the object into the ego became imperative" (p. 56). The authors derived their terminology from Abraham (1924), who introduced the concept of primal depression due to a severe narcissistic injury to the infant in the later oral stage. They relate their findings to Jacobson's (1946) reference to "observations of children up to three years with depressive symptoms which reflect disturbances of the pre-oedipal mother–child relationship" (p. 145) and to Bibring's (1953) suggestion that the earliest and most frequent factor in the mechanism of depression probably lies in the young ego's lack of power over the object. It should be noted, however, that John I., as described by Putnam, Rank, and Kaplan (1951, p. 53) did not have depressive symptoms but "atypical" (psychotic) functioning. The authors emphasize that "the primal depression—with its concomitant regression—which ensues as a reaction to major traumata is the decisive turning point in the production of the arrest" (p. 57); that is, they consider "primal depression" a causal determinant of atypical disturbances in children.

Similar difficulties beset us in our attempts to clarify the concept of apathy and to distinguish it clinically and theoretically from depressive responses. The main clinical difference appeared to us to lie in the different affective states. Apathy is marked by an absence of conscious suffering. In the preliminary survey of our material, however, we had already noticed that this clinical affective difference cannot readily be deduced from observation alone. Some children looked very dejected but, in their analyses, were found not to feel sad or hopeless. It was even harder to assess the affective experience with preverbal infants and toddlers.

We also failed to define apathy metapsychologically and to determine the theoretical connection between depression and apathy. The different views expressed on this subject in the literature served as a basis for our discussion and comparison of clinical findings. In contrast to depression, apathy is relatively neglected by psychoanalytic authors. Several analysts working with infants describe manifestations of apathy which follow a period of overt weepiness. The term apathy, however, is not specifically stressed, and the relationship between the two stages of response is noted in a temporal sequence rather than in metapsychological terms. For example, Spitz (1946) views "anaclitic depression" as a psychiatric syndrome resultant upon the specific deprivation of loss of mother during the second half of the first year. Although he has no observations of the exact period of the mother's leaving the infant, his data show a progression from despair, weepiness, and desperate crying when approached by another person, to a later period when affect is bland and interactions with people are not responded to. There is increasing evidence of loss of appetite, developmental retardation, "stupor." The apathetic response is not seen as protective or adaptive, as it threatens the child's very existence. Bowlby (1960a) describes a different form of circumscribed apathy which affects specifically the child's interaction with the mother after a period of separation from her. After the overtly angry and dejected phases of "protest" and "despair" the infant enters the phase of "detachment" in which he fails to respond to the mother but shows no sign of unhappiness or suffering: "He may remain remote and apathetic" (p. 90). A. Freud (1960) speaks of this phenomenon as withdrawal and stresses the fate of the child's libidinal cathexis of the mother.

A member of our group had observed a baby ten months old who had all the overt manifestations of a "depressive reaction" during his hospitalization and of a period of apathy following it, although his very supportive and responsive mother remained with him throughout. Another clinical example concerned a child of four and a half years of age who was abandoned by his adoptive parents while he was hospitalized, ostensibly for observation. The child therapist worked with this child in the hospital at the time and did not notice a depressive reaction. On the day when the boy's package of belongings was delivered, he fully realized that his parents had given him up. He became physically sick, refused food and literally turned to the wall. Two days later, just as the hospital personnel expected him to die, he suddenly changed, began to reinvest himself and the world and made a gradual recovery. It appeared that the child's sudden upward trend was due to a basic sufficient libidinal investment of his body image which was, at that point, threatened by his extreme apathy.

Bibring (1953) regards apathy as the result of a special "blocking" of the depressed affect, that is, a defensive measure employed against feeling. Greenson (1949) observed apathy in adults who were in the armed forces during World War II. He views apathy as the outcome of deprivation in the widest sense, which brings with it a restriction of ego activities, including lack of interest in relationships and a regression to primitive bodily, especially oral, needs. He distinguishes it from depression by pointing out that there is no internalized conflict between ego and super-ego, which he accepts as characteristic of depression. He does not consider depression as a stage prior to apathy. In his patients, apathy served a defensive adaptive function and could be relieved by restoration of those satisfactions of which the patient had been deprived. Greenson did not see patients whose apathy led to ultimate interference with survival for lack of restoration of satisfactions nor did he have an opportunity to observe or analytically reconstruct the symptomatology preceding apathy.

Our group quoted experiences with adult prisoners in whom, in some cases, apathy affected the body libido and led to death; in other cases, the opposite held true.

It seemed to us that apathy as a clinical manifestation may range over a wide area of intrapsychic conditions. It may be an adaptive almost conscious or preconscious attitude; it may be an unconscious defense mechanism; it may be the expression of a kind of withdrawal which ultimately threatens the very existence of an individual.

Our own clinical material was too limited to enable us to adopt any one specific theoretical definition. In relation to both depression and apathy we therefore decided to use only the descriptive clinical manifestations and to avoid the terms as such. We set ourselves the following task: we would make a concentrated effort to spot the periods in the analytic treatment when a bereaved patient showed any or all of the characteristics of the clinical pictures of depression or apathy. We would describe and hopefully understand such situations, paying special attention to evaluating the patient's affect and noting the incidence of other manifestations and variations that might accompany the depressive or apathetic response. We would also study those intrapsychic conditions in our patients which, according to different authors, evoke such responses and observe whether our patients reacted to them with or without depressive or apathetic signs. Toward the end of our project work we would review and discuss our collected data on the subject.

We hoped that such an effort would alert us to the actual incidence of periods of depression or apathy in our patients, help us get a clearer idea of clinical pictures of depression and apathy in different phases of childhood, and enable us to gain a better metapsychological understanding of the phenomena.

When we returned to the topic of depression and apathy almost two years later we found that our earlier difficulties were not resolved. Our material did not conform to any of the theoretical definitions we knew. At the same time it was still too limited to enable us to gain a comprehensive metapsychological understanding or to construct a developmental line on depression or apathy. We present our findings in the hope of contributing, in Mendelson's words (1960), to the "great investigation" rather than to the "great debate" on the subject.

Danny, a well-developed infant, experienced a week's hospitalization at eleven months. During that week his father died and his mother was unable to visit him (see analyst's report on p. 198). On leaving the hospital, and for several months to come, Danny appeared apathetic. He had lost his motility, speech, and interest in the world. His expression was bland. He clung to his mother physically but was unresponsive to her affective overtures. With help Danny gradually regained his speech, affective response, and perceptiveness by age four. Brief periods of the dull, blank expression persisted for another year or two, restricted to times when Danny did not feel well bodily. Danny's motility picked up very rapidly by seventeen months, turned into hyperactivity of a heedless nature, and persisted in this form. In his analysis it was seen primarily as a defense against sadness and loneliness for his mother. In response to this interpretation the hyperactivity gave way to periods characterized by depressive manifestations. Danny curled up on the couch, sucked his thumb, looked and felt dejected, and withdrew interest from his surroundings. The analyst related these periods to his feelings during his hospitalization. Some of Danny's poignant memories of the hospital, recovered during the analysis, served as partial evidence. With this work the depressive manifestations subsided without recurrence. Although Danny had difficulties with aggression, material and interpretations of ambivalence did not come up in relation to the sad periods.

Hank, aged five years two months, was referred three months after his father's death (see analyst's report on p. 129). The symptoms were manifestations of partial apathy and depression—withdrawal from social contacts, whining and whimpering when approached, lack of pleasure, marked restriction of interests and motility. The mother dated the onset of this behavior to Hank's third year, when his sister was adopted. One additional symptom started following the father's death, a tendency to roll on the floor and repetitively kick a foot. When the mother became able to encourage Hank to share his feelings, he began to cry bitterly about his father's death and, at a later time in the work, expressed concerns about his sister's adoption. As Hank's overt sadness increased, his apathy, dejection, and repetitive motor activity subsided and his functioning improved rapidly. Hank's aggression, both to the mother and to the deceased father, did not appear to be a main aspect of the apathetic and depressive responses.

Jim, aged nine and a half, was referred for excited hyperactivity and "depression" (see analyst's report on p. 88). These symptoms had started after his mother's sudden death two years earlier. The frequent periods of depression were characterized by Jim's sitting almost motionless for ten to thirty minutes, usually staring out the window but not taking interest in anything. He did not respond readily when approached. When these periods occurred in the analysis it became clear that they represented apathy rather than depression in that Jim was unaware of any feelings or thoughts at such times. Analysis revealed that they warded off deep sadness and longing for the dead mother. As Jim was able to experience these feelings and memories consciously, the periods of apathy gradually subsided and did not recur at later times of great sadness. Jim's anger at his mother was difficult for him to face and express. It was worked on in the later years of his treatment and did not seem related to the earlier apathetic periods. His hyperactivity had several meanings; among them was a defensive reversal of affect. He used excited "happiness" accompanied by frantic bodily activity to ward off unhappy feelings and thoughts.

Geraldine started analysis in her twelfth year (see analyst's report on p. 69). The main symptom was a hysterical amnesia that extended back to the time just before her mother's death when Geraldine was eight years old. She had two circumscribed periods of depressive symptoms during her analysis. There is no evidence that she experienced this kind of difficulty in her earlier life or subsequently. The first depressive reaction occurred at age thirteen, coinciding with the anniversary of her mother's death. The depressive response was preceded by a period of frantic busyness and severe acting out. Finally she appeared in her analytic hour deeply dejected, helpless, and withdrawn. She was told that these feelings, which she had warded off until then, belonged to her experience of longing, sadness, and helplessness after her mother's death. Geraldine acknowledged this and sobbed bitterly that day. Her depression lessened and subsided altogether as she became able to express this sadness consciously over a prolonged period of work. The second depressive period occurred when Geraldine was eighteen years old, several months before the anticipated end of treatment. This depressive response extended over many weeks, characterized by feelings of worthlessness and dejection, crying spells, sadness, lack of interest in work and people, neglect of her appearance, and restriction of motility. The analytic work traced the onset of these manifestations to Geraldine's having noticed that an unmarried peer was pregnant. This observation was linked to Geraldine's repressed knowledge that her mother had conceived her before she married her father. Although the imminent loss of the analyst and the possible loss of her boyfriend played a part, the main factor in the depressive reaction appeared to be the identification with the unconscious image of the debased mother and the need to relinquish the idealized mother representation. When this material became conscious, Geraldine's depressive symptoms ceased. Her severe difficulties with aggression were not a part of the material during the analysis of the depressive periods.

Lucy was close to fifteen years old and in the fourth year of analysis when she experienced a depressive period (see analyst's report on p. 219). It was marked by feeling dejected and hopeless and being unable to wake up in the morning, losing interest in social activities, and not attending school and analytic sessions. She seemed immobilized bodily and mentally—a characteristic she had never shown before. In addition, old difficulties were exacerbated; she gained weight, experienced increased physical symptoms and, on one occasion, scratched her wrist. Consciously, Lucy linked her difficulties to her disappointment at her first boyfriend's withdrawal. She was less aware of her rebellious wish to be independent of the love objects of childhood, including the transference relationship. Her greatest despair stemmed from not having an image of her dead mother from which she could divorce herself as a child and with whom she could choose to identify, or not identify, as an adult woman. During the following two years Lucy searched out independently enough detailed knowledge of her mother to form the coherent picture she had always lacked. Then, on her own and for the first time, she visited her mother's grave. These achievements marked the end of her depressive symptoms. Lucy's struggles with ambivalence played a part in her reaction to the boyfriend's rejection of her and in her difficulty in taking the developmental step of "rejecting" the parental figures. Equally, if not more, important appeared to be the deprivation caused by the lack of a real mother and of an internal mother image during the developmental phase of object removal and the search for an adult self-image.

From this limited case material we gained the following impressions:

1. The clinical manifestations of apathy and depression appear to cover a variety of metapsychological constellations and, on the other

hand, comparable psychological conditions within different personalities do not always manifest themselves in clinical apathy and depression.

2. From observations alone it is difficult to distinguish apathy from depression if the patient's affective state is taken as the main criterion for differentiation. The patient may not feel the way he looks to the observer. Psychoanalytic work appeared to be the only avenue toward a differential diagnosis.

3. In our patients, apathy was seen as a defensive measure warding off overwhelming sadness.

4. The role of object loss as a precipitating event or determinant of a depressive response was not clear. Among the patients with depressive or apathetic symptoms were some who experienced serious physical illness and medical procedures at the same time as the loss of the parent. The relative importance of each of these factors was difficult to ascertain. In others the depressive manifestations were not linked to the death of the parent but to other factors which could only to some extent be viewed as object loss. For example, Hank's difficulties followed the arrival of his adopted sister when he perhaps experienced his mother's care of the sister as her partial withdrawal. Geraldine's second depressive period related to an unconscious identification with her "devalued" mother and, in part, to her need to give up an idealized aspect of the mother image. Lucy experienced the rejection by the boyfriend and the developmental need to turn away from the maternal figure as a loss of love object. However, she also struggled with a lack of positive narcissistic investment and a difficulty in integrating her self-representation that appeared to be of at least equal importance. Some of these children had experienced separations and object losses in their first and second years of life but, apart from Lucy, these were not traced as genetic antecedents of their later depressive responses. By contrast, a number of the bereaved children showed no signs of depressive or apathetic reactions but, in addition to the death of the parent, they had also experienced separations and losses of love object as infants and toddlers.

5. The effect of pre-oedipal and oedipal ambivalence in relationships was similarly uncertain either as a current or genetic factor in the depressive response. In some children there was no evidence that aggression to the love object determined the depressive reaction or played a part in its course. In Geraldine, primitive ambivalence

was an important factor in her early childhood and later personality difficulties, but it could not be detected as a factor during the analysis of her two depressive periods. Ambivalence appeared to play a significant part only in Lucy's case. The early ambivalence of several bereaved patients strongly affected both their personality development and their reaction to the parent's death, but they did not show depressive manifestations or tendancies.

6. Pathological discharge of aggressive drives, in the form of an inhibition, restriction, or turning against the self, was noted only in some instances of depressive response. In these it appeared to represent a concomitant or contributory factor rather than a major one. Such was the case with Lucy and, in a different form, with Hank, whose motility might have been affected by his difficulty in neutralizing aggression. This was not evident in Geraldine's depressive periods although she harmed herself at other times. The aggression of several children was severely inhibited or turned against the self, but they showed no depressive manifestations.

7. Loss of narcissistic supplies, unattainability of narcissistic aspirations or of a state of well-being, appeared to play an important part in some cases but not in others. Danny's and Lucy's and, to some extent, Geraldine's apathetic and depressive responses could be seen in this light and were important aspects of the analytic work. This did not apply to Hank and Jim. There were several other children for whom these factors were very prominent but who did not show depressive or apathetic reactions.

8. Motility was strongly affected in all our depressive or apathetic patients, though not in a uniform manner. Only Lucy's behavior was characterized by immobility during her depressive period, without any signs of hyperactivity at other times. All the others used hyperactivity, or limited repetitive motoric discharge, or frantic "busyness," at least in part to ward off sadness and despair. By contrast, their motility was markedly slowed down or altogether inhibited during their apathetic or depressive periods. Hyperactivity and busyness were frequently noted as defenses against sadness in other bereaved patients who did not show depressive responses.

9. The only factor common to all our depressed or apathetic patients was their lack of conscious awareness of sadness or of its true ideational content. In each case the treatment process had to uncover either the underlying affect or content or both, and, with the help of

interpretation, assist the child in gaining conscious recognition. The patient's ability then to tolerate and express his deep sadness in relation to its real content depended not only on his conscious recognition but also on the availability of a person who could empathize with him and maintain a relationship that could support the child in his task. The analyst could fulfill this role with the older children. For prelatency children, direct help or at least "permission" from the surviving parent was necessary. Although the ability and opportunity to feel and express great sadness were crucial in all our cases, most of the children did not have depressive or apathetic responses. The only exception to this finding was Geraldine's second depressive period. In that case the analytic work also had to enable her to become aware of her unconscious knowledge of having been born out of wedlock. Geraldine could integrate this content consciously, and her depressive response ceased without her experiencing pronounced affects. She was developmentally ready to restructure her object and self-representations and ideals.

10. In several of our cases either the deceased or the surviving parent had manifested symptoms of depression. Although the parental depressive symptoms affected the children, they did not react with depressive symptoms themselves nor with defenses against them insofar as the analytic work could ascertain. For example, Addie's mother had suffered from chronic depressive symptoms for years before her death when Addie was four years old. Addie's extreme difficulty in allowing herself to be sad actually led to the recovery of her memories of her mother's depression, but Addie's hyperactivity was not a defense against a depressive reaction. When she could eventually tolerate sad feelings Addie was not depressed.

*Danny and Lucy suffered the death of a parent during their first year
of life. The treatment reports trace the effects of this tragic event on
their development. Neither experienced the loss at a time when the
child was developmentally capable of mourning. For each the circumstances at the time of bereavement and subsequently were very
different. Both, however, had to cope with the reality of a dead, not
merely absent, parent and with the special hardships this entails.*

DANNY   by Eleanor S. Fiedler

Danny was the youngest in a family of three children, having a
brother Ted five years older, and a sister Kathy three years older.
When Danny was eleven months old his father developed a virus infection, became seriously ill, was hospitalized, and died forty-eight
hours after admission to the hospital. The rest of the family was ill
also, and Danny was hospitalized at the same time as his father. After
father's sudden and unexpected death, the mother, shocked and distraught with grief, returned to their former home state to arrange and
attend the funeral, leaving Danny in hospital. She was away from
Danny for one week, and in the following week was very much oc-
cupied with selling the home and moving with the children back to
their original community to live with her parents.

Mother was unable to visit Danny throughout his week-long hospital stay. Before she left town she arranged for two neighborhood
friends, whom Danny knew, to visit him daily, and she also took
some of his favorite toys to him before she left. As for medical
procedures in the hospital, it is known that Danny was tied to the crib
by one leg; that he was X-rayed at least once daily and possibly of-
tener; that medication was given him intravenously; that he underwent repeated blood tests; that he was in an oxygen tent part of the
time; and that his bronchial passages probably were suctioned.

When mother picked him up at the hospital upon her return he was
pale and listless, did not smile or respond to her. He was no longer
outgoing and emotionally responsive as he had been before his illness. He no longer tried to walk or crawl, nor did he speak the few
words he had been using prior to his illness. He was limp and apathetic and clung to his mother in an infantile fashion. He had been an
unusually expressive child before—taking much pleasure in his motility, beginning to walk and talk. He had been close to mother as well
as to the father and siblings and had taken a lively interest in everything around him. There had been no previous separations.

The new home with maternal grandparents offered many advantages: security for the mother, a nice father figure for the children, and it enabled mother to stay at home while the grandmother went to work to augment family income. But there were also disadvantages: it was a completely new ambience for Danny, and the grandmother maintained meticulous order and cleanliness and was inclined to make frightening statements to the children in relation to what she considered their misbehavior.

The mother contacted Miss Barnes (the child therapist who had worked with her earlier) for help a month after the father's death. The initial work with the mother centered on helping her to share some of her grief with the older children and to work through with them some of the realities about the father's death. The mother's own mourning continued over a period of several years. She was fearful of being overwhelmed by sadness, allowing herself to grieve only in piecemeal fashion in an attempt to integrate it. She had difficulty in answering the children's questions clearly, particularly Danny's. Although mother was often sad, she did not withdraw from the children. With Danny particularly, she maintained a close relationship, regarding him as a representative in some ways of her deceased husband. Danny bore his father's name and there was a striking facial resemblance.

Miss Barnes's work with the mother concerning Danny's problems centered primarily on his infantile clinging to the mother and his unresponsiveness. The mother linked this with his having been left at the hospital. She reassured him that this would not happen again. Danny was seventeen months old before he began to walk again or even to crawl. In spite of the mother's active efforts to engage him in emotional interaction, he continued to lack affective expression or response and he resumed the beginnings of speech only in the latter part of the second year. Lack of affect, response, and speech made him appear mentally retarded by the age of two. Testing, however, showed him to be of at least average ability.

The last half of the second year was marked by a change from immobility into hyperactivity. Danny was constantly on the go—into everything, climbing precariously—frequently coming to minor harm himself or upsetting or destroying things. The mother never firmly restricted or crossed him. She offered him substitutes and tried to protect him by being with him. This approach was characterisitic of the mother.

Toilet training was begun at two and accomplished with some difficulty within a few months. Miss Barnes helped the mother to be consistently and reasonably firm in this area. When Danny was two and a half the mother took a nine-day vacation. Danny (and siblings) stayed at home with the maternal grandparents. Reportedly he was quite comfortable, and he delightedly welcomed his mother back. There was no regression, not even in the recently achieved toilet training.

At two years and eleven months Danny began to attend the Hanna Perkins Nursery School. His speech was still quite poor, his accident-proneness and hyperactivity marked. His separation anxiety in the nursery school was extreme; gradual withdrawal of the mother was accomplished only after six months. His symptoms were the same at school as at home, and the teachers found it impossible, as the mother had, to protect him from coming to harm in his often sudden and precarious hyperactivity. Danny had overheard many of mother's conversations about father with the older children. As he began to show verbal comprehension, mother talked directly with him. By the time he entered nursery school he had some concept of death, of the cause of his father's death, that he had been in the same hospital as his father, and that the father was buried.

In the nursery school Danny showed much preoccupation with death: dead birds; the death of his great grandmother (when he was about three) and of his uncle (when he was three and a half) caused him to react with acute fear of dying himself. He pled with his mother, "Don't let me die"; and after the death of his uncle he played at being dead. When a child got sick with a minor illness, he announced, "She's dead now." He feared going out to play lest he catch cold and die (as maternal grandmother had warned him, in just these words). He equated death with sleep and had particular difficulty at nap time when he would become especially loud and hyperactive. Death, sickness, and being left in the hospital seemed tied up in his mind, and he dealt with his fear of dying in various ways: by anticipating it excitedly (to avoid being surprised), as in announcing that people were dead when they were only a little sick; by denying death in some instances; by becoming hyperactive and accident prone when he feared he might be left; by denying pain; by ensuring himself against death by wanting to take medicines.

By age three and a half he no longer clung to mother, but his fear reached panic proportions if he thought she would leave him suddenly. In one situation in a store he momentarily lost sight of her. He screamed in panic to the point of turning blue, and the mother had to resuscitate him with mouth-to-mouth breathing. Another time a similar panic overcame him when, as he was walking behind her, he got his shoe stuck in the mud and feared he would not be able to catch up with her.

He had several accidents—a tooth knocked out, a hand cut by putting it through a glass door—as well as constant cuts and bruises. He was an excellent patient, always allowing his mother to care for his hurts, never crying. In time this could be seen as reaching the point of denial of pain. For example, on a walk with mother and his uncle at age three years and nine months, they stepped into a wasps' nest. The uncle was stung and was quite upset. When they got home, the mother found a dozen or more wasp stings on Danny's head and neck under his hood. He had not said anything.

When Danny was three years and seven months the mother and children moved to a house of their own. Danny was upset and blamed mother for taking his grandfather away from him. When mother, shortly after this, began to have dates, Danny developed a night problem and, on seeing the man, started to cry in a special baby way which the mother recognized at once as the cry at the time of his hospitalization, and he sobbed. "Didn't you know how scared I was? Why did you leave me?"

Along with this memory there were evidences of other memories. Danny would go into a panic when he was to have his picture taken, the same panic reaction occurred at age one and a half, again at two, and again at three years. Mother then remembered the repeated X-ray pictures taken in the hospital, for which he was tied down. She discussed this with him, assured him of the differences, and Danny cooperated very well with the photographer after that. He played a repeated game with blocks and with a small boy doll: the doll would be high up on the roof or on a high cliff; he would fall and his daddy would come and catch him. This exciting and apparently pleasurable game appeared to relate to Danny's memories of the father playing with him by tossing him up in the air and catching him.

Some time after Danny's fourth birthday Martin Luther King was assassinated. Danny became very upset, asked many questions, and declared that he would never believe that his father was dead unless he saw the grave. For the first time the mother took the children to see the grave. Danny took along toys "to play with daddy." He became even more anxious and confused at the grave; he found his own name on father's gravestone; the still-living grandparents had erected stones for themselves next to father's. His mother felt overwhelmed both with sadness and with Danny's anxious questions.

Miss Barnes referred Danny to me for psychoanalysis shortly after his fourth birthday because of his extreme fear of injury and/or death resulting in his denial of pain, as in his failing to react to the multiple wasp stings or to a smashed finger etc.; his panic at the prospect of separation, as illustrated in the breathholding incident; his constant preoccupation with death and his extreme anxiety over illnesses; the difficulty of identification with a masculine figure; and his fear of growing up because it meant being closer to dying. In addition, Danny's physical activities were most unsafe, resulting in many falls and accidents. He was loud, bossy, and aggressive in play with other children; he frequently sucked his finger and occasionally stuttered. Certain ego functions seemed to be imparied—memory, distinguishing colors—and he had trouble concentrating.

Analysis began when Dan was four and a half and I maintained weekly contact with his mother. Separation from mother in the treatment room was relatively easy, compared with the very long period that she had had to stay with him when he started nursery school. The first day he came in with an air of self-confidence and assurance that was most convincing on the surface. He preceded me from the waiting room as if he knew exactly where to go. But his fears and anxieties about the new situation were evident underneath this exterior.

During the first week or so he did much testing of what he could do in my office—what I would permit, what I would stop, whether I would protect him. Not until the second or third week did he have difficulty in leaving his mother in the waiting room. This was typical of Dan's delayed reactions to trauma. Several times he needed to have his mother in the treatment room or he would have to run out to assure himself that she was there and had not deserted him. This was apparent at first when he felt anxious or unsafe, and again later, after he expressed angry or aggressive thoughts toward his mother. By the fifth month he no longer had to run out of the office for this sort of reassurance but could stay and hide himself under the desk or couch briefly when he felt anxious or "bad."

In general Dan was a pleasant, responsive little boy when he was successful in mastering feelings of anger, sadness, or anxiety. He never showed the kind or amount of hyperactive out-of-control behavior in the treatment sessions that was so apparent in the nursery school and kindergarten.

Castration anxiety shown by his great concern over small hurts (bumps and scratches) was prominent from the beginning. The first few months he was preoccupied, almost obsessed, with the need for large supplies of Band-Aids and with their magical curative properties. He would often appear with them on face, arms, and/or legs, covering even the most minute of scratches. One of his first questions of me was whether I had Band-Aids, and he soon made it necessary for me to get some. On the fourth day, as Dan ran ahead of me to the office, he teasingly ran into the toy closet and slammed the door behind him, catching his finger painfully in the door. At first he couldn't look at it, being sure it was gone, but he could cry hard from pain and fright. He needed a Band-Aid and his mother. Months later in a conversation between Dan, his brother, and a neighborhood boy when they were discussing treatment, mother overheard Dan advising the boy that if he ever went to see a "talking lady," he shouldn't be scared, explaining how he had been so scared when he first started coming that he sometimes ran into the toy closet to hide, and one day he did a "very silly thing," he slammed the closet door on his finger.

Several months later he reminisced about this incident with me and said he'd been afraid I might get mad at him, hurt or kill him, which seemed to represent his old fears of death, and of what scary things can happen to you in a hospital when mother leaves.

Dan played with the window and heating register and worried that "a boy could lose his finger out the window, or down the radiator"— yet he was fascinated with these "dangerous" objects and had to keep opening and shutting them. When I would wonder why he played with them if he thought such dangerous things could happen, he countered that it was ok—if his finger got lost out the window he would go out there, climb up on the next-door roof and retrieve it, put it back on with a Band-Aid. He dropped many Band-Aids into the register and for many months tried in one ingenious way or another to retrieve them.

Much of Dan's early, dangerous physical activity in the office (climbing, jumping, purposeful falling) was to see if I would be able to protect him, to keep him safe, as he felt that mother could keep him safe. It also had a counterphobic quality, and he often said with great glee after a fall: "See, I didn't get hurt," or, "It didn't hurt me." When I said to him that he seemed to have to do these dangerous things to prove to himself that he didn't get hurt, but wasn't he afraid he might go too far, he looked at me incredulously and said, "But my mother's a nurse." We could then begin to understand how he felt that his nurse-mother could keep him somehow from *really* hurting himself—or could make any hurt well—and so he didn't have to take good care of *himself*.

What became increasingly clear during the first five or six months was the amount of underlying feeling of sadness, anger, fear, and "badness" which Dan tried in a variety of ways to avoid.

His defensive maneuvers included a state of high hyperactive excitement in which he wanted to play exciting, active games with much hiding, surprising, and scaring. This kind of activity quickly led to out-of-control throwing of objects (toys) or of himself. He tried over and over to get me to hunt for him or to chase him, and he reacted with anger at me when I failed to participate in these exciting scary games or when I tried to help him stop them. At times he was able to stop himself with a verbal suggestion from me, but then he would often hide himself under the couch or under the desk, after which his whole mood would change remarkably into a faraway sadness, his finger in his mouth. At these times he was unreachable. They were reminiscent of an infantile way of trying to comfort himself.

Dan had a persistent interest in magic and magical thinking. Magic could bring his father back to life. This was understood as a remnant of his earliest experience—as a defense against the narcissistic injury and shock—as well as an expression of the confusion of "disappearing and finding" mother, but also "disappearing and not finding" the father and his old home.

Dan used neutral activities such as making pictures or working with scissors and crayons (in which he did very good work from the beginning) for defensive purposes, i.e. as a way to keep himself in control—to keep away feelings. He spent many entire sessions in such activities. Once when I commented that he seemed to use his very good abilities in making pictures to keep himself away from his worries, he replied, "We have airplane-making days, picture-making days; today will be hat-making day and day after tomorrow will be worry day."

Dan also tried to control others rather than himself—a trait well known in the nursery school. One way of gauging how close to the surface his worry feelings were was the extent of his demandingness and his attempts to control me or "order me around."

Also he was very accomplished at changing the subject under discussion if it began to be uncomfortable for him, or at "turning off" (appearing not to hear).

Within the first half year Dan's sad and angry feelings were gradually more often in evidence. There were more forlorn lost-looking times when he seemed to be wrapped up in his own thoughts and feelings, when he withdrew, sucking his finger and seeming quite unable to verbalize. He appeared to be very much like a baby who could not put feelings into words, and his behavior must have represented his old baby feelings in the hospital. He made valiant efforts to ward off these feelings, but they often failed. In addition, there was much preoccupation with death and killing which he *did* often verbalize. He feared that he might die as a result of his frequent bruises and hurts, and he played out his hostile killing thoughts with toys. While at times he could speak of his daddy's death when he was a baby, and his mother's leaving him alone in the hospital, at the same time he countered the fact of his father's death with denial—he *had* a daddy (grandfather), or, in play, he showed how things that died always came back to life. While he remembered visiting his father's grave, and this was occasionally mentioned without affect, he once said, "My mother knows where my daddy is but I don't." I understood this to mean at the time, "My mother understands about it but I don't."

His angry and sad feelings centered mainly around the memory of his mother's leaving him, and at times when these thoughts and feelings were uppermost, he had a most difficult time with his controls. At my first vacation time he made "millions" of airplanes to take home with him; he wrote me cards and implored me to be careful, when he was not denying my approaching departure. He brought a story book, *Everything Happens to Aaron,* and could say it felt like everything happened to him.

Occasionally Dan was overwhelmed with feelings. Once upon coming into the clinic (two weeks after my vacation), for seemingly no clear reason he cried hysterically in despair, repeating over and over, "I want to go home." As this went on one could observe its turning into an angry, demanding attempt to control his mother. After he had pulled himself together with mother's and my help, he told me, "Only babies cry!"

On another occasion he told me he had tried to choke himself in school. "I could have killed myself," he said. I thought he must have had some terrible feelings and he said, "Sometimes I always want to be dead—then I'd be dead like my daddy." Or, "I wish I was dead—then I would be with my daddy, I would know him." There was also talk about his daddy being black, having black skin, which was not understood until much later in the analysis.

Real feelings were expressed in his anger, both verbalized and acted out, against mother for leaving him when he was little. On several occasions he would say vehemently, "I hate her—she didn't have to [leave me]," and once or twice he ran impulsively from the office to the waiting room to hit his mother. One day he came late, sad and despairing, finger in mouth, hanging back, trying to prevent his mother from coming into the clinic. Rather suddenly, as he saw me, his face brightened and in excitement he ran away from both of us, out to the front of a nearby building facing a busy street. After this was over and he was back in the office, I told him I thought he was trying to show us something. Still gleeful, he said, "Wasn't that funny?" I didn't think it was funny—rather I thought he was trying to make mother and me feel scared the way he had felt scared and mad when mother left him. And he sobered, saying with anger, "She ran away from me and left me in the hospital—and she was a long time—fifty-five minutes, even one hundred minutes. Why did she have to? She didn't have to." We could talk then, and subsequently, about how all alone and scared he felt in the hospital and about scary things the doctors and nurses did to him; how he was so little that he couldn't understand why mother had to leave him, or why all the scary things were done. With great seriousness he said about the doctors and nurses: "They made me little." And this, too, was not understood until much later.

The verbalizing of his anger toward his mother for leaving him in the hospital, and for letting his father die (she should have known how to help father as she knew—being a nurse—how to help him) brought changes in Dan's general behavior, some settling down in school.

By the end of the first year of treatment Dan's teasy, excited, hyperactive behavior almost entirely disappeared from the treatment sessions. While he still liked at times to play hiding, searching, and finding games, these no longer led to anxious out-of-control behavior. He was much more often able to let his underlying feelings show via the occasional sad, desolate-looking times when he quietly sucked his finger and seemed far away and unreachable; or when he more and more verbalized his angry, frustrated feelings toward his mother or a teacher, his brother or another boy. He rarely acted in an angry way in the sessions although he was apt to act out his angry feelings at home where he was far less able to verbalize them, as mother has always found verbalized anger difficult to take.

The need for Band-Aids completely disappeared by the end of the first year. His dangerous climbing, jumping, and falling in the sessions and elsewhere diminished noticeably after some interpretations, particularly one regarding my concern at his seeming not to like himself well enough to keep himself safe. This appeared to have considerable meaning to him, and I occasionally would hear this repeated by him in connection with others who hurt themselves.

Oedipal material came into prominence in the treatment following Dan's fifth birthday, and the birth of his dog's puppies. Dan had looked forward to his fifth birthday, counting the days, and was very proud when it came; proud of how much he knew, of how big he was, and of all the five-year-old things he could do. His previous teasy, demanding, controlling behavior, ordering me to do this or that, was now more and more replaced by a kind of gentleness and a rather charming seductiveness toward me. He felt he would soon be as big or bigger than I, measuring his height against mine. He made drawings for me, shared his candies with me (especially those he didn't like too well); he had pretend dinner parties to which he invited me and fed and entertained me royally, and he invited me to his house, enumerating the things he and I could do together—''talk, go ice-skating, have parties.'' He showed off his new accomplishments—headstands and back somersaults (very carefully executed), his drawings and art work (which were indeed often clever and original). We could talk about his wish to be big and do grownup things, and how hard it was to wait to be grown up.

With the doll family (usually consisting of a father, mother, and three children) he played house, often assigning the mother's role to me and directing what she should say and do. The father was consistently a strong, masculine, active man, able to do many things the mother couldn't do. He was able to control and settle the "bad, mischievous baby boy," who was always getting into trouble. Frequently the boy and the mother got into dangerous predicaments—about to fall over a cliff or be attacked by wild animals—and the father would come to the rescue in the nick of time. (This differed from his previous doll play in which the main activity was falling over the cliff or off the buildings and being killed.) Sometimes the father doll got quite punitive with the rest of the family, but he was always able to establish order. His family play showed how much Dan missed a daddy, and what an important role he attributed to the father. Once he quietly and seriously remarked that a boy would want to have a daddy in his house.

After the puppies were born, Dan could speculate on how the puppies got out, and this led to how they got in, and what part the father played in putting his "spur" into the mother. He knew before the puppies were born that he could not keep any, but he tried pathetically hard to change his mother's decision (and nearly succeeded). He brought his favorite puppy to his treatment session. He was appropriately sad when the puppies were sold, especially his favorite. He then thought (hopefully) that their dog might have some more, and if she had a girl he would name it Miss Fiedler. If she had two girls, he'd name the other one Miss Eleanor Fiedler. Some time after the puppies' birth (and after the birth of a sibling of one of the nursery school children) Dan, in playing with the doll family, sneaked a baby into the bed of the father and mother doll while they were sleeping. The mother woke up and upon discovering the baby, exclaimed, "God, look what we got in the night!" Father, equally surprised, "Well, I'll be! How'd he get here?" to which the mother replied, "Well, I guess it just slipped out during the night." In a further elaboration of this play the baby grows up over a period of time, being replaced from time to time by an older boy until finally he is a man and takes over the original father's place with the mother. The original father, he explained, "got lost." I thought that a little boy might sometimes think that this could happen, but he might also wish very much that the daddy would not get lost. He agreed with this, but told me that this was "only just pretend." He wouldn't want to have a new baby at his house—that would be like having other kids come to see your talking lady—or like when new kids came to the school. Then he assured me it couldn't happen at his house because "you have to have a daddy to get a new baby."

The other side of his feelings about fathers was amply illustrated in his jealous, angry, and often frightened feelings toward older boys and men—his brother Ted and his friends, or mother's gentlemen friends, or, in the transference, the big man whose office was next to mine. While he looked up to and tried to emulate Ted (five years older), he also got very angry at Ted's interference, expecially when mother did something with Ted. Ted spent a week's spring vacation visiting an aunt and uncle in another city and Dan was frankly glad to have him go, sorry to have him return, but very worried and solicitous of him when he was sick after he returned. Dan was openly angry at mother's boyfriends and would bluntly ask them to leave— even repairmen. He bragged, showed off, and talked big in front of Ted and his friends, as well as mother's men friends, then would be hurt and indignant if they teased him back. There was an incident in which Dan, who was with his mother, acted in a very boastful and cocky way in front of three men at a filling station. They, in turn, teased him with a blowgun and Dan was both scared and angry. "They could have killed me!" he told me. On another occasion, with me, he was showing off and talking about Dr. S. in the next office who, he said, was dumb. He threw a few blocks at the wall, then got scared that Dr. S. would come in and throw him out.

There was some material in the treatment about his father and his father's death. While he could express sadness in relation to other people's losses through death, he did not at any time express sad feelings around his own father's death. Once he told me if I ever met his aunt on the street I shouldn't say anything to her about *her* daddy, because her daddy died and it made her very sad to talk about it. I learned from mother that this aunt was seventy-four, and that her "daddy" died before Dan was born, but it *was* true that it was difficult for *mother* to talk about daddy's death.

Toward the end of the first year of treatment Dan had the flu and missed five treatment hours. He was quite ill for a while, with a persistent high temperature. During his illness he was "an excellent patient," taking all his medicines with no fuss and doing everything mother and the doctor suggested. After he was better he showed clearly how worried he had been that he would die, and how relieved he was when assured that he was almost well again. He told me later, "I was afraid I might die," and after his illness there was some temporary regression to the old dangerous behavior at home and in the sessions—throwing himself around carelessly, falling, etc.

He brought several snapshots to show me when he returned; one of his father holding him when he was three months old, and two of him at eleven months taken in the yard of his home. He told me this was his daddy, but he couldn't remember him, he was too little. He thought his daddy looked like a nice daddy; he also thought that his face looked like an artist. The other two pictures of Dan alone, he thought, were taken by his daddy before he died. He then told me that he had been very sick, so sick that he didn't want to talk with anyone over the telephone, but he missed me and he missed school.

There was considerable growth and development in the area of Dan's ego functioning during the first year, especially in learning. He became very interested in writing (his name and certain letters), could recognize certain letters and numbers, and could count. He became able to distinguish colors accurately. He could do simple addition and subtraction and seemed capable in other cognitive functions. At five years, two months, an IQ test showed him to function in the superior range.

During the second year of treatment there was further elaboration of Dan's oedipal development and its vicissitudes, particularly his attempts to cope with some very real rivals. Connected with this was further work around his father's death and his feelings about it or, more accurately, about not having a father.

At my month's vacation at the end of the first year, Dan (five and a half) could express his oedipal feelings in the transference through frank love letters (dictated to his mother or to me); for example: "It's been a long time since I saw you. I do love you, Miss Fiedler. Sincerely, Dan." or "Dear Miss Fiedler: Will you come to my party? Where are you? Are you on a date or something?"

Along with his continuing concerns about ghosts and monsters (although, as he said, he knew very well there were no such things) Dan developed a real concern about his father's picture (a framed portrait photograph) which sat on his mother's dresser. Several times mother found him looking intently at the picture, and he always acted embarrassed or guilty at being discovered; or, more often, mother would discover the picture turned face toward the wall. Once he brought this picture, carrying it carefully under his jacket, to an analytic session and explained to me how the eyes (which looked directly into the camera) scared him. "They look at you real mean; they have monsters in them," he said, and he thought somehow the monsters might get after him. This led to Dan's fears of sleeping alone in his room and his wish to sleep with his mother—and to his not infrequent nighttime wanderings when he would wind up sleeping on his mother's bed where she would find him in the morning. At this point mother was convinced of the importance of closing her bedroom door. After this he turned his nighttime attentions to Kathy, his sister, slipping into her room at night where he would sit on her bed and talk, or together they would go downstairs and watch TV. He was often both sad and mad, having ideas of blowing things up with time bombs, etc. When I told him I thought he was really so mad about mother's closed door and that she forbade him to come into her room at night, he readily agreed that this made him very mad. He produced a dream: *Mother let him sleep in her bed, then she carried him to his bed and left him there. Then there were monsters and thunder as in "Dark Shadows"* (a scary TV show) *and he was very scared.* We talked then about his wish to sleep with mother as a daddy would, as *his* daddy did before he could remember. This would be like a little boy doing big-man things and it scared him very much to think he might be able to do big-man things. Then he had to be scared by monster thoughts.

Before long, Dan's analytic material suggested that his mother was having a more seriously intentioned suitor. Dan became more and more demanding of mother—in knowing just where she was going and with whom. He was very curious about and openly jealous of the older adolescent boy I was seeing in the hour following Dan's. He referred to this boy as "that man who comes after me," or, sometimes, as a "hippie," whom he considered very dangerous. One day he drew a picture of a house where children and a father lived. "The mother died," he said, "just like *my* house, only my *father* died." Later I learned from mother that this was, in fact, the family situation of the man who was then showing much interest in her. When I had asked Dan, in reference to the picture-story, what had happened to the mother, he said sadly that he didn't know, but *his father* died a long time ago—"I don't remember what he died of; you know, he caught something—a virus—from someone else who was sick; I don't remember who."

Later on he observed, "If you saw your mother kissing someone, you might think she didn't love you anymore." He then added that his mother kisses *her father* (his grandfather), and he wished *his* father was alive, then he, Dan, would kiss him. I thought maybe he was also thinking that then *mother* would kiss his daddy, at which he burst out that he "hates" Mr. T.—"Yuk, she won't marry *him!*" I thought he so much wished his father could be here to help him with these feelings.

His troubles and his rivals increased; soon there were two men vying with each other for mother's attention. "Now," said Dan, disgustedly, "there's Mr. T. and a new one," whose name he could never remember, and he was convinced, no matter what mother said, that marriage was imminent. He wished and feared alternately. Now he openly wished his own daddy hadn't died. *He* was good; these interlopers were *bad* because they took up all mother's time. I thought his own daddy, if he had lived, would also take up a lot of mother's time, and he shouted at me, "NO!" He closed himself off in a "little house" made with chairs in the corner of the office and was very, very sad. Shortly after this, around the time of his sixth birthday, Dan made what mother referred to as a "last stand, all-out try." At bedtime one evening he asked for a bedtime story, and after she'd read it and kissed him goodnight he asked her seriously, *"Now* won't you sleep with me?" She declined and as she was leaving his room, he called, "Mom, won't you marry *me?"*

After this he seemed to be more accepting of the sad fact that mother would not marry or sleep with him. For some time he seemed to be torn between his wish for a new daddy and his fear that he would get one, with what seemed to me to be slightly more emphasis on the former. He drew another house, this time with four bedrooms, one for the mother, one for the father, and one each for the two boys of the family. "There's something wrong with this house," he said, "there shouldn't be a father in it." I said he felt both ways about a father in the house. Again he reiterated, "Four bedrooms; one for each member of the family." I said I thought that the "something wrong here" was that he somehow knew that most mothers and fathers share the same bedroom. "Not this one," he retorted, "I don't need no papa!" We could also see that Dan was afraid that if a new father moved into his house (which was a four-bedroom house) that someone, maybe he, would be displaced.

Several months after Dan's sixth birthday, mother told all three children that she definitely was not going to marry Mr. T. Dan was both relieved and disappointed: relieved in that he had all along clearly disliked Mr. T. but disappointed in a way because as long as there were two suitors, it seemed safer, as if he had a faint hope that they might somehow cancel each other out. This left only Mr. M., whom Dan had never rebuffed as he had Mr. T. and other potential "rivals." He seemed especially fond of Mr. M's younger son, who was Dan's age and, according to mother, very much like Dan. Dan's puppet shows, stories, and plays continued to include a good, wise father who knew how to do many things—the added quality being that the father and the boys in these pretend families did many things together while the mother did the housework—and when they all went to bed at night, the mother and father shared a bed. The father, in his play, sometimes punished and maintained order, but there was no longer the dangerous, punitive aspect to him. He seemed to be more like someone for the boys in the family to admire and emulate.

For a while Dan seemed to have to prove himself with Mr. M.; for example, if both families were picnicking together, Dan would suddenly climb the highest tree or in some fashion call attention to himself. Mr. M. seemed able to deal with him calmly and reassuringly, and this kind of behavior soon disappeared. The two families spent much time together, doing the kinds of things the children enjoyed.

During the winter and spring following Dan's seventh birthday, the third year of treatment, as Dan talked about his mother's approaching marriage to Mr. M., he seemed mainly to look forward to it, even though it would mean, he said, that they would have to move again into a larger house; there would be six children. He and Paul, Mr. M's youngest child, hoped to share a room. In the spring he announced to me one day, "You know what—my mother's finally going to marry Mr. M." Dan was quite taken up with ideas about the wedding, playing out numerous variations of the wedding ceremony—for example, one of his favorites: "Do you take this man for your *awful* wedded husband? (I do.) Do you take this woman for your lawful wedded wife? (I d-d-d-d-do.) Then I pronounce you man and wife—now kiss!"

During the last year of the analysis several things were worked through or more fully understood. During Dan's kindergarten year, glasses were prescribed for him. He steadfastly refused to wear his glasses in school (kindergarten and most of first grade) as he was certain that other children would tease him. The fact that other children wore glasses made no difference to him; he adamantly refused to discuss the subject. Similarly, he refused to work on some isolated incidents of urinating on the floor at home. He was most reluctant to go swimming because of his extreme modesty about undressing in the locker room. He was always very modest about undressing although not averse to looking at others—i.e. peeking in the school toilets. At home, Ted teased Dan. I learned belatedly from the mother that Dan had an unusually small penis. It had always been very small so that he even had trouble holding onto his penis when he was learning to urinate in the toilet. Dan's fear of being teased about wearing glasses was understood as a displacement from his concern over his small penis. This material helped us to understand his (much earlier) remark when complaining about his early hospital experience: "They [doctors and nurses] made me little."

Around the time of his seventh birthday Dan began wearing his glasses in school as well as at other times, reporting that if other kids teased him it was because they didn't know any better. "Ted said I looked silly, but that's not true—my glasses don't look any different from his!" Also, there were no more reports of his urinating on the floor, although this remained not very well understood. His mother reported having seen Dan without his clothes on—a rather rare occurrence—and that he seemed to have grown in all respects, but particularly that his penis seemed more normal in size for a boy of his age and stature. It was my impression at this time that Dan regarded himself well in relation to his peers.

There was occasional doctor play throughout the analysis, often related to real doctor visits. Earlier, he had often used a white lab coat he found in the closet to dress up the couch pillow into a "stuffed doctor," which he then punched and mistreated. On one occasion, for the first time he put the coat on himself, saying, "The doctor's got something up his sleeve"—pulling out a toy saw or a pair of scissors. He then acted out with play tools all kinds of horrors on the couch-pillow patient. Suddenly, he stopped, took off the coat as if to say that it was too much for him. He guessed he'd draw the operation instead. He drew a picture of a man lying on an operating table with a doctor standing over him, administering penicillin with a spoon. A baby was trying to crawl up to see what was going on on the operating table. Then he added a tarantula sitting on the patient's abdomen. I thought this must represent his confused thoughts about what the doctor did to his father in the hospital when he was so little and couldn't understand; and also what he feared may have been done to him to "make him little." Concurrent with this Dan made a fifteen-page picture book entitled "The Dopey Doctor." Each picture, carefully executed, was described. The book was the story of his illness and hospitalization, the mother's abandonment, and the father's illness and death. The titles of the pictures (with Dan's verbal explanations) were: "This is the Dopey Doctor's office. This is the Dopey Doctor; The Dopey Doctor—The dopey doctor is very, very, very, very, very, very, smart!!! This is the dopey doctor's patient [a baby]; The big one is the baby; The little one is the mother [she's little because she's far away and you can't see her very well]. The doctor is helping the patient; The patient is better. This is the ambulence!!! *He* is in the hospital! [he is another patient.] Now the [baby] patient is betor; But there is a nother one. The patient [other one] is going to die. The patient is bettor; There is a nother one. The patient might die—the grass groo long!!!" [the grave]."

From time to time Dan brought what appeared to be screen memories from the time he was in the hospital. For example, he talked about his "lost little red rooster" in a very affectionate, nostalgic way. He had a toy rooster with him in the hospital, he said, and his father gave it to him. It was his favorite toy. He thought it was left at the hospital. He had me draw a little rooster for him which he colored, and he took it home and hung it in his bedroom. His mother was amazed to hear he had remembered this toy, as she had not seen it since his hospitalization. She confirmed that it had been given Dan by his father and had been one of his favorite toys.

Another memory concerned his often-repeated memory that his father was a black man. One day toward the end of his analysis, after talking about some black boys in his class, he reminisced that he had used to say his father was black, and I said we'd never really understood about that —did he think he ever knew a black man that he might have got mixed up with his daddy? To my surprise, he replied, "Yes"—then, as if unable to speak out loud, he formed the words: "You know—the doctor!" He meant, he said, the *black* doctor when he was in the hospital when he was a baby. Again, as with the red rooster, mother verified that the doctor who took care of Dan in the hospital was a dark-skinned Indian. Dan brought only pleasant memories of the black doctor who played with him, although it will be remembered that in some of his picture stories of doctors and what they did to "patients," doctors were not so kindly.

Dan's spring school report from his first grade teacher corroborated my impression that Dan was dealing successfully with the resolution of his oedipal conflicts and that he was able to use his good mind for learning. The end of his analysis was in sight and Dan, now aged seven and a half, worked to finish by the time his mother was married. The very great gain in having a father whom he liked and admired and a brother his age whom he knew and liked appeared to outweigh the losses inherent in the change—most particularly the loss of his old home and neighborhood and the sharing of his mother and siblings with the new family members. A follow-up visit initiated by Dan in the summer after termination indicated that he had made a good adjustment within his new family.

Dan's analysis is not an illustration of a boy's mourning the loss of his father. For him the early hospitalization experience and separation from mother appeared to be much more significant in the genesis of his disturbance than the loss of his father, although the fact that father had died and that he was without a father played a prominent part in Dan's subsequent development.

Dan's whole life prior to analysis seemed to revolve around avoiding and fearing a repetition of the separation–hospitalization experience and the fear that the event that had caused all this (the father's death) would happen to him. This early great fear of death was rooted in his fear of annihilation and feeling of lack of protection during his hospital experience. Subsequently, Dan's own aggression greatly enhanced his fear of danger from inside and outside himself. Knowledge of the father's death and, later on, of the deaths of other adults (great grandmother and uncle) contributed.

Dan's tremendous difficulty in accepting the death of his father (his denial, confusion, magical thinking), as well as his other defenses against the fear of death, was due in part to his difficulty in differentiating himself from his father. His own immature personality structure, the many similarities between himself and his father, may have contributed to this. Further, a death represents not only a loss, but a threat: "This could happen to me." The intensity of the threat varies according to the age and cause of death of the deceased. For young children the threat is so great that extensive defenses have to be utilized.

It is important to note that Dan's mother kept the image of the father and of his personality very much alive in her children's minds, especially as these were years when she herself was preoccupied with the mourning of her husband. Her difficulties with aggression in general had some negative effects upon Dan's ability to deal with aggression, but it had the positive effect of keeping up a very wholesome, loving, and protective picture of the father. Further, Dan had the benefit of his close relationship with his maternal grandfather as a father substitute. For Dan, father and grandfather became fused, and as he accepted grandfather as his father, he thought of him as alive. This supported his denial of father's death, which, to some extent, may have been an age-adequate way of maintaining memories of the father. His "daddy will come and catch the baby" games lead one to think that some memories of father were retained.

Dan's reaction to the separation–hospitalization experience, the regression in the ego functions of motility and speech, could be viewed as directly related to the level of development in his object relationships. On the one hand, assuming that at eleven months his object relationships were still at the level of primary identification, the ego function then is both part of the self and part of the object, and when the object is withdrawn, the function cannot survive. On the other hand, assumed that Dan had achieved the beginnings of object-constancy prior to his hospitalization, he may well have maintained some of it throughout his experience, as evidenced in his immediate recognition of his mother and intense clinging to her. The loss of motility and speech, then, would be explained in terms of their very recent tentative acquisition and close dependence on the mother's libidinization. The mother's distraught and preoccupied mental state, together with the total change in physical and emotional family milieu, may have accounted for Dan's temporary loss of affective responsiveness.

Dan's unsafe and uncontrolled behavior had many determinants. Among them were the restraints and hurts imposed upon him in the hospital and the mother's characteristic tendency *not* to clearly limit or restrain overly active behavior. This behavior gained momentum and significance when bodily injury became linked to castration with the beginning of the phallic phase. His castration fear was very early drawn into the area of fear of death, both through his many minor and major injuries, and through living with his brother Ted, whose main problems centered around his own extreme castration anxiety which he tried to handle in part through teasing of Dan.

The grandfather represented a positive influence in Dan's phallic and oedipal development as did the mother's excellent handling of this phase. These factors, plus the eventual appearance of Mr. M., greatly enhanced the analysis of Dan's oedipal conflicts.

Dan's early memories of the hospitalization—his memories of the little red rooster and of the black doctor—were of quite different quality from other memories such as the games of being caught in the air (reminiscent of games with father) and his fear of being photographed (reminding him of hospital X rays). It would seem that the cathexis of these memories (red rooster and black doctor) may have occurred during subsequent weeks and months. Many other memories of the hospitalization were lost but certain ones "chosen" for retention. These very early memories may serve some defensive purposes, e.g. maintaining something pleasant in order to counteract all the unpleasantness of the experience. They may also have served to "bind" otherwise traumatic experiences, and, in this way, enhance mastery. They may resemble the last vivid mental contact prior to a traumatic experience, such as Freud described in aphasia. In this sense the mind keeps intact a small area of functioning in the face of overwhelming disaster. In Dan's memories the feeling of longing for a treasured something, the red rooster (object or partial object), was very pronounced and appeared to be evidence of a strong libidinal cathexis of the lost rooster and, to some extent, even of the black doctor. Both probably represented the dead father and absent mother.

Lucy was ten weeks old when her mother died. The interferences in her subsequent development resulted from the indirect, more than the direct, effects of the death due to the unfortunate events following it. During her analysis, which began in her eleventh year, it was possible to trace some of the influences on her character development that arose from the loss of the mother and what came after it. Her intense conscious longing for a mother of her own, her fantasies and conflicts, were stimulated primarily at the age of five, when she was separated from the cousin with whom she lived. She failed to establish a satisfactory relationship to her new mother.

While her parents were out celebrating her birth, Lucy's mother fell dead. An autopsy led only to the verdict of unexplained death. Her father was stunned by the mother's sudden death and in his grief withdrew to another city. Lucy was left in the home of maternal relatives. They could not bear the thought of becoming attached to her and then having to give her up, so when she was five months old she went with her father to live with a paternal cousin who had a child a little older than Lucy. Lucy shared a room with her father and the other child. Because of overcrowded conditions, the family moved twice in Lucy's first four years. The father's job took him out of town a great deal, and he and the cousin fought over Lucy's upbringing. The cousin was warm and permissive but overly volatile and emotional. Lucy was overweight and enuretic, having never achieved nighttime control. Both of these qualities were common in the family and were not regarded as problems.

When Lucy was not yet six, and halfway through kindergarten, the father married a woman with three children, all older than Lucy. The cousin's strong reaction to losing Lucy led to a permanent rift in the family. The child had little preparation for the move. Her school was changed and her way of life drastically altered. The new mother's high standards contrasted with the comfortable sloppiness of the old home. Her attitude toward Lucy's wetting and weight varied markedly from that of the cousin. Lucy was ill at the time of the move, and the father immediately went out of town, leaving Lucy and the stepmother with no support in getting accustomed to each other.

Lucy never made a satisfactory adjustment to her new home. At the age of ten she was still enuretic and overweight. At home she was practically mute, but at school she was excessively verbal, disruptive, and unable to settle down in the group, though she was intellectually bright. Her relationship with her stepmother had steadily worsened, in spite of their mutual efforts to get along better. Outpatient therapy failed to help, and at age ten and a half she was placed in a residential center and began her analysis a few months before her eleventh birthday.

Lucy's father was a well-intentioned man who was hit very hard by the death of his wife. He was a person who kept an emotional distance from his own and others' feelings. He handled stress by avoidance and denial. Lucy described him as "putting things out of his mind, as if you won't have feelings about things you don't mention." This was the way he coped with the death of Lucy's mother. In addition, he traveled on his job and was often absent. He cared deeply for Lucy, but taught her that anything can be solved by will power. This left her with the idea that she should have conscious control over all her difficulties, and had only herself to blame if she didn't. He expected Lucy and her new mother to be as close as a real mother and daughter, though they both knew this was not possible. Lucy's stepmother had suffered much adversity during her own life. She was a frank, outspoken woman with good super ego values and high standards. She often showed warmth and appropriate feeling for Lucy. Though they both tried hard, neither she nor Lucy could overcome the obstacles between them.

Lucy knew the circumstances of her mother's death and had a vivid memory of a snapshot in her father's room. She "always knew" her cousin was not her mother, but did not recall how or when she learned this. Lucy's father could not allow her to ask questions about her mother and she learned quickly not to ask. She was always told she could see pictures "when you are older." The image of the mother was never brought "alive" for her through the recollections of others. Later, when she was helped to seek information about her mother, she found it hard to integrate because she missed the impression she would get if someone would "just talk" about mother.

Lucy took in her father's prohibition so thoroughly that she never attempted to look at the pictures of mother, though she knew where they were kept. An inhibition of curiosity spread from the subject of mother to many other areas. This applied more to people and events around her than to formal learning. She accepted plans made for her without question and could never ask about any absences or activities of mine. She viewed her wish to know as wrong, and finally she could ask me directly if it were wrong to want a picture of her mother. Sexual curiosity was treated much like "mother curiosity." She defensively demanded sexual information from me with the words, "I'm old enough and I have a right to know." Sexual curiosity was further inhibited by having showered and slept with her father until she was five. Since he could not acknowledge or answer her questions in this area either, she handled observations of his penis by "not noticing." This mechanism became prominent in relation to all other perceptions that aroused anxiety.

Originally Lucy's affect toward the dead mother was contained in her statement, "I didn't know her, so how could I have feelings?" Later she could recapture sadness about not having a mother. She told me at once that the problem with which I could not help was her relationship with her current mother. I viewed this as a displacement from my inability to help with the fact of the dead mother. Her greatest wish was that her mother had not died so early, because the "hardest thing" was never to have known her and to know she never could. There was an "empty spot" because there was nothing to remember. Her father's reticence about her mother left her with no secondhand knowledge. She thought girls who were adopted were better off. If a mother is still alive you can think about her, "somewhere leading a good life."

Lucy could recall no sadness about leaving her well-loved cousin, but she spoke with intense longing about many things she had lost— baby clothes, toys, and houses—all of which she could remember in great detail. When my office was moved she longed for the old cozy office, hated the new modern one, and worried that I had no consideration for the feelings of the furniture that had been dislodged from its familiar place. The change of place also brought a fear of change of person. When the office was moved she expected to have a new therapist or to be left behind, both old feelings from the time of her father's remarriage. Changes in familiar surroundings always brought feelings of distress and disequilibrium similar to those she must have experienced during the moves in her first five months. A change in her bedroom resulted in "missing" feelings and an inability to invest in the new room, so that an unkempt messy room became an area of strife between Lucy and the caretaking adults.

Affects were also displaced to less important people. She could have no feelings about my vacation times, but her sadness and tears when other people left were very genuine. When a girl she knew left town she cried all night. In reality, this friend had been quite cruel to her, but Lucy idealized her memory and could allow no aggression toward it. In a letter to her friend, Lucy wrote, "You left at night without saying good-bye." She referred to the short time they had had together. Both things were true of the real mother but not of the friend. She explained that the depth of her feeling was great because this girl was the first person she had met when she came to the residence.

Lucy denied having fantasies about what her real mother was like. In the transference she wished that I would be the always available mother who would listen to mundane things and take pride in her accomplishments. Fantasies about gaining an ideal mother were connected with her father's remarriage; she had looked forward to a new all-giving mother and was terribly disappointed. Part of her lack of sadness around leaving her cousin was due to her hope that she was regaining her mother through her father's remarriage. Other therapists were idealized, while I was rejected because she had "no choice" about me. I was just assigned, which reflected feelings about real mothers who are not assigned, as well as about stepmothers who do not choose you. As Lucy put it, "I was part of a package deal; she had to take me to get my father." Lucy felt that her trouble lay in not knowing what a mother is like at all. Losing a cousin is not the same as losing a mother. Visits to her own home were very hard because they revived the longing for early mothering from the stepmother, and they inevitably ended in anger and disappointment.

One fantasy about treatment was that I would make it possible for her to return home to a loving real family. When the time came for her to leave the residence, it was recommended that she go to a foster home. Though she had asked for this plan, she became immobilized, and her functioning deteriorated. To her it meant giving up forever the idea of regaining her own family. She reacted with desperation, projecting and externalizing all her problems, and casting about pathetically for a place to go. First she decided to return to her cousin, viewing this as going back to the early preschool years and denying the current realities of this home. Then she tried to make herself very "good" so she could live with her father. She could make no decision out of fear of making the wrong one. Her immobility arose from her inability to face the sad reality and the unfairness of having no real mother. To decide on the foster home meant accepting the irrevocable fact that she would never have her own mother.

The greatest obstacle in Lucy's treatment was her inconsistent attendance. The work was continually interrupted by her absences, which were often unpredictable and resulted in a lack of continuity and integration. All her relationships were characterized by this withdrawal or absenting of herself without explanation. For example, she would periodically refuse visits home, or would suddenly drop out of a class. She always felt that the other people involved would understand why, without the need for any discussion of her motives with them. She had never been a participant in changes in her own life. She had a tendency to let relationships with others drift off, rather than really ending them. Lucy had to fight the wish to see me because it contained the desire to get more from me than I, as her therapist, could give. Sporadic attendance also put separations under her control. I was the one who waited and never knew when she would appear, just as she had earlier never known when her father would leave or return from his trips. The inability to control life and death, the comings and goings of other people, and her own bodily functions contributed to her being a very controlling girl in her relationships. Though it was evident she wanted help and was dissatsified with herself, she continually refuted everything I said and could not consciously want anything from me. She warded me off as if fearing the repetition of painful disappointments if she invested in our relationship. She told me she would not form close friendships with staff because they left too often. This was reminiscent of her father's instructions to her cousin not to get attached to Lucy because she was not her daughter. Lucy found her father's idea ridiculous. Her maternal relatives had also given her up to avoid coming too close to her.

The early object loss and the separations thereafter pervaded much of the material. Penis envy, masturbation, bedwetting, oedipal wishes, all made her view herself as a "bad girl" who had deserved to be abandoned, and all object relations were colored by the wish for the early mother. Relationships for Lucy always contained the hope that what she had missed would be forthcoming. To make a new friend was tantalizing in its possibilities; she tantalized me with intriguing material, after which she failed to show up for a number of sessions. Her sporadic mothering was reflected in her characteristic way of working hard, then losing interest and giving up, as she must have felt her mother substitutes had done with her. As they had disappointed her, she disappointed me.

During the course of the treatment, Lucy's bodily reactions to mental stresses were notable. Her weight problem, respiratory ailments, and severe gastrointestinal upsets pointed to remnants from the earliest losses. She had been a colicky baby, had frequent colds, and had been ill at the time of leaving her cousin. During placement, a move to different living quarters coincided with abdominal pain and extreme tiredness. She worried that she would lose her breath. This may have been a fear of being like her mother, who had to rest after her birth and who lost her breath when she suddenly died. When Lucy was convalescing from an illness, she would become anxious about returning to school, being afraid she would become sick again if she went out.

When there was any change in her life, in either people or surroundings, Lucy would develop abdominal or respiratory symptoms. Frequently she would lose her voice, connecting this with aggression, "If you have laryngitis and can't talk, you can't get in trouble." She remarked that even when a slight acquaintance left, it "felt like death" to her, and when those important to her left, she could not maintain an interest in self-care. She would overeat, suffer many accidental injuries and, on occasion, inflict a self-injury.

Lucy was not successful in losing weight, despite a very strong conscious wish to do so. Losing weight meant a loss of her body image. She feared she "would not be Lucy." The extra weight was a companion, something no one could take away, unlike people who come and go. It was also a way of retaining the cousin in whose home everyone ate pleasurably and everyone was fat. Eating became compulsive when it represented taking in the object, destroying it, and then having to take it in again. She gave me custody of a huge lollipop in the hope that I would protect it from her incorporative wishes. It was too beautiful to be destroyed and "could never be replaced." She ate a little each day and was very sad when it was gone. Before coming to see me, Lucy would eat in order to avoid needing anything from me. Her greatest success with dieting came when she felt cared for by her stepmother, but when she felt no one took an active interest, she reverted to overfeeding herself. Overeating was also connected with fears of death. She told me that she ate to keep alive.

Lucy felt she would not have been fat if her mother had lived. She recognized that what little she had known of her mother was the feeding experience. To feel lonely and empty was to feel hungry. At these times not eating meant to face unbearable lonely feelings, while eating brought a sense of contentment, but also a self-loathing. Food was a substitute for narcissistic supplies from people. It was a consistently available comfort, while the feeder was not. Lucy knew she ate when she was not hungry. She would be overcome by a "frantic feeling" of having to eat as if she might never get the chance again. In reconstruction, we felt that she may have been fed to quiet other forms of distress, as well as suffering early periods when her hunger went unnoticed and untended. The early shifts in the need-fulfilling person led to a predisposition for bodily distress to become easily involved in subsequent stressful periods. Her first five months were spent with adults who were undergoing their own painful reactions, which may have made them less attuned to her needs. The frantic feeling of hunger was also related to the change in family eating patterns when she moved to the stepmother's home, where the continual snacking of the cousin's family was not practiced.

Lucy's bedwetting stopped in the third year of her analysis. She attributed this to becoming aware of and experiencing her sadness about having no mother, and to being able to cry about it. In the treatment it became permissible to have feelings which had not been allowed expression in her family. She began to understand that she had internalized her father's problem of not permitting curiosity or feelings, or preparation for important events. When she no longer had to tune out her own affects or wishes, she could become more of a participant in her life and could assume more control over her body.

Initially she regarded wetting as something very bad, and told me she had never wet, not even as an infant. Then she decided it had started when she moved to her stepmother's home. It is probable that it became a source of conflict at that time because of the difference in attitude toward it, and because other channels for expressing feelings were not available. Lucy had not been permitted to cry at home. She also viewed her wetting as "part of being Lucy," and felt giving it up would be to lose herself. It too was a link to her cousin's home and a way of holding on to early objects, as well as an identification with her father's family, all of whom had been enuretic. Lucy's unpredictable attendance in her treatment had seemed a repetition of father's comings and goings in her life, but she also connected it with the wetting which, to her, came and went unpredictably. Periods of dryness in the past had been related to separations. When she was two, her family went on vacation, leaving her behind. For a time afterward, the enuresis stopped, just as it did not occur later on overnight visits to this family.

Lucy's lack of self-esteem was extreme and was accompanied by a feeling of not deserving better. Her harsh super ego was directed mainly toward affects and instinctual pleasure. She treated herself in a critical manner, similar to her family's criticisms of her, and said that part of being Lucy was being criticized. When she began analysis, she viewed feelings as bad and "sick," and would have an angry outburst if I so much as mentioned a feeling.

There were indications that she blamed herself for her mother's death. She spoke of her whole life as a punishment. She castigated a girl who had lost her foster parents as being entirely to blame because of her demands for their attention. She told me she had been offered attention as a baby but she never took it. She thought the rift between her cousin's family and her current family was her fault. Her very existence had caused them to fight.

Lucy lost many things that were of value to her, including several watches which she felt she did not deserve to have. With great feeling she longed for a lost watch her parents had once given her. "The first watch is the best," and it could never be replaced. Both her words and her affect were more appropriate for the loss of a person. Much later I learned that the father still kept the mother's watch. This came to light after Lucy again lost a watch her father gave her, then worried it might have been mother's watch. A preconscious fear of having caused her mother's death appeared after she broke up with her boyfriend. She wondered if it were her fault that so many people left her, adding "of course, not my real mother. I was too young." By this time she had overcome her prohibition against asking about her mother. Through various sources she had obtained information and pictures. She learned that her mother had wanted a girl and was pleased with her birth. The mother had anemia after Lucy was born and was supposed to stay home and rest. Lucy felt that if she had not been born there would have been no outing; mother would have rested and not died. Lucy should have been the one to die since she had no life yet and would not have missed it, while mother had a lot to live for.

Lucy often protected others from her aggression by leaving them. Much of her aggression was invested in the super ego and turned against herself, resulting in, for example, school failure. When someone left she got the feeling that people were reacting toward her as if she had been bad. Since they did not punish her, she would punish herself.

At times of separation, Lucy identified with the person leaving and used a passive into active defense. She left me first at holiday times and failed to return, or became excessively critical of me, as if I had left her out of dissatisfaction with her.

Her most prominent defense was isolation, which in many ways seemed to point to an early interference in integration. In addition to the silence he maintained about her mother, Lucy's father supported splits in the family through family feuds. He did not get along with the cousin, did not maintain contact with Lucy's maternal relatives, and made it hard for her to have continuing relationships and to put the pieces of her life together. Lucy felt disloyal to him when she wanted to know her relatives, feeling she had to choose between them and him, and that contact with one person led to loss of another. The father was quite unaware of the way he conveyed this feeling to Lucy. She struggled with her despair as she tried to put together an image of her real mother; she failed in this as there was no opportunity to integrate her bits of knowledge through the conversation and reminiscences of those who had known her mother.

The father's characteristic of avoiding stressful feeling through not talking about it resulted in Lucy's seldom being prepared for changes in her life, nor being able to master them through verbalization. She felt a lack of influence over her own life and attempted to handle her feelings by tuning them out and not noticing difficult outside happenings over which she had no control. She seemed at the mercy of events, moving from one place to another, taking in what that place offered, and remaining a "here and now" person. Lucy isolated the "bad" parts of herself, as well as unpleasant situations, from treatment, keeping them from her own awareness as much as from mine. Isolation was pervasive. She did not relate one session to another; when on a diet she couldn't notice herself eating until it was too late;

and she ignored important school projects as if they would have no effect on her grade. Many disappointments resulted from this, since not connecting her own actions with the outcome of a situation often kept her from getting what she wanted.

Lucy had great compassion for children who were motherless or in some way deprived. She liked to help other girls be more attractive, using her talents to fix their hair or design their clothes, and often giving up competition in their favor. Her altruism was thought of as a defense against her envy of and aggression toward her "siblings": her cousin's and her stepmother's own children. It appeared to have its origins in never having been the "own" child in any of her homes. She thought of her siblings as more fortunate in their possessions and achievements, as each had a mother of her own.

Lucy's personality revealed primitive identifications and contained contradictory attitudes side by side in comfortable coexistence. Her lack of consistent early mothering was reflected in the way she took in bits and pieces of the various people who had cared for her. She enjoyed being messy and relaxed just as much as she enjoyed being neat and clean. Super ego and ego ideal attitudes seemed to belong to the stepmother, while affects and instinctual pleasure belonged to the cousin. Lucy quickly took on traits of other people; for example, she adopted my vocabulary. She lectured herself as her father lectured her, held up to herself her stepmother's moral standards, was permissive as her cousin had been. At times she fought any agreement with my opinions, as if she feared she would lose herself in becoming like me.

She had great difficulty deciding what kind of person to be. Who was the "real Lucy"? This affected her identity as a boy or girl. She saw herself as having been raised a boy and becoming a girl when she moved. She showed me that she wore shorts under her skirt and was still a secret tomboy. As puberty approached she had a great deal of worry about how she would turn out. She searched for any resemblance to her father, as the only person she knew she might resemble. She couldn't know what she would be like because she didn't know what her mother had been like. She was afraid to grow up and have children for fear she would die and leave them as her mother left her. Once, uncharacteristically, she bleached a streak in her hair. Much later, when she obtained the early picture of mother which she had always dimly remembered, the mother's hair looked bleached in front. When a favorite teacher left, Lucy talked in the teacher's voice.

Lucy and her father had been very close in the preschool years. They went places where he and mother used to go. During treatment she cried over the loss of this early special closeness with her father. When he remarried she lost him as her exclusive object. She remembered her own possessiveness at that time and her anger toward the new wife for taking her father away. This represented not just an oedipal loss but the loss of father as a mothering figure, the only person who was family of her own. This double loss was an additional factor in her inability to form a satisfactory relationship with her stepmother. At the stressful time of moving to the new home, Lucy's father left immediately on a business trip, arousing her strong aggression toward him for this desertion.

Her father's promises of expensive gifts and trips alone with him if she would lose weight or improve her grades were influential in her lack of success in these areas. Her stepmother's active support of her dieting was helpful in counteracting her feeling that the stepmother wanted her fat and unattractive. She admired her own mother's very good figure, as revealed in pictures, and this too played a part in the oedipal prohibition against losing weight. At times Lucy hid weight loss from me, worrying that I might disapprove if she lost weight without my help.

In adolescence, Lucy established a strong and long-lasting relationship with a boy. She couldn't let her parents know about him, and she hid the flowers he sent her when father visited. She looked upon this boy as the person who would stick by her forever, and she was heartbroken when the friendship ended. She recognized that her feelings for him were of extra importance because of her early losses. They were not just feelings toward a boyfriend but toward a long-awaited person who would care only about her. The boy, like her father, was unpredictable in his whereabouts and often disappointed her. When he left town she experienced severe stomach pains, lost interest in her own progress, and became dejected and hopeless for some time. Though they continued to correspond, she felt the relationship had lost its important meaning. Her love for him depended on their living in the same place and sharing their daily life, and a "boyfriend" relationship could not serve the same purpose. While this friendship was often a repetition of her interaction with her father, it also contained her longing for the lost mother.

Lucy's approach to school was always one of lack of interest and intrinsic motivation. Schoolwork provided no pleasure. Low grades were due to such omissions as not turning in work, or to unkindness to herself in losing work she had prepared. She would interfere with her own success through misplacing her books, forgetting her homework, or isolating mathematical concepts from their application. Her attendance at school followed the same sporadic pattern of her attendance in treatment. When Lucy began analysis at age ten, she did not know the months of the year in succession, had no idea of geography, and had a poor sense of time. When I went on vacation, she didn't know where I was, how long I would be gone, or when I would return. If I left in August and returned early in September, she did not know how many months intervened. She explained that "mothers are supposed to teach you the months," and since she changed homes in the middle of kindergarten she lost her chance to learn. The libidinization of learning was lost in the move. Her parents' attitudes perpetuated poor performance, as the father overexpected and the stepmother underexpected. Lucy connected lost learning with lost people. She felt she no longer had the ability to draw since she had left the cousin who taught her and the teacher who helped her. She spent a lot of time drawing girls while telling me about past girls she had drawn, which were always better and had always been lost. We had to make an identity for each of these girls: name, family, occupation. She wished she could make the pictures come alive at will. She became anxious if she changed the appearance of a drawing for fear she would forget what it looked like originally. Once she drew a picture of me and secretly kept it in her room, just as she used to secretly look at mother's pictures in father's room. Taking in learning was a forbidden secret activity, with roots both in the father's secrecy and in secret sexual knowledge from the time of shared bedrooms.

When Lucy was nearly fifteen she began to talk about leaving the treatment center which had been her home for several years. This introduced a period of depressive manifestations. She developed a dejected hopeless mood and lost interest in school and social activities. She couldn't get up in the morning, fell asleep in school, and eventually stopped attending. Though she had often felt hopeless in the face of inner and outer obstacles, she had never before appeared manifestly depressed or had seemed so immobilized. Old difficulties arose again. Physical symptoms were prevalent, she gained more weight, and on one occasion superficially scratched her wrist. Her boyfriend, who was preparing to return to his own home, had broken up with her, and she viewed her depressive response as due to his withdrawal.

In the analysis at that time, Lucy was working on material related to her toilet training. She rebelled against the wishes and expectations of adults. She often left her analytic sessions early because it was pointless "to sit here and do nothing." At this time her main characteristic was a demanding omnipotence. She wanted special privileges and was furious if they were not granted. Though physical examinations had revealed no medical reason for her symptoms, she felt she should not be expected to do such things as clean her room or go to school since she was "sick."

While genetically this material related to her toilet training, currently it seemed to represent a wish to be independent of the love objects of childhood and, in the transference, of the analyst. Unfortunately, a full understanding of the period was precluded when she left the analysis. She gave up attending her sessions after she had expressed the wish to move to a home for older youngsters and the fear that if she did not like that home she could not return to the treatment center.

She did not officially terminate the analysis but retained the idea of returning once she had left the center. She desperately cast about for a place to go, alternately wanting to return to her own home and to the early home of her cousin. She became immobilized and could make no concrete plans. At the same time her daily life functioning deteriorated to the point where her readiness to leave was in question.

After a few months Lucy decided to resume her treatment on a twice-weekly basis with the stipulation that she would not always be able to attend. She was then able to proceed with plans to move to the home for older adolescents. Her provocative behavior and her depressive symptoms lessened in intensity. The content of her sessions focused on her despair that she could not live with a family of her own, and the great handicap of never having known what her mother was like. From remote sources she sought out information about her mother, and on her own located and visited the grave. After Lucy moved she continued to accumulate knowledge about her mother and was able to enlist her father's cooperation in this. She lost a great deal of weight, resumed her former interests, and began to invest herself in school. She increased her contacts with her own family and was able to establish a good relationship with her stepmother, who was most helpful in supporting Lucy's efforts toward independent strivings and knowledge.

The developmental step of object removal was most difficult for Lucy because there was no external home from which to break away and no internal image of a mother from which she could distance herself. In addition, she had no adult woman model on which to pattern herself. Since she had not known her mother she could not choose to identify or not identify with her adult characteristics. Thus she desperately tried to reestablish a home (with her cousin or father) from which she could become independent. The object of her struggle for independence ultimately centered on the analyst and the treatment center. Only after she had achieved the break from them could she resume progressive growth and identify with some aspects of the adults there.

Her struggles with ambivalence played a part in her difficulty in taking the developmental step of rejecting the parental figures and in her strong reaction to her boyfriend's rejection of her. But more important seemed to be the deprivation caused by the lack of a real mother and of an internal mother image during the developmental stage of object removal and the search for an adult self-image.

Though Lucy's conflicts contained meanings from all levels of development, the early loss of the mother remained a continuing influence which pervaded her personality. This was especially true for her because of the unfortunate circumstances of her life following her mother's death. The lack of a consistent ongoing replacement for the mother deprived her of sufficient love and left her with little opportunity for unimpeded growth.

9. Relating This Work to Other Studies of Mourning

Initially we had attempted a cursory survey of the literature by singling out psychoanalytic writings on bereavement in childhood. We encountered a great diversity of views, many at variance with our clinical material and theoretical thinking. We therefore formulated our own concepts and defined them to the best of our ability. To a limited extent I collected and reviewed the literature during the years of our group meetings but the main portion of it was held over until the conclusion of our studies. It was hoped that this would better enable me to explore and clarify the differences in views and to correlate our findings with those of others.

In recent years death, dying, and bereavement have received constantly increasing attention from analysts and, even more so, from workers in related disciplines. In some ways this makes it difficult to encompass and integrate the literature. In the psychoanalytic field reviews of the literature (Pollock 1961; Siggins 1966; Miller 1971), indexes (Grinstein 1956–72; Hart 1972) and content lists of journals are helpful. Many articles, however, include the topic of death in the title but do not deal with dying or bereavement (Sachs 1942; Natanson 1959). Many more discuss the effects of object loss and mourning on their patients but do not specify this in the title (Lewin 1937; Wittels 1939). Some of the most pertinent child analytic contributions do not stress the aspect of bereavement or discuss its theoretical implications (Meiss 1952; Root 1957; Bergen 1958; Gyomroi 1963). Theoretical and clinical contributions tend to be isolated from one another.

The professional literature in the other disciplines presents a different problem. It is so numerous and diverse that its mere study constitutes an extensive independent project, well beyond the scope of this review (Kalish 1969; *Archives of the Foundation of Thanatology* 1969–70; *Journal of Thanatology* 1971–72; Vernick 1972). Many of

233

the articles and books are most relevant, observant, and insightful; written by nurses, doctors, social workers, and ministers of different religious denominations, they stem from the experiences of those who, day in day out, care for the dying and the bereaved. Considering the great personal stress such work involves, one is particularly admiring of the many who explore the topic with feeling and understanding. Clinical in orientation and practical in application, many of these publications are of great interest and help to the analyst as well as to the layman (e.g. Ottenstein, Wiley, and Rosenblum 1962; Chaloner 1962; Grollman 1967; Paul 1969; Kubler-Ross 1969; Benolie 1971). For practical reasons I did not include creative writers' discussions of death and bereavement in spite of the excellent and insightful contributions such artists had made.

My search of the professional literature was halted when my efforts yielded increasingly diminishing returns. The final list of close to two thousand publications does not nearly represent the available literature to date. I felt certain that I had missed many psychoanalytic contributions and would be unable to include the majority of nonanalytic articles.

Faced with an unwieldy number and variety of literary contributions it became necessary to leave out some and to organize others around selected aspects of the subject matter. It was not an easy choice. All aspects are interrelated and many explorations of an apparently tangential area bring insight to the focal topic. S. Freud (1913, 1915a) used anthropological data to illumine the problems af ambivalence and narcissism in our attitude to death. Other writers studied social and cultural manifestations to highlight the individual's needs (Irion 1954; Van Gennep 1960; Krupp 1962; Gorer 1965; Fulton 1967; Steiner 1970). Some included data on animal behavior to validate theories of human mourning reactions (Bowlby 1961; Pollock 1961). Many brought an understanding of the dying patient to bear on our empathy with the role of the survivors (Eissler 1955; Joseph 1962). Nevertheless, the topics had to be narrowed down. Among those set aside were all books and articles relating to the dying patient as well as the substantial literature on the dying child and his parents' bereavement. Also excluded was most of the sociological and anthropological work dealing with bereavement customs in Western cultures and other societies, as well as all studies of bereavement in animals.

The main body of this chapter is divided into a theoretical part and a clinical part. The first compares and correlates definitions of mourning and views on the processes of mourning, the role and nature of the accompanying affects, the assessment of the outcome, and the forms and causes of pathology. It concludes with a brief summary of different authors' views on mourning in childhood. The second part examines the clinical contributions on death and bereavement in childhood which form the basis for general and theoretical statements—data on the development of the concept of death, studies of childhood losses of love objects other than parents, and reports of work with bereaved children and with adults whose parent died in their childhood. A section on ways of assisting bereaved families concludes the discussion. With each subject the discussion will focus mainly on the psychoanalytic literature and include only limited references to the contributions from other disciplines. In view of the deep emotional significance of the subject of death and childhood bereavement, it seemed appropriate to start with a discussion of attitudes to death in our culture.

Some Attitudes to Death

The rapid recent increase in scientific and popular publications on death, in memberships in memorial societies, and in attendance at lectures on this subject all suggest that there is a change underway in our attitudes to death. It would appear that we begin to look at death more realistically and allow ourselves more empathy with the dying and the bereaved. I am not qualified to judge the validity of this impression, to guess at the complex nature of its causes, or to assess the future course of these cultural developments. A glance at the content of many recent articles bids caution and points to the fact that, for most of us, the topic of death is personally and socially as obscured by defensive reactions as it was almost sixty years ago when Sigmund Freud addressed himself to it in the midst of World War I: "Should we not confess that in our civilized attitude towards death we are once again living psychologically beyond our means, and should we not rather turn back and recognize the truth? Would it not be better to give death the place in reality and in our thoughts which is its due, and to give a little more prominence to the unconscious attitude towards death which we have hitherto so carefully suppressed?" (1915a, p. 299).

Sterba (1948) described some of the differences between the Middle European and American attitudes to death and bereavement. He stressed the greater prevalence of denial and other primitive defenses in this country. Gorer's (1965) more recent work, however, decries the intensified denial of death in the United Kingdom, especially the tendency to suppress feelings and to isolate the bereaved. In the United States much of the recent interest in death focuses on our widespread denial, magical thinking, and rationalizations concerning death as well as our insensitivity to the dying and the bereaved which follows in the wake of such defenses (Mitford 1962; Lipson 1963; Fulton 1967). Psychiatrists and psychoanalysts are not exempt from these difficulties. Wahl wrote, "It is a surprising and significant fact that the phenomenon of the fear of death, or specific anxiety about it (thanatophobia), while certainly no clinical rarity, has almost no description in the psychiatric or psychoanalytic literature. . . . anxiety about death, when it is noted in the psychiatric literature, is usually described solely as a derivative and secondary phenomenon, often as a more endurable form of the 'castration fear.' There is good clinical evidence that these kinds of displacement occur, but it also is important to consider if these formulations also subserve a defensive need on the part of the psychiatrists themselves" (1958, pp. 215–16).

It seems that in one area our denial of death and bereavement is particularly strongly entrenched, namely vis-à-vis our children. Many authors note that the adults' difficulties with the acceptance of death reflect especially in their inability to explain the realities of death to children and to acknowledge children's concerns and suffering in bereavement. For example, Becker and Margolin (1967) worked for several years with seven surviving parents and their nine young children following the death of one parent in each family. Six parents informed the older children within twenty-four hours of the other parent's death, but the younger children were not told for days or months. Six parents explained the death only in terms of "going to heaven," although three of them did not believe in heaven themselves. None of the children attended the funeral services and some were told of burial only two years later. Gorer (1965) found that, according to his survey of bereaved families, 41 percent of the parents told their children under sixteen nothing about the death and did not discuss the subject; half of the remainder told them "fairy tales," i.e. beliefs they did not hold themselves; the other half told their children something consistent with their own belief, but this only rarely included the concrete facts of death. Jackson stated, "Instead of trans-mitting information and the capacity to cope with crises in compe-tence, adults tend to pass on mainly their anxiety and other negative attitudes about death. This means that the open and honest inquiry so natural with children is doubly thwarted, for in response to their questions they get not only denial of information but also the hazard of anxiety which tends to be cumulative with the years" (1967, p. 172). Wahl, in his perceptive discussion of the barrier between the child's interest and the adult's defensiveness, compares the current attitude to death with the earlier attitude to sexuality: "Clinical expe-rience abundantly proves that children have insatiable curiosity not only about 'where people come from' but also 'where people go to.' In his efforts to find an answer to this conundrum he is met today, as his questions about sexuality would have been met in the 1890's, with evasion and subterfuge" (1958, p. 221). Such views are voiced by others (Eliot 1930, 1955; Flugel 1940; Peniston 1962; Gorer 1965) and are supported by clinical findings, including our work with pa-tients.

Parents, as well as authors, have difficulty in observing the child's experience with death and deny his need for realistic information. Harrison, Davenport, and McDermott (1967) described how, on a child psychiatric ward, the staff's upset over President Kennedy's death interfered with their ability to observe the children's reactions and to handle them appropriately. The authors suggest that bereaved adults' observations of children may be quite misleading. Some ad-vocates of a frank and honest approach with children to the subject of death exclude the prelatency children (Jackson 1967; Gibney 1965). Many reports of psychoanalytic and psychotherapeutic treatments of bereaved children indicate that the analysts refrained from helping their patients to face the contrast between the factual realities of death and their fantasies and misconceptions (Meiss 1952; Wallach 1961; Shambaugh 1961; Gauthier 1965; Wolfenstein 1969).

Could it be that, in spite of our genuine interest in children's thoughts and reactions to death and our wish to help them, we find it too difficult to give up our defenses? Do we tend to exchange one set of defenses for another, as is often the case with our attitudes to in-fantile sexuality where such defenses as exposing the child to nudity and overwhelming him with intellectual explanations supplanted the earlier prudery and denial? In that case perhaps much of our increased awareness of death and its problems represents merely a shift in our defensive patterns. In her introduction to her recent book, Sylvia Anthony recalls Flugel's introductory comments to her much earlier publication: "In this he touched on a fact which I had scarcely considered: that the subject of death was generally taboo. His observation was not only true and important but in a sense prophetic, for a taboo may he attacked, even with cheers from onlookers, without necessarily disappearing. What tends to disappear, at least temporarily, is the missile launched against it" (1972, p. 7). The fate of oblivion which befell her work on the child's discovery of death illustrates the point, but repression and denial are not the only means at our disposal to ward off anxiety-arousing events or to uphold taboos.

S. Freud (1915a) shows that, unconsciously, we maintain a double attitude toward death. We are as convinced of our own immortality as we are murderously ready to annihilate others. We acknowledge death for others but not for ourselves. Some authors, for example Rochlin (1967), stress these narcissistic omnipotent attitudes to death in adults and particularly in children. Others, including this study, address themselves to our difficulty with death at another level (Zilboorg 1943; Wahl 1958; Rochlin 1961; M. Stern 1968, 1968a). In some ways we are all too aware of the threat of death to ourselves. Denial (Geleerd 1965), narcissistic omnipotence, and magical thinking help us to ward off this danger, but the very nature of these defenses suggests the intensity and early origin of our fear. Brandon (1962) claims that the discovery of death usually precedes that of birth in individual experience, but the effect of the original shock quickly disappears. With young children this threat tends to be exaggerated because of their insufficiently differentiated object and self-representations, ready use of primitive identifications, and helplessness in the face of internal and external overwhelming. McDonald (1963, 1964) finds that prelatency children could come to terms with the death of a peer's mother and allow themselves to feel sympathetic only after they had been able to express their immediate basic concerns: "What is death? Who will take care of Wendy? Can it happen to my mother? Can it happen to me?" Wolf (1958) and R. A. Furman (1970) relate very similar experiences with children under five years of age. We can more readily acknowledge the death of others when we are assured of our own safety.

It is in the nature of our relationships with children, and our mutual empathy with them, that we extend our narcissistic investment to them and detect our own childhood in them. This makes it especially difficult for us to observe in them objectively those aspects which arouse anxiety in ourselves. All of us who study reactions to death, particularly in children, are more or less handicapped by our cultural and individual attitudes to this troublesome topic.

Concepts of Mourning Compared

Mourning is a very complex subject as yet explored insufficiently for us to understand it in all its ramifications. It is also difficult to construct a single theoretical model that unifies all the different approaches and serves to explain the many diverse clinical pictures. These difficulties limit our understanding of adult mourning but are even more pronounced in our attempts to assess bereavement reactions in childhood. Several reasons for this stand out.

Many discussions of bereavement in childhood focus on the differences between the mourning of children and adults. Such a comparison is handicapped since each author chooses a different adult model as his basis for comparison. Adult mourning is sometimes erroneously viewed as an established entity in terms of its exciting causes, manifestations, processes, and outcome. As R. A. Furman points out, "In underlining a child's inability to mourn, it has seemed to me as if some have idealized adult mourning, which would mean a denial of the inability of so many adults fully to master the demands of mourning" (1973, p. 228).

Another difficulty arises from the fact that the nature of the loss is not always comparable. Usually, children's reactions to the death of a parent are compared to adults' mourning of love objects in general, without taking into account the differences in libido distribution and effect on the mourner's life.

There is also a tendency to attribute to developmental factors all differences between adult and childhood mourning as well as all the children's difficulties in coping with bereavement. This leads to a neglect of other important factors, such as the effect of the loss on the child's actual (not merely felt) state of need fulfillment; the weaknesses and strengths of his personality prior to the loss; the impact of the form of the death and of coincident stresses; and the role of the surviving love objects in caring for him physically and emotionally in presenting the realities of the event and in serving as a model for coping with it. An underestimation of these factors interferes with the task of exploring and understanding the true role of developmental criteria.

In regard to the developmental capacities for mourning there is considerable divergence on all questions. When can a child understand the concept of death? Does a child relinquish cathexes more readily or more reluctantly? When is he capable of internalizations and in what form? When does longing begin and when do primitive affects become modulated? To what extent can the child tolerate painful feelings? In which form does he discharge them? What is the role of need fulfillment and narcissistic injury or depletion? What constitutes a normal outcome of childhood mourning? What pathologies are encountered? Can they be helped in the family or in treatment?

Last, but not least, our difficulties stem from using very different data. The views of many authors on childhood mourning derive from studies of related clinical situations rather than from their work with bereaved children: for example, temporary or permanent separations often accompanied by hospitalization or loss of home, pathology in the mother–child relationship resulting in withdrawal of the mother, partial loss of a parent owing to divorce; or in studies of developmental processes or of adult pathology such as depressive illness. It is important and valuable that we apply to our understanding of mourning all that can be learned from the investigation of such situations, but it is erroneous to equate them with real bereavement and to disregard the important differences.

Those who do base their conclusions on direct work with bereaved children, or with adults who suffered bereavement in childhood, tend to err in other directions. Little distinction is made among data gained from questionnaires, interviews, short- or long-term observation, once- or twice-weekly psychotherapy, and analysis. All data need to be utilized but their validity and chances of providing psychoanalytic understanding cannot be equated. Even the thorough analysis of an individual child contains so many variables that it can only contribute a measure of understanding and does not provide a basis for generalizations. Although, in psychoanalysis, understanding has traditionally proceeded from pathology to normality, the additional value of direct analytic observation of normal development has been stressed. In studying bereavement we still largely lack this type of data.

It is in the nature of a difficult topic that different aspects are explored separately, and the underlying links are found only gradually to enhance fuller understanding. Many differences of opinion in the literature are no doubt due to this. However, they also appear to stem from premature conclusions, based on insufficient data and applied to all of childhood instead of to some children at certain stages of development.

All psychoanalytic authors utilize S. Freud's observations on mourning and relate their views to his formulations. Their selective emphasis on certain papers in some instances suggests, however, that some analysts, like ourselves, found it difficult to gain a comprehensive understanding of the development of Freud's thinking on bereavement.

The importance of Freud's contribution to the understanding of mourning was matched perhaps only by that which mourning made to the course of his own life and to his psychoanalytic insights. We learn from Jones's biography (1953) that psychoanalysis owes a special debt to Freud's own mourning for his father who died on October 23, 1896. Freud handled this event realistically, simply, and with utmost dignity (Karpe 1961). In a manuscript, dated May 31, 1897, he noted the role of hostile impulses against parents, their repression at times of the parents' illness or death, and reemergence in mourning in the form of self-reproaches or identification with the deceased parent's illness. In July 1897 Freud began his self-analysis and in October 1897, less than a year after his father's death, he announced his discovery of the Oedipus complex in a letter to Fliess. It was not the only bereavement to be suffered by Freud and to influence his private life and professional thinking. In addition to the deaths of older relatives, he endured the loss of a younger sibling when he himself was only a toddler and, in his later life, the loss of a daughter and beloved grandson, Heinele.

Unfortunately, the influence of Freud's clinical work with bereaved patients on his theoretical expositions is as yet insufficiently detailed and integrated. He himself never undertook such a synthesis explicitly and, for that matter, never addressed himself specifically to the topic of mourning in a comprehensive single paper. Pollock (1961) and Siggins (1966) admirably reviewed and summarized the trends of Freud's theoretical views. *Mourning and Melancholia* (1915) does not represent his main thinking on this topic and can therefore be misleading if considered by itself. It was written during a period when Freud's investigative efforts focused on the understanding of narcissism and of the "critical faculty," and when he tried to clarify the mental processes in melancholia. For this purpose "he sets up a model situation for mourning" (Siggins 1966, p. 16) but does not attempt to portray actual mourning processes in their full clinical complexity and theoretical implications. These were well known to him. He described them repeatedly before 1915, in *Studies on Hysteria* (1893), *Notes upon a Case of Obsessional Neurosis* (1909), *Formulations on the Two Principles of Mental Functioning* (1911), *Totem and Taboo* (1913), and later in *From the History of an Infantile Neurosis* (1918), *Inhibitions, Symptoms and Anxiety* (1926), *Fetishism* (1927), and *Dostoevsky and Parricide* (1928). No doubt there are others with which I am not familiar. A detailed comprehensive account of the relationship between Freud's personal and clincal experience and his theoretical thinking on mourning still awaits an author. Jones (1953–57), Pollock (1961, 1972), M. Stern (1968a), and Schur (1972) have made important contributions to this topic.

What Precipitates Mourning?

The majority of analysts holds the view that mourning follows specifically the permanent loss of a love object in the external world. Many authors state this explicitly (Abraham 1924; Klein 1940; Lindemann 1944; Anderson 1949; A. Freud 1960; Mahler 1961; Pollock 1961; Lipson 1963; R. A. Furman 1964; Siggins 1966). Some refer to S. Freud's (1915) definition, but in their work concentrate solely on object loss and disregard Freud's inclusion of certain abstractions (Deutsch 1937; Wolfenstein [1] 1966, 1969; Laufer 1966; Nagera 1970). Several authors do not actually define what precipitates mourning but their expositions clearly imply that they have in mind a permanent external loss of love object (Fenichel 1945; Jacobson 1957, 1967). Most of these writers do not consider whether the per-

1. Wolfenstein does not always adhere to the concept of mourning relating to the loss of a love object. In 1965 she compared children's reactions to the assassination of President Kennedy with the normal adults' "mourning" for him. With adults, outside the circle of family and personal friends, the mental representation of the President consisted of a complex amalgam of narcissistic and displaced object libidinal cathexes. It did not correspond to the object representation of a loved person with whom a mutual personal relationship was maintained. Wolfenstein recognized that the President's image did not represent a love object for the latency children and that it included displaced parental cathexes for the adolescents, but she did not note that for the adults too he had not been a loved person in his own right. Her comparison of reactions therefore refers not to the mourning of the loss of a love object but of a mental representation of a public figure which is invested differently.

manent loss occurred through death or separation, but the context in which they discuss the topic implies that they refer to death or that they do not consider the difference significant. Only Lindemann (1944) and Pollock (1961, 1962) point to the difference between permanent loss through separation and through death in its potential effects on the mourning process. Lindemann draws attention to clinical instances where the confusion between death and separation, due to external circumstances, caused difficulty in the later reestablishment of the relationship that was presumed to be lost. Pollock notes, "Usually we assume that mourning and the reaction to permanent loss without death are equivalent. This equation, though not rejected, requires further demonstration" (1961, p. 343). Our work showed considerable differences between reactions to death and other permanent losses.

There are notable exceptions to the majority's view on the relations of mourning to the death of a loved person. Bowlby (1960, 1961, 1963) initially defines mourning in terms of object loss but later includes such losses as relinquishing a major goal. Bowlby also does not distinguish between temporary and permanent loss. His main body of clinical observations derives from the study of infants and young toddlers to whom the lost object, the mother, was restored. Rochlin (1953, 1959, 1961) also came to the topic of mourning from his work with very young children who suffered temporary and partial (withdrawal) separation from the mother. He extends Freud's loss of object and abstractions, stating, "The conditions which produce a narcissistic injury, or hurt self-esteem, or circumstances when the person is devalued, produce the same reactions and the same responses and conflicts seen in object loss in which the self-esteem has been affected" (1961, p. 452). Rochlin's definition resembles that of Engel (1961) as quoted and utilized by Solnit and Stark (1961, p. 526): "Grief is the characteristic response to the loss of a valued object, be it a loved person, a cherished possession, a job, status, home, country, an ideal, a part of the body, etc." When Solnit and Stark speak of a mother's need to mourn the hoped-for healthy infant before the real defective child can be accepted, they extend the concept of loss to a narcissistic fantasy. Jacobson (1965) uses a similar concept when describing two patients' fantasies about a parent they never knew as their reactions to "object loss."

It seems pertinent here to add a word on some authors' views on developmental losses, that is, losses of some aspects of an object relationship which are inherent in the individual's emotional maturation; for example, the loss of the oral-libidinal relationship with the mother, the relinquishing of oedipal attachments, the adolescent object removal. Rochlin (1959) includes certain developmental losses in his considerations of the "loss complex." As his case vignettes illustrate, he refers to developmental losses in the prelatency age group, especially to those complicated by pathology in the parent–child relationship. Wetmore (1963) extends the concept of mourning to all developmental losses. He includes the analytic process during which the analysand mourns his earlier maturational losses and, if successful, carries his mourning to sufficient completion.

Klein, Winnicott, and Wolfenstein view certain developmental losses as mourning experiences per se and as prototypes of all subsequent mourning reactions. Klein (1935, 1940) stresses the crucial role of the oral phase. She claims that, following the real loss of a loved person, the normal mourner goes through a modified and transitory manic-depressive state. In this way he repeats under different circumstances and with different manifestations, the processes which the child normally experiences in the "depressive position," that is just before, during, and after weaning. The actual loss of a love object in later life activates these early struggles so that the mourner has to work through the current as well as the early loss. The "depressive position" is evoked by the loss of the breast and all the love, security, and satisfaction it stands for. It is characteristically fraught with guilt and anxiety and with unconscious fantasies of having lost the "good" object and being in danger of inner disruption. In normal mourning, as in normal early development, these psychotic anxieties are overcome with the help of reassuring experiences in reality, with the establishment and reestablishment, of "good" introjected objects, and with a sufficient degree of drive fusion. Winnicott (1954) takes a similar position insofar as he regards the successful achievements of the "depressive position" a prerequisite for grief and mourning.

Sugar (1968) speaks of mourning in normal adolescence. Root (1957), A. Freud (1958), Lampl-de Groot (1960), Frankl and Hellman (1962), Jacobson (1964), and Laufer (1966) liken the processes of adolescent object removal and restructuring of the personality to mourning, but they do not consider it identical. Wolfenstein assigns a special role to the developmental losses of adolescence: "The adolescent, subject to the necessity of seeking a nonincestuous sexual object, is for the first time forced to undergo a radical decathexis of his first loves, the parents . . . Once this major transition has been achieved, it is as though a pattern has been established for decathecting a beloved object if the need arises, as when the individual is confronted with losses in later life. Having been initiated through the trial mourning of adolescence he is then able to mourn'' (1969, pp. 457–58). Wolfenstein does not consider the differences. Loss through death is an external loss whereas the adolescent process involves an internal one. The adolescent is unaware of what exactly he is losing in his development, while a loss through death is consciously perceived. There also is a difference between giving up an object and having it taken away. Pollock comments on the difference between mourning and mourning-like reactions during analysis: ''This concept of ego depletion in mourning may assist in differentiating the reaction after the death of an object from that of the loss of an object not through death but through growth . . . This latter is a living process leading to a particular goal of detachment. This process is different from the mourning following the actual death of a significant being'' (1961, p. 347). Loewald (1962), Fleming and Altschul (1963), and R. A. Furman (1968) make a similar point about developmental losses.

Our clinical experience and theoretical thinking led us to view mourning as a response solely to the loss of a love object through death. We considered other forms of loss and acknowledged many similarities in their effect on the ensuing mental processes. The differences, however, appeared to us so significant that a specific delineation seemed indicated.

Recognition and Acceptance of the Loss

Most authors agree that the initiation of the mourning process depends on the bereaved individual's perception of the loss and his inner acceptance of it as permanent and irretrievable. S. Freud (1915) points out that the continuous confrontation with the reality is the most important factor inducing the bereaved to detach his love from the lost object. Klein starts her 1940 paper with, ''An essential part of the work of mourning . . . is the testing of reality'' (p. 125). Many authors stress how difficult it is for the bereaved to accomplish this first step and suggest that the individual's failure to recognize and accept the loss causes various pathological forms and outcomes of mourning. In contrast to other forms of loss, the death of a love object represents an unequivocal external reality, starkly confronting the bereaved. Nevertheless, certain circumstances may make it difficult to grasp and accept the fact. The most commonly cited example of this is the occurrence of a sudden, quite unexpected death. This takes the bereaved so much by surprise that it is impossible for him to integrate at once the magnitude and intensity of stimuli (Lindemann 1944; Lehrman 1956; Engel 1961; Pollock 1961; Lipson 1963; Gorer 1965).

Sometimes the bereaved has no concrete evidence of the death, when testimony is not available from others, or when the sad news is withheld from him or misrepresented. Several authors (Wolf 1958; Benda 1962; Bowlby 1963; Gorer 1965; Fulton 1967) point out that the bereaved person's capacity to acknowledge a death is considerably diminished because, in our present-day society, people usually die away from home and alone. The interference caused by lack of evidence is even more pronounced when relatives are informed of deaths that occurred in wartime, in prisons, or in concentration camps, or when the loved one is reported "missing" and only time can confirm the fact.

Analytic and other writers stress how hard it is for children to recognize and accept death when they are deprived of the opportunity to participate in the funeral rites and visits to the cemetery, which confirm the concrete aspects of death, or when they remain uninformed or misinformed about the death (Keeler 1954; Root 1957; Bowlby 1963; R. A. Furman 1964, 1970, 1973; Jacobson 1965; Becker and Margolin 1967; Fulton 1967; Grollman 1967; Nagera 1970).

Another specific circumstance that influences the individual's ability to recognize and accept the death is the actual form it takes. Some deaths occur in such a way as to pose intense threats. The bereaved cannot accept the death because he cannot cope with the manner in which it came about; for example, murders, mutilations, suicides, debilitating and disfiguring illnesses. There is, to our knowledge, no literature on the role of this factor except for a brief statement by Siggins (1966).

In our experience, the traumatic impressions connected with the form of death were particularly difficult for child patients to face and were usually augmented by the tendency of the surviving adults to lie about such deaths. The adults were themselves so upset by the horror of the form of the death that they could not truthfully discuss anything about it.

Among the effects on mourning we noted difficulty in achieving the appropriate degree of differentiation from the deceased and obstacles in the path of adaptive identification with the lost loved one. Some authors describe the psychic havoc created by the threat of such circumstances but do not specifically evaluate its effect on the mourning process (for example, Anderson 1949; Bergen 1958; Kearney, in Nagera 1970; Chethik 1970).

Many writers omit from their case reports the pertinent details regarding the circumstances of the death and their patients' reactions to them (Deutsch 1937; Meiss 1952; Pollock 1961; Shambaugh 1961; Fleming and Altschul 1963; Wolfenstein 1966, 1969; Altschul 1968). Scharl's case may serve as an illustration: Linda, aged eight, and Nancy, aged five, "witnessed their father's violent death by decapitation in an automobile accident" (1961, p. 471). There is no report of the details of the accident or whether the event was discussed by the surviving mother. Linda's first interview with the therapist, six months later, is described: "She had great difficulty separating from her mother . . . instead of talking to me she repeatedly drew a man without a head, hanging from a tree. She left these pictures with me and rushed back to her mother . . . When Linda in her first hour drew a decapitated man, she confessed her constant preoccupation with killing her father" (p. 472). Linda's material is at no point related to the horror she witnessed or to the fears engendered by her own narrow escape.

In all discussions of interference with the recognition of death it is taken for granted that the bereaved person's reality testing has reached a sufficient level of development and is intact. When and how children acquire a concept of death is therefore important and will be discussed later.

Frequently an inability to recognize and accept the death of a loved one is caused by internal obstacles. According to Freud (1915b), reluctance of the libido to give up cathected objects is the most important obstacle to relinquishing the internal object as well as to accepting its nonexistence externally. This may result in "a turning away from reality" or even a "hallucinatory wishful psychosis" (1915, p. 244).

Some analysts stress that the pain accompanying libidinal detachment may interfere with the acceptance of the loss. Anticipating the pain of sadness and grief, and finding it impossible to bear, the ego denies the death or denies it in part. Some consider this an especially prominent obstacle in childhood (Mahler 1961; Wolfenstein 1965, 1966, 1969; Jacobson 1967). Others take it also to be characteristic of the adult ego under certain circumstances (Deutsch 1937; Pollock 1961). Fleming and Altschul (1963) and Altschul (1968) distinguish between acknowledging the reality of the death and denying its meaningfulness.

Many authors discuss the importance of a conflict over ambivalence in the relationship to the lost love object and the guilt resulting from fulfillment of unconscious death wishes. To some this is an essential feature (Klein 1940). To others it represents a developmental, characterological, or circumstantial variation leading to lasting or intermittent denial of the loss (S. Freud 1909, 1928; Lindemann 1944; Bowlby 1961, 1963; Pollock 1961; R. A. Furman 1964a, 1967; Jacobson 1965; Siggins 1966; Wolfenstein 1969).

The threat to the bereaved person's narcissistic equilibrium is also viewed as a major obstacle to the acceptance of the death. Pollock (1961) states that the initial shock phase of mourning results from the fact that the bereavement is always experienced as a narcissistic loss and accompanied by an upsurge of primitive separation anxiety, leading to intermittent or permanent denial of the reality. Klein (1940) suggests that, since actual object loss revives the anxieties of the depressive position, it always entails the threat of the loss of self. This in turn tends to engender manic omnipotent defenses which distort the perception of reality.

In writing about childhood bereavement several authors address themselves to the danger of lack of need fulfillment, withdrawal of narcissistic supplies, and loss of parts of the self, which the child feels as a result of his developmental dependence on the deceased parent (R. A. Furman 1964, 1964a; Jacobson 1965; Wolfenstein 1966, 1969; Chethik 1970). Lindemann (1944) mentions the similar effects on the bereaved adult in instances where the lost loved one played the role of provider. Geleerd (1965) points to the essential use of denial in the service of survival in situations of major threat to the self. R. A. Furman (1968) relates the use of adaptive denial specifically to the situation of the bereaved child in certain circumstances.

It seems pertinent to note that no author explores the interferences which result from the coincidence of a bereavement and other stressful experiences such as illness, destitution, or other threats to survival of the bereaved or of his other love objects. The use of denial in such situations may be regarded as adaptive. When coping with these experiences absorbs a person's available energies it may be impossible for him to begin the task of mourning, and it constitutes an interference with his recognition and acceptance of the loss. Siggins (1966) briefly refers to such conditions. We encountered them frequently and were impressed by their inevitable and detrimental effect on the bereaved person's ability to mourn.

Some authors focus on the particular narcissistic interference that stems from the bereaved person's fear that he may die himself or from his relief or guilt at not having died like the love object. Klein (1940) traces this "triumph" to unconscious ambivalence and relates it to denial of the loss. Rochlin (1953, 1967) stresses the need to maintain the unconscious belief in one's own immortality. Siggins points to the guilt over the common "relief that the death is someone else's and not one's own" (1966, p. 18). Deutsch (1937) notes the fear of identification with the dead which may result in suicide and therefore has to be warded off by denial of the loss.

One topic, relatively neglected in the literature, concerns the specific obstacles posed by the nature of the lost relationship—its role in the life and libido economy of the bereaved. *Who* is lost accounts for many variations in the nature of the narcissistic injury, degree of ambivalence, guilt, etc. We found these differences important both in children and adults. Some authors draw attention to this topic but do not fully explore the implications (Lindemann 1944; Engel 1961; Pollock 1961, 1962).

Wolf (1958) and R. A. Furman (1970) discuss some of the pertinent differences in relation to a child's loss of his parent, sibling, or grandparent. Most often, however, the distinction is made, in general, between losses in adulthood and losses in childhood, without due emphasis on the specific type of relationship.

In working with our bereaved patients and their families we noted all these interferences with the recognition and acceptance of the loss. We were especially impressed with the interdependence of general and specific, and internal and circumstantial factors and the need to understand how much each contributes to the individual's handling of this phase of mourning.

Clinical observations and analyses of bereaved persons of all ages show frequent difficulties with recognition and acceptance of the death. Many authors therefore agree that this step is taken only over a considerable period of time and that it is initially and intermittently accompanied by the use of defensive measures which afford the bereaved protection against excessive hardship (S. Freud 1915; Lindemann 1944; Pollock 1961; Siggins 1966; R. A. Furman 1968, 1970). For some writers the initial denial of the death is so characteristic that they consider it the first phase of mourning (Bowlby 1960, 1961; Engel 1961; Lipson 1963).

Our experience confirms the frequent and necessary use of defenses to ward off the recognition and acceptance of death in cases of normal mourning. We found, however, that a large variety of defensive measures was used, rather than any single response or mechanism, and their duration and intensity varied considerably. It depended on who died, how he died, and on the mourner's personality. For example, the need for defensive activity differed when an old grandfather died after a long sickness or when a young parent died suddenly; or when the bereaved person's character was of a hysterical or obsessional type. For these reasons we decided against including the defensive activity in our definition of the mourning processes but acknowledged it as a normal accompaniment in many situations of mourning.

Whether or not authors include the use of denial or of other defenses in the work of mourning, it is generally agreed that the indefinite delay in recognition and acceptance of the death of a love object interferes with the normal course of mourning. Bowlby (1961, 1963) views even melancholic disturbances primarily as an attempt to preserve the object and to deny its irretrievable demise.

Internal Means of Adaptation to the Loss

According to Anna Freud, "The process of mourning (*Trauerarbeit*) taken in its analytic sense means to us the individual's effort to accept a fact in the external world (the loss of the cathected object) and to effect corresponding changes in the inner world (withdrawal of libido from the lost object, identification with the lost object)" (1960, p. 58). This definition succinctly summarizes also S. Freud's views on the processes by which the inner adaptation is achieved (1915, 1923). The majority of analytic writers accept this basic approach (Abraham 1924; Klein 1940; Fenichel 1945; Jacobson 1957, 1967; Pollock

1961; Loewald 1962; Lipson 1963; Fleming and Altschul 1963; R. A. Furman 1964; Siggins 1966; Laufer 1966; our research group, chapter 4).

Deutsch (1937), Wolfenstein (1965, 1966, 1969) and Nagera (1970) are, as far as we know, the only writers who consider decathexis a normal process of mourning but exclude identification. Deutsch and Nagera do not mention identification at all. Wolfenstein (1969) claims that the child tends to fear that he himself may die if he becomes like the parent and, more important, "The image of the self and of the parent remain too disparate for identification . . . the relationship appears not one of likeness, but a complementary one, of the needy child and the parent as the source of supplies" (p. 456). Wolfenstein here refers to children of all ages, including adolescence.

By contrast, Rochlin (1953, 1959, 1961) considers identification the only process and excludes decathexis. He views fear of abandonment as the basis of the universal conflict which provokes these identificatory processes. Developmentally, Rochlin considers identification the prevailing process after the oedipal phase. According to him, all earlier object relationships are predominantly narcissistic, so that loss of object results in increased narcissistic cathexis of the self-representation, accompanied by regression to part objects. Scharl (1961) and Shambaugh (1961) follow Rochlin's theoretical formulations. Rochlin (1953), however, also notes the persistent need for love objects. He mentions two ways of establishing new relationships without a process of decathexis: "Before when the figures were given up, the child does what was done to him. He abandons those whom he lost and takes up with others" (1961, p. 461). Rochlin refers here to the pre-oedipal child and apparently describes the use of turning passive into active as a means of relating to a new object. In regard to older children and adults he finds that internalizations are not sufficient: "The need to project and to transfer object relationships is equally indispensable" (pp. 462–63). Here the establishment of a new relationship is viewed as the outcome of projections of introjects while a "transfer" suggests a displacement of a defensive nature. It may be that Rochlin's neglect of decathexis relates to the nature of his data. We also found that children who suffer partial and temporary losses rather than bereavement keep the cathexis of the love object and use identificatory means to deal with his temporary absence or withdrawal.

Greene (1958) worked psychotherapeutically with patients with leukemia and lymphoma. He suggests that, in normal mourning, different means of internal adaptation may be utilized. Decathexis, accompanied by manifest affective discharge, may constitute the appropriate process for some, but others may use "the mechnisms seen in melancholia or hypochondriasis or the proxy mechanisms" (p. 349). The proxy mechanisms are described as a particular combination of introjection and projective identification, resulting in the adoption of a vicarious object. An individual's choice of mourning mechanism may, according to Greene, be determined by his role in the family and may interact with the mourning processes of other family members in such a way as to maintain the family unit. Deutsch (1937) describes such a process. In that case, however, it reached pathological proportions. Bowlby (1963) considers the adoption of vicarious objects a pathological outcome and suggests that it is usually found in girls.

Some writers view the mourning process in different terms altogether. They emphasize clinical manifestations and behavioral adaptation and concern themselves less with the intrapsychic processes (Lindemann 1944; Engel 1961; Bowlby 1961, 1963; Parkes 1967). Their data derive from observations, questionnaires, psychiatric interviews, and psychotherapeutic contacts. Bowlby prefers ethological concepts to explain the psychic work of mourning. According to him, the individual's attachment to the love object is mediated by a number of instinctual response systems and manifested in behavioral sequences. After the "protest" phase, the response system ceases to be focused on the lost object and no longer tries to recover it. The resulting disorganization of personality is accompanied by despair. This is a prerequisite for the third phase, in which reorganization takes place. Bowlby comes closest to describing the working of the mind when he discusses the "broken down patterns of behavior" during the despair phase, "Just like a child playing with Meccano must destroy his construction before he can use the pieces again so must the individual each time he is bereaved . . . accept the destruction of a part of his personality" (1961, p. 335). Bowlby refers to identification on two occasions (1961, 1963). He notes that his data do not provide an opportunity to study identification. He adds, however, that the role of identification in mourning is overrated, that it is too complex a subject to discuss in the present papers, and that he will devote future publications to it, which have not yet materialized at this writing. Parkes (1967) favors Bowlby's concepts.

Decathexis in Children

Most analysts agree with S. Freud's view on the tenacity of libidinal cathexes. He assumed that, following loss, the object representation is hypercathected and then gradually and painfully decathected.

Opinions vary on how this applies to children. In their discussion of infants' and young toddlers' reactions to separation from mother and home, Burlingham and A. Freud (1942) note that, after children reach the beginning of object constancy, their affective reaction is intense but relatively short-lived. The youngsters' pressing needs force them to withdraw cathexis from the representation of the mother and, under favorable circumstances, to accept need fulfillment from a stranger. The authors observe, however, that young children sometimes maintain the cathexes of the father and of inanimate objects longer than that of the mother. Spiegel suggests that all children, even adolescents, have an "extraordinary mobility of their libido" as well as "availability of other external objects" (1966, p. 88). This enables them to short circuit the work of mourning. He suggests that the same quick decathexis is "often seen in the young adult mother whose baby has died. The birth of another one usually consoles her" (pp. 88–89). Bowlby (1960, 1961, 1963), by contrast, stresses that the toddler, in reaction to separation, clings to the object representation of the lost mother but wards off contact with her after reunion. He notes that mourning in early childhood frequently takes a pathological course because of defenses against yearning and protest. A. Freud (1960) and Nagera (1970) point to the possible differences between separation from mother and home and a loss through death after which the toddler remains in his home and is cared for and emotionally supported by surviving loved ones.[2] We found considerable variations in the course of decathexis among bereaved toddlers, depending on differences in personality growth, circumstances, and nature of the lost relationship. Our experience suggests that object cathexes may be maintained for several years, and decathexis may occur slowly and painfully in bereaved children from as early as sixteen months on. Our knowledge of one-year-olds is insufficient to warrant a general statement.

2. J. and J. Robertson's (1971) studies of toddlers, temporarily separated from the mother but living in their homes or foster homes, confirm this. The authors found a variety of behavioral responses, but these differed sharply from the severe distress of toddlers brought to institutions.

With older children, above the toddler age, the opposite difficulty is sometimes stressed, namely an inability to decathect the object representation of the deceased (Pollock 1961; Jacobson 1965; Wolfenstein 1966, 1969; Nagera 1970). Several reasons for this are mentioned. There is a developmental lack of tolerance for pain and, in the case of parent loss, there are the child's need for a parental love object and the threat of narcissistic loss. R. A. Furman (1964a), however, reports on a six-year-old whose decathexis of the dead mother occurred during the first year after bereavement and could be followed in his analysis. Some of our children had difficulty with decathexis, others did not. There were great individual variations in personalities and circumstances.

A child's decathexis of a parent has to be distinguished from his decathexis of other lost love objects. The care and support of the surviving parent as well as the eventual availability of a new parent affect the course of decathexis. These variables applied in many instances to adults as much as to children. When a parent lost a child through death, decathexis was in many cases most difficult. Pollock (1961) suggests that decathexis tends to be especially difficult in early and late life. It depends, however, at all ages on who is lost, on the individual personality, and on opportunity for recathexis.

Some writings deal with measures which circumvent or facilitate decathexis. Abraham (1924), Fenichel (1945), Pollock (1961), Loewald (1962), Lipson (1963), and others stress that the initial introjection of the deceased preserves the object internally and enables the bereaved to effect a gradual decathexis. Different ways of avoiding the overwhelming upset and pain of decathexis are by defensive displacement (Deutsch 1937; Lindemann 1944; Jacobson 1965), by turning passive into active (Rochlin 1961), or by using a vicarious object (Greene 1958). Wolfenstein (1966) describes a particular form of "adaptation" which she calls a shift of cathexis. Her case report suggests, however, that either a defensive displacement or a normal painful decathexis occurred. According to most writers, except Spiegel (1966), such primitive cathectic shifts are not characteristic of a normally developed ten-year-old such as she describes.

Other aspects of decathexis will be discussed in connection with the outcome of mourning.

Processes of Internalization

In his earlier observations on mourning, Freud considered the pathological aspects of identification (1897, 1915). Later he described its developmental and normal role (1921, 1923). Similarly, Abraham (1911) studied introjection in the context of manic-depressive disturbances, but his experience with bereaved patients led him to view introjection as a process in normal mourning. Jacobson (1954, 1967) pointed out that both Freud and Abraham did not sufficiently distinguish the various forms of, and reasons for, identificatory processes. These differences decide, to a significant extent, whether a particular internalization contributes to the personality in a constructive or pathological manner. Although authors differ in their use of the terms, many have attempted to clarify the differences and relations between the various processes of internalization. With many, the term introjection has come to denote the process of internalization as well as a primitive total form of identification, whereas identification, or ego identification, stands for a more advanced, selective process which achieves a full integration into the ego and self-representation.

As mentioned above, many authors consider introjection a necessary step in mourning. Their emphasis varies in discussing the nature, purpose, and course of this type of introjection and its relation to pathology. Fenichel stresses the primitive nature of the introjection and its role in facilitating gradual decathexis. According to him, initial identification in mourning is ambivalent and accompanied by guilt. It is "subjectively perceived as an oral incorporation occurring on the same level as in psychotic depression but of lesser intensity" (1945, p. 394). Lipson (1963) also stresses that introjection preserves the object and represents a step toward giving it up. He, however, does not relate introjection in mourning to the type that occurs in psychotic depression or in other forms of pathology.

Pollock (1961), Loewald (1962), and Jacobson (1957, 1967) concern themselves with the course of internalization in normal mourning. Pollock states that in the healthy personality, introjection as a process results in identification, or total assimilation. Pathology results when the course from introjection to identification is interrupted. Loewald compares the course of internalizations in normal development and in mourning. He views it in terms of degrees of internalization or distances from the ego core. Jacobson similarly observes that in grief the identifications "may start—and possibly always start—at a magic fantasy level; but they gradually progress to the ego level and eventually bring about solid, selective ego alterations" (1957, p. 106). According to her, the pathological outcome of an identification depends on its primitive form, narcissistic nature, or underlying conflict of ambivalence. Smith (1971) relates introjection to depression and identification to grief. Klein (1940) stresses the effect of the ambivalence conflict in early internalization: "In normal mourning the individual reintrojects and reinstates, as well as the actual lost person, his loved parents—who are felt to be his 'good' inner objects" (p. 146).

The literature appears to contain no reference to two aspects of identification in mourning which we found quite significant. One concerns the nature of the model—that is, the personality of the deceased and his form of interaction with the bereaved. The other deals with the proportion of decathexis and identification and how it affects the outcome of mourning. In some of our cases the pathological effect of identification stemmed from the deceased parent's behavior difficulties as they actually were or as the child perceived them. In several instances the children's identifications with the parent's pathology were not based on hostility or guilt but represented an important, admired, and loved aspect of the deceased and of the relationship with him. R. A. Furman (1967) describes such a case. The integrative and adaptive functions of the ego determine to some extent which aspects are selected for identification. Observation in analysis shows how, in mourning, an attribute or trait of the deceased is temporarily "tried out" and then given up in favor of another.

The proportion of decathexis and identification needs to vary according to the type of loss and the developmental stage of the bereaved. It is almost impossible for a parent to identify adaptively with his dead young child. Decathexis, in such cases, has to be far greater than identification. When an adult loses his spouse, the proportion between decathexis and identification may vary widely within normal limits. He may decathect extensively and remarry, or he may primarily identify and remain a widower. In the case of children, especially before adolescence, it is important that identification not become the predominant means. This can interfere with the capacity for recathexis of a new parent figure and progression in the development of relationships and structuralization. In contrast to Wolfenstein (1969), Birtchnell (1969) and our group found that children are developmentally inclined to deal with loss by identification, so that this frequently presents a danger to the resolution of mourning. Meiss (1952) suggests that her young patient, three years old at the time of his father's death, effected a premature super ego introjection. S. Freud (1928) relates some of Dostoevsky's difficulties to identification with his dead father. Bonaparte's (1928) autobiographical account also illustrates the role of identification, and Zilboorg (1937) considers it especially in connection with suicide.

Affective Responses

Many clinical studies of normal mourning show manifestations of pain, sadness, grief, anger, and guilt in varying intensity (Klein 1940; Lindemann 1944; Fenichel 1945; Bowlby 1960, 1960a, 1961, 1963; Pollock 1961; Engel 1961; R. A. Furman 1964, 1964a, 1970; Gorer 1965; Parkes 1965). S. Freud discusses these affects in his clinical studies of bereavement as well as in theoretical articles (1913, 1926). Our experience also shows that each of these feelings can be part of a normal mourning. Deutsch (1937) and Wolfenstein (1966, 1969) equate the work of mourning with the affective experience and especially with affective discharge. Others (Spiegel 1966; R. A. Furman 1968) view the work of mourning and the grieving state as separate aspects of the process. Most writers agree that the affective experience accompanies the mourning process and that discharge is most helpful. Much discussion centers on children's capacities in this regard. There are differences on the definition of grief, and some writers explore certain affects in detail, emphasizing such aspects as their source, development, range of normality, and modes of expression.

Following perhaps the multiple meanings of Freud's use of the German word *Trauer*, many authors use grief as synonymous with mourning or with some of its processes (Lindemann 1944; Engel 1961; Solnit and Stark 1961; Parkes 1967). Others have found it helpful to regard grief as an affect, a feeling of deep sorrow which accompanies mourning but occurs also in situations which do not involve a mourning process (Abraham 1911; Pollock 1961; Wolfenstein

1965, 1966, 1969; Siggins 1966; Nagera 1970). By contrast, Deutsch (1937), Mahler (1961), and Jacobson (1957) relate grief specifically to object loss.

S. Freud (1915, 1926) questioned the reasons for the peculiar and intense pain of grief and addressed himself to the problem primarily from an economic point of view. Pollock compares Freud's views on pain (heightened undischarged cathexis) with Federn's (1952) hypothesis of libido avulsion which leads to the impoverishment of the ego. He suggests that "further study is necessary to find specifically which is more significant" (1961, p. 347). Fenichel (1945) and Wolfenstein (1966) favor Freud's concept. Spiegel states that pain following object loss is "brought about by internal discharge of object cathexis into the barrier separating self and object" (1966, p. 88). He distinguishes this pain from grief and links the latter to the ego's recognition of the reality of the loss.

Some authors have concerned themselves especially with the instinctual components of grief. Jacobson stresses the libidinous nature of grief: "Unlike depression, sadness as such does not involve an aggressive conflict, whether with external reality or endopsychically" (1957, p. 87). Klein (1940) and Winnicott (1954) also consider the degree of instinctual fusion the main demarcation between normal mourning and depression. S. Freud (1913, 1915, 1915a) discussed the effects on normal mourning of ambivalence in the relationship to the deceased and the resulting guilt. He stressed the universal nature of ambivalence and ascribed pathological mourning to special difficulties with ambivalence, for example in obsessional neurosis and melancholia.

Pollock (1961) and Bowlby (1960, 1961, 1963) regard anger and frustration in grief as inevitable, relate it to the initially primitive and insatiable nature of the yearning for the lost object, and attribute a special constructive role to the presence and discharge of this anger in the mourning process. These authors and others (Lindemann 1944; Siggins 1966) helpfully distinguish between anger at the death and ambivalence in the relationship to the deceased which preceded his death. They also observe that the specific circumstances of a death heighten or lessen both forms of aggression. Our experience confirms Pollock's view. We found also that children, more easily than adults, acknowledged anger at the dead, both for having died and for their shortcomings when still alive. Sometimes young children's anger and guilt stemmed not only from these sources but was augmented by inadequate independent reality testing. When a child's surviving loved one failed to clarify the real causes of the death, the child was forced to fall back on his infantile reasoning and could not advance toward a more appropriate understanding. Mahler (1950) refers to this.

Several writers address themselves to genetic factors in grief and to modes of affective discharge. Fenichel (1945), Bibring (1953), Bowlby (1960, 1961, 1963) and Pollock (1961) relate the initial intense anguish of mourning to the infant's reaction to separation from the mother and point to the similar discharge manifestations of wailing and shrieking in both situations. They contrast this behavior with the more advanced attenuated grief, expressed in crying, contained sadness, or verbal expression. Jacobson (1957) describes the different types of discharge, suggesting that intense and uninhibited sadness, accompanied by weeping and sobbing, leads to relief.

Developmentally, Burlingham and A. Freud (1942), A. Freud (1960), and Mahler (1961) date the experience of grief and sadness to the second half of the first year, coincident with the beginning of object constancy. Klein (1935, 1940) and Winnicott (1954) concur with this timing although they view the psychic process of the emergence of grief differently.

Much literary discussion focuses on the importance of the ego's capacity to bear the stress of strong feelings and its means of, and opportunities for, discharge. Clinical observation of bereaved adults suggests that difficulty in tolerating feelings is rather common (Lindemann 1944; Marris 1958; Gorer 1965; Parkes 1965). As mentioned earlier, Deutsch (1937), Siggins (1966), and our research group found that, at all ages, specific conditions related to a bereavement may weaken the mourner's ego or absorb its energies in such a way as to impair his tolerance for affects. Most writers emphasize the child's developmental inability to tolerate intense feelings (Deutsch 1937; Burlingham and Freud, A. 1942; Freud, A. and Burlingham, 1944; Freud, A., 1960; Mahler 1961; Pollock 1961, 1962; Bowlby 1961, 1963; Flemming and Altschul 1963; R. A. Furman 1964; Wolfenstein 1965, 1966, 1969; Jacobson 1965, 1967; Nagera 1970). There is divergence, however, as to which phase of childhood this applies to and whether there are variations in terms of personalities and external factors.

Observers of infants and toddlers note the overwhelming initial wail-like discharge that follows the mother's disappearance (Burlingham and A. Freud 1942; Spitz 1946; Bowlby 1960; A. Freud 1960). Even in this age group, however, there are instances where the child does not respond in this fashion or does so only intermittently or belatedly. Bowlby (1963) considers the very young child's need to ward off sadness and anger as a major cause of his inability to mourn successfully and of his predisposition to later pathology in dealing with object loss. Mahler (1961) and Jacobson (1967) state that the very young child's handicap lies in not being able to sustain and express affects in a modulated piecemeal form over a long period. All these authors assume a gradual increase in the child's capacity to tolerate feelings as he matures. Kliman et al. (1969) imply a similar view.

We worked with two children very shortly after they had lost their mothers in the middle of their second year. During the initial period they showed no affective expression but appeared intent on gaining some understanding of the changes in their lives and some mastery over how they were affected by them. Then they experienced overwhelming sobbing outbursts while sleeping. After a few such episodes they could allow the surviving parent to hold them, sympathize with their hurt, and talk about the lost parent. The sobs turned into crying, and sadness and anger became expressed in daytime without interfering with their sleep at night. In our patients beyond this early age group, difficulties in tolerating and expressing feelings were caused by factors other than developmental immaturity.

A. Freud (1960) notes that the bereavement behavior of youngsters in the Hampstead Nurseries lasted for hours, weeks, or even a few months. R. A. Furman (1964a) and Barnes (1964) report on children under five and in early latency who could sustain deep sadness over periods of several months. R. A. Furman (1964, 1968, 1970, 1973) stresses the role of the surviving love objects in supporting the child's tolerance and expression of sad and angry feelings. Deutsch states, "It is of great interest that observers of children note that the ego is rent asunder in those children who do not employ the usual defences, and who mourn as an adult does" (1937, p. 14). Wolfenstein (1966, 1969) holds that children of all ages, including adolescence, are unable to express apportioned sadness and anger and ward off overwhelming feelings of rage and despair. This inevitably jeopardizes their mourning. Nagera (1970) expresses a similar viewpoint. Pollock

(1961) and Fleming and Altschul (1963) do not specify an age range.

R. A. Furman (1964, 1968, 1970, 1973) discusses some of the difficulties encountered in gaining data on the affective reactions of children. His comments coincide with our findings. In latency and adolescence children often consider crying babyish. Among a variety of different reasons for this are fear of loss of control, sometimes unconsciously related to wetting and soiling; fear of exposing himself, which tends to be linked to phallic conflicts; fear of infantile dependence on adults; internalized parental demands for containment of feelings; identification with the parents' manner of expressing affects. Many children cry repeatedly but only in private. Even adults close to the child have no opportunity to observe the child's feelings or their discharge. Some of the same factors can be found with preschoolers but the conflict is often an external one. The adults hide their own expressions of grief from the child and, in part to protect themselves, do not welcome manifestations of the child's affects. The child senses this and responds by suppressing his feelings and by adopting the same defenses. We noted repeatedly that the prelatency child needed "permission" from his surviving parent before he could allow himself to experience, and particularly discharge, sadness and anger in regard to object loss. R. A. Furman (1964) points out that a child's overt sadness also does not necessarily indicate his grieving for the dead love object. It may represent an identification with the mourning relatives or his reaction to the withdrawal of grieving adults. From clinical observation we cannot gain reliable information about a child's feelings. Understanding can come only through the use of analytic tools—interpreting defenses, tracing their origins, and affording support for expressing affects.

Sometimes, however, at all times of life, the difficulty in affective expression stems simply from not having anyone who shares feelings or toward whom they can be expressed. Moller (1967), R. A. Furman (1968), Kliman et al. (1969), and Solnit (1970) give examples of such situations. The importance of meaningful love objects who empathize with and accept the mourner's feelings, and the help of social and cultural customs related to this, is frequently mentioned but not explored in theoretical terms (Klein 1940; Lindemann 1944; Peniston 1962; Ottenstein, Wiley, and Rosen 1962; Steiner 1970; Paul 1969).

One difficulty in assessing children's tolerance for and discharge of affects arises from comparing them to an ideal adult norm which is usually not found in bereaved adults clinically. Moreover, the children's affective responses are mostly studied in regard to parent loss whereas adults grieve for love objects who are cathected differently. This affects not only the intensity and amount of feeling but also the personality of the bereaved in a different way.

Outcome of Mourning in Adults

Freud touches upon several factors that determine the outcome of normal mourning. Most obviously, he addresses himself to the nature of decathexis. The end of mourning coincides with the decathexis of the lost object and the reinvestment in a new one, perhaps even "more precious." He qualifies this, however, by inserting the clause "in so far as we are young and active" (1915b, p. 307). Later Freud finds that at a more advanced age and following specific losses, decathexis is not complete. A new object is not an improvement over the lost one. On the contrary, the new relationship may be less satisfying or it may be impossible to achieve a recathexis, even if another love object is available. On the anniversary of his dead daughter's birthday he writes, "We know that the acute grief we feel after a loss will come to an end, but that we will remain inconsolable, and will never find a substitute. Everything that comes to take the place of the lost object, even if it fills it completely, nevertheless remains something different" (Binswanger 1957, p. 106). Freud raises here the question of normal variation in decathexis and introduces several other factors: the ability to invest in a new relationship, the opportunity for doing so, the significance of the object that was lost, the age and stage in life of the mourner.

He also implies normal differences in the nature of the narcissistic cathexis. In 1915 he considers "the narcissistic satisfactions it [the ego] derives from being alive" (p. 255) as the main impetus for the withdrawal of cathexis from the lost love object. Later he shows how certain losses, or losses occurring at certain periods in a person's life, can result in depletion of narcissistic libido to such an extent that living ceases to be pleasurable. In a poignant letter (1926) Freud writes that since his grandson Heinele's death he can no longer care for his grandchildren or find joy in life (Jones 1957).

Although he focuses especially on decathexis and recathexis, he includes other forms of outcome from the start. In 1915 he speaks of the ego becoming free and uninhibited again, suggesting new interests and activities. In 1923 he discusses the role of identification in the building of the personality. The duration and manifestations of mourning are also considered. Initially Freud viewed mourning as a period of drastic personality changes. He suggested that one would regard these as symptoms of disease if it were not known that they stem from a specific cause and cease after a predictable self-limited course. Later he qualifies this by showing that in certain phases of life or with certain losses, the course of mourning extends over a much longer indefinite period.

In their discussion of the outcome of normal mourning, writers tend to single out one or another of the aspects Freud mentioned. The task of achieving decathexis is emphasized by Deutsch (1937), Fenichel (1945), Bowlby (1961), Wolfenstein (1966), and Nagera (1970). Lindemann (1944) includes adaptational criteria—readjustment to the environment in which the deceased is missing. These authors do not address themselves to the question of normal variation in decathexis—residual cathexis, decathexis depending on the age of the mourner, significance of the lost love object, opportunities for recathexis. Pollock, Siggins, and Nagera touch on some of these aspects. Pollock (1961) notes that older people tend to invest fewer object-directed activities, and more narcissistic withdrawal occurs. He also observes, "In the instance of the loss of a very significant object, the total mourning process may never be completed" (p. 354). He considers this especially in the case of the death of a child. Siggins points out that, in one sense, "mourning is never really over, for new life-situations may appear at any time which evoke for the mourner aspects of the lost relationship insignificant at the time of bereavement" (1966, p. 18). As an example she uses those who lose a parent early in adolescence. Nagera (1970) discusses the latency child's need for a parent figure, which prevents decathexis if no new parent is available. We noticed this most in children at the phallic and oedipal levels.

Several analysts relate the normal outcome of mourning especially to the nature and form of internalization. According to Loewald (1962) successful mourning consists of the internal substitution for an externally lost relationship and the resumption of early boundary-setting processes between object and self-representations. Klein (1940) refers to the necessary re-introjection of the "good" parent and introjection of the "good" current lost object. Jacobson (1957) emphasizes the importance of selective advanced forms of identification which contribute to the structuralization of the ego and new sublimations. Pollock (1961) similarly stresses the transition from introjection to identification. Rochlin (1959, 1961) also considers identification the keystone in adapting to loss. These authors discuss developmental and pathological aspects of internalization. They do not concern themselves with those variations in mourning that make the amount of identification appropriate or that depend on the personality of the lost object or the circumstances of his death. How and to what extent can a mother identify with her dead young child, a grandfather with his grandson, or a child with a parent whom he knew only as sick? When does identification preclude cathexis of new love objects?

Freud's emphasis on the narcissistic satisfactions derived from living is considered by some authors in terms of depletion. Federn (1952) and Pollock (1961) discuss the narcissistic depletion that results from the loss of a love object and the ego's protective mechanisms in this respect. Pollock (1961) and Siggins (1966) apply this particularly to bereavement in old age. K. Stern et al. (1951) stress ego weakness in old age and mention among other factors the tendency of the aged mourner to identify with the deceased as well as the self-isolation and increase in somatic illness. Young, Benjamin, and Wallis (1963) confirm this in their study of mortality in widowers. Jacobson (1965) points out that for young children the death of the parent represents a narcissistic loss as well as an object loss. Wolfenstein (1966, 1969) speaks of the narcissistic injury the child suffers when his parent dies.

Freud's reference to mourning as a normal self-limiting illness is echoed in the views of several writers (Engel 1961; Parkes 1964). They consider mourning a disease or a process of wound healing, the course of which is influenced by preexisting conditions. Klein (1940) also includes the concept of disease in her view of mourning but in a different manner. According to her, the mourner goes through a modified and transitory manic-depressive state and overcomes it. Anderson (1949) and Winnicott (1965) illustrate this concept clinically.

The normal duration of mourning is assessed variously. As mentioned above, Freud, Pollock, and Siggins point to the fact that sometimes, or in some ways, mourning is never completed. Lindemann (1944) speaks of several months of mourning in adults, following different forms of bereavement. Clayton, Desmarais, and Winokur (1968) conclude that, in normal adults, the course of mourning is self-limited after about four months. A. Freud (1960) implies that she expects adult mourning to last much longer than a few months. Barnes (1964), R. A. Furman (1964a, 1967) and our experience with adults and children suggest a period of one to two years or more. There are, however, innumerable individual variations in personalities and circumstances. It is very difficult to pinpoint the end of the chronic phase and the beginning of sporadic mourning. Therefore an average time span seems at best misleading.

In keeping with the different approaches to assessing the normal outcome of mourning, there are varied views on what constitutes pathology in this respect. Pathology is relatively easy to assess when the patient suffers from psychiatric illness of a neurotic or psychotic nature which can be traced to the bereavement. Since Freud's and Abraham's early investigations, many analysts have explored the connection between loss and manic-depressive illness, neurotic depressions, and obsessional and hysterical reactions (Klein 1935, 1940; Deutsch 1937; Jacobson 1946, 1957, 1967; Bowlby 1961, 1963). These writers further trace the genetic origins of their patients' diseases in childhood events which predisposed them to later pathology in reacting to object loss, but their views differ on the nature and timing of the crucial early determinants.

Some authors consider mourning pathological when it is unduly delayed, protracted, or very brief, or when the characteristic clinical manifestations are unusually intense or subdued or absent (Lindemann 1944; Fleming and Altschul 1963; Siggins 1966; Wolfenstein 1966, 1969; Nagera 1970). As Siggins points out, assessment of these conditions "is, of course, a matter of degree: while extremes are readily classified, the dividing line is often unclear" (1966, p. 20). Further, the assessment of pathology here depends on observation of manifest behavior and provides no reliable guide to the understanding of the underlying psychic processes and their effect on the personality.

As mentioned earlier, many authors explore the pathological outcome of mourning in relation to personality factors that precede bereavement. Many stress the effect of a conflict over ambivalence (S. Freud 1909, 1913; Klein 1935, 1940; Deutsch 1937; Lindemann 1944; Jacobson 1957; Pollock 1961). Many discuss developmental factors—affect tolerance, stability of object cathexes, prevalence of narcissistic libido in object cathexes, capacity for different forms of identification (Deutsch 1937; Rochlin 1953, 1959, 1961; Fleming and Altschul 1963, R. A. Furman 1964, 1964a, 1968, 1970; Jacobson 1965, 1967; Wolfenstein 1965, 1966, 1969; Spiegel 1966; Nagera 1970). Pollock states that "ego defects, distortions, or arrests cannot result in healthy mourning processes" (1961, p. 335). There is relatively little emphasis on characterological defenses. R. A. Furman (1964), Barnes (1964), and McDonald (1964) discuss the effect of adults' defenses on the young child's mourning efforts. Our experience suggests that the bereaved person's defense structure has a significant effect on his ability to cope with mourning.

As mentioned earlier, pathology is often associated with difficulties in various stages of the mourning work: the recognition and acceptance of the loss; the presence or absence of certain mental processes (e.g. the presence, content, or nature of internalization); different ways of investing freed energy or inability to do so. In relation to pathology, as with other aspects of mourning, there is little consideration in the literature of aspects that are specific to each death and influence the bereaved person's experience and resolution of the mourning task. These include *who* died; to what extent other love objects are invested and share in grieving; whether other stresses coincide with the bereavement.

As far as we know, most publications do not discuss the need to assess the mourner's total personality in relation to his mourning work. In our experience all parts and functions of the personality interrelate in affecting the bereaved person's handling of this task. His relative success or failure depends on how all parts of his personality respond and adapt to the complex specific circumstances of a particular bereavement. It is difficult, and perhaps erroneous, to assess the outcome of mourning primarily in relation to one aspect. Criteria for the normal outcome of mourning seem as difficult to pinpoint as those for the satisfactory end of an analysis. In the latter case, particularly in child analysis, it has been helpful to assess the total personality and to view its phase-appropriate progressive maturation as a basic sign of health (A. Freud 1945, 1962, 1965). R. A. Furman (1968) utilized this approach to assess the normal outcome of mourning. He shows that this makes it possible to focus on metapsychological understanding of mourning in different age groups throughout life instead of comparing them in terms of behavioral characteristics. Our study adopted the criterion of progressive maturation within the context of a metapsychological understanding of the personality to assess the normal outcome of mourning. This avoids exclusive emphasis on any one aspect or process. It allows for the many individual variations in mourning which are appropriate to specific personalities and situations. For example, in relation to the duration of mourning, it substitutes developmental for chronological time; in regard to decathexis, it does not preclude a young child's prolonged cathexis of a deceased parent as long as this aids his development and does not interfere with ultimate recathexis of a new parent; similarly, it allows for a parent's prolonged cathexis of his dead child as long as this does not interfere with his cathexis of his living family and work, and does not prevent him from becoming a parent again. The developmental approach avoids the need to determine to what extent decathexis and identification should be employed but allows for appropriate variation depending on age, character, and circumstances; it makes it less crucial how affects are experienced and discharged and whether their manifestations can be observed. After the work of mourning, a varying proportion of investment in new love objects or in sublimations can be taken into account.

Outcome of Parental Bereavement in Childhood

Many authors do not consider the death of a parent as necessarily pathogenic and find that, under favorable circumstances, children cope with it successfully either by means of mourning or through other adaptive measures. Several clinical reports confirm this (Barnes 1964, R. A. Furman 1964a, 1967; Gauthier 1965; Wolfenstein 1966, 1969). There are also studies of adults who suffered early parental bereavement and made a normal adjustment (Hilgard, Newman, and Fisk 1960). The professional literature inevitably describes persons who could not master the stress of bereavement and this influences the sample.

No author, however, minimizes the difficulty of the task of coping with a parent's death. There are numerous reports of pathology associated with parental death, both at the time and in its later effects on adult mental health (see the section on data below). Treatment reports on bereaved children indicate a variety of symptoms, personality disorders, interferences in functioning, and neuroses. The diversity is so great that it is impossible to link any specific pathological outcome directly to the event of the parent's death. Studies of larger groups of children corroborate this.[3]

Some studies of adult patients suggest that parental bereavement in childhood is a significant factor in the etiology of various forms of mental illness and adult maladjustment (Zilboorg 1937; Birtchnell 1969, see also section on data). The link between pathology and bereavement often appears certain. It is very difficult, however, to determine which aspect of the bereavement most significantly contributes to a specific problem. Sometimes preexisting personality factors seem primarily responsible; at other times the circumstances of the death or aspects of the mourning process cannot be handled; in still other instances events that coincide with, or follow, the bereavement increase the stress to unmanageable proportions.

Several writers focus on a category of disturbances in which childhood bereavement leads to an interference in development and results in arrest, regression, or distortion of the personality. Difficulty in object relationships is most often referred to, but there is diverging opinion on whether it is caused by arrest or regression and to what level regression proceeds. Some authors stress the effect on the structuralization of the personality or on certain ego functions. It is as yet unclear which kinds of arrest or regression occur in specific phases of childhood and under certain circumstances. Our study deals with some aspects of this topic. A. Freud, commenting on observations in the Hampstead Nurseries, notes the permanent "impairment in the capacity for and quality of object relationships which can be observed in cases where repeated changes of mother figure have taken place" (1960, p. 60). In addition, many children showed temporary instinctual and ego regression. Rochlin (1953, 1959, 1961) worked with preschoolers who, from the first year on, suffered from the mother's temporary absences and emotional withdrawal. He finds that the usual outcome of loss in this age group is regression of object libido to narcissism and investment in part objects. Shambaugh (1961) and Scharl (1961) worked with bereaved children in weekly psycho-

3. Keeler (1954) interviewed eleven bereaved latency children and adolescents. He found symptomatology of depression, anxiety, suicidal attempts or preoccupations, delinquent behavior, and autonomic disturbances such as vomiting. Shoor and Speed (1963) noted delinquency among recently bereaved children. Arthur and Kemme's (1964) study shows a high incidence of intellectual and emotional problems which the authors relate directly or indirectly to the loss of the parent.

therapy. Shambaugh notes temporary arrest in development, regression in attitude to schoolwork, and demandingness in his seven-year-old patient. Scharl's five-year-old girl showed regression in intellectual and social achievements. Wolfenstein (1966, 1969) bases her conclusions on psychotherapy with latency children and adolescents who lost a parent through death. She frequently sees an arrest in development at the point the child reached at the time of the parent's death as well as regression to earlier phases in object relationship and instinctual fusion. Nagera records Kearney's and Novick's analyses of bereaved children, and his own observation of a four-year-old whose grandfather died. It is difficult to relate these data to his conclusions. He speaks of bereavement in childhood as a developmental interference that leads to "simultaneous symptom formation and the creeping character distortions" (1970, p. 198).

Pollock, Fleming and Altschul, and Remus-Araico base their conclusions on analyses of adults who suffered parental bereavement in childhood at different phases of development. Pollock (1961) notes especially an interference in the integration and structuralization of the ego and super ego. Fleming and Altschul (1963) and Altschul (1968) find arrests in many ego functions, especially in the area of ego-object relations, and a failure to resolve developmental conflicts. Remus-Araico (1965) sees various forms of developmental arrest.

Can Children Mourn?

At this point it seems appropriate to summarize briefly the different authors' views on whether and when a child can mourn—setting aside differences in concepts of mourning and its processes.

Klein (1935, 1940) and Winnicott (1954, 1965) consider the resolution of the depressive position in infancy to be the first experience of mourning and the basic pattern for all later bereavement reactions. They date this to the period roughly between six and twenty months of age.

A. Freud (1960) states, "the nearer to object constancy, the longer the grief reactions with corresponding approximation to the adult internal processes of mourning" (p. 59). R. A. Furman (1964, 1968, 1970, 1973) uses Freud's definition of mourning and her terms but is more specific. He considers the normal personality achievements of the phallic level to be the developmental prerequisites for mourning. Laufer (1966) shares Freud's and Furman's views. Furman stresses, in addition, that the child can utilize his capacity for mourning only when additional factors obtain. Among these he lists the realistic education about the concept of death; consistent adequate fulfillment of physical needs; acceptance of the child's feelings, fears, and realistic evaluations regarding the dead parent; and help in mastering anxiety related to the form of the death. Kliman et al. (1969) express this outlook in their clinical work without stressing theoretical implications. Our experience basically confirms Furman's views but extends them in several areas. Bowlby (1961, 1963), Mahler (1950, 1961), and Jacobson (1967) similarly hold that normal mourning is impossible for the youngest children and that their capacities develop gradually, but they do not state specific phases.

Rochlin (1959, 1961) considers mourning possible for children above the age of early latency. Scharl (1961), Shambaugh (1961), and Wallach (1961) share Rochlin's opinion.

Wolfenstein (1965, 1966, 1969), Nagera (1970), and Miller (1971) state that mourning cannot take place till adulthood is reached. Pollock (1961) and Fleming and Altschul (1963) express a similar though less categorical viewpoint.

Let us now examine some of the clinical data on which these views are based.

Clinical Data on Childhood Bereavement

Development of the Concept of Death

The first step in the mourning process consists of the bereaved person's recognition and acceptance of the love-object's death. The child's capacity to understand the reality of death is therefore crucial and warrants our need to understand the development of this concept and the factors that facilitate or impede it. Except for Barnes (1964), R. A. Furman (1964, 1968, 1970, 1973), Nagera (1970), and a brief comment by Bowlby (1963), papers on mourning do not discuss the child's ability to understand death and do not relate it to his bereavement reaction. Sometimes the young child's assumed incapacity to grasp the concept is used as a reason for not telling him about a death. Some dwell on the child's inability to accept the death of a loved one for emotional reasons but do not consider his capacity and opportunity for factual understanding (Pollock 1961, 1962; Scharl

1961; Fleming and Altschul 1963; Wolfenstein 1966, 1969; and others). Data on the concept of death therefore come largely from studies that explore it independent of bereavement.

The literature varies greatly in its views on the child's concept of death. Some authors, for example R. A. Furman, find that children two to three years old are capable of mastering the meaning of "dead"; Gibney (1965) states that children under six cannot conceive of death; Piaget claims that the concept is not established till the prepuberty or puberty years. This wide divergence stems from investigators referring to different levels of conceptual development, studying the child's use of the concept in different contexts, and utilizing varied methods of gaining and evaluating data. The development of the intellectual concept of death extends over many phases. The initial stage comprises the child's interest in and capacity to learn the differences between dead and alive. Later stages include verbal symbols, knowledge of the different forms and causes of death, rites and customs regarding disposal of the corpse, inevitability of death for all living beings, and ability to think of death in abstract terms and in relation to religious and philosophical concepts.

It is most difficult to isolate the cognitive aspects from other factors. Since we study the concept of death in relation to the child's capacity to recognize the death of a love object, I shall not detail studies that consider it only as part of a general investigation of thought processes. Anthony (1972) summarizes these different views, especially Piaget's, and considers parallels between the concept of death and the development of related concepts. Gesell and Ilg, for example, discuss death under the heading "Philosophical Outlook." According to them, the five-year-old's attitude to death is "matter of fact and unemotional. Bodily actions may come in, associated with death: avoids dead things, or may enjoy killing" (1946, p. 449). They find that, at four, the child has a very limited concept of death and, by nine, accepts all aspects of death.

The child's grasp of death does not depend solely on the maturation of his thought processes. It is affected by many factors from within his personality and from without. Among these are the child's instinctual impulses at each developmental phase with attendant anxieties and defensive measures, the nature of his experiences with death, his adaptation to, or identification with, adult attitudes to death, and the amount of correct or incorrect information he receives.

When we assess a child's concept of death at a specific point in his development, or in the context of a specific situation, we actually assess a complex amalgam of factors. Unless we have very thorough knowledge of that child's total development and personality, including the determinants of the immediate situation, we cannot reliably single out the significance of any one factor.

Keeping these criteria in mind, R. A. Furman (1964, 1970, 1973) and this study group find that the older toddler shows interest in "dead" and "alive" in connection with observations of dead animals or insects and can, with educational help, gain realistic understanding at this level. We consider the intellectual mastery of this cognitive stage as the minimal prerequisite for recognizing the death of a love object. It is helpful, however, when the child has a more advanced concept of death. Also, the child acquires this concept, at any stage, more easily when he learns about death in situations which do not involve the death of a love object and when he is given realistic concrete information suited to his level of understanding. Other factors, such as anxiety, defenses, and instinctual conflicts, need to be considered at the same time. An advanced intellectual concept of death does not necessarily enable a person to recognize and accept death. Adults have a fully developed cognitive concept of death but some may be unable to look at a dead animal or explain to a child the concrete difference between what is dead and what is alive. By contrast, a nursery school child may not be able to define "dead" in reply to an adult's question, but when he sees a dead fly or bird he may correctly assess its state.

A few observations record two-year-olds' interest and understanding of death (Nagera 1970; Anthony 1972; R. A. Furman 1973). A. Freud (Nagera 1970) comments that the two-year-old frequently approaches injury and death not with horror but with fascination.

There are many more data on three- to five-year-olds, but few analytic records. Barnes (1964) discusses her two young patients coming to terms with the concept of death, as does Bergen (1958). M. Stern notes that his adult analytic patients "reveal worrying about death already at three, most often connected with the death of relatives or of animals" (1968, p. 24). Many authors derive their data from the observation of young children's play, conversation, or behavior. Such records are most instructive when the observing adult is not blinded by his own emotional involvement yet maintains a relationship with the child, or knows his earlier experiences and understands the immediate context. The work of several analytic observers illustrates this (Issacs 1930; Moellenhoff 1939; Burlingham and A. Freud 1942; Mahler 1950; Bender 1954; Wolf 1958; McDonald 1963, 1964; R. A. Furman 1969; Kliman et al. 1969; Nagera 1970). These authors note preschoolers' interest, knowledge, and concern about death as well as their struggles in coping with contradictory adult information. Hug-Hellmuth's (1912) conclusions are an exception in that she disclaims the young child's capacity to understand death and considers his ideas solely related to instinctual conflicts. Her data consist mainly of excerpts from a couple's conscientious diary of their young son's childhood. They reveal indeed many misconceptions but impress the reader with the child's intense interest in his many encounters with death and his struggles to reconcile his own observations and feelings with his parents' evasions and untruths.[4]

Rochlin (1967) used interview-play sessions in his office to study children's attitudes to death. He selected well-developed three- to five-year-olds with minimal observational, emotional, and educational experience with death. The interview records show that these youngsters thought a lot about death, were aware that it represented the end of vital functions, and concerned themselves with the causes of death. The method of this study highlights the children's fantasies and defenses. Rochlin comments on their—and adults'—narcissistic magical thinking and use of defenses to counteract fears and helplessness in face of the knowledge of death.

Many writers note how much adults interfere with the child's developing understanding of death. A. Freud (Nagera 1970) comments that adults protect themselves from the young child's sadism by avoiding his contact with and questions about death. R. A. Furman (1973) suggests that in this way adults also ward off their own conflicts over sadism, activated by the child's attitude. McDonald (1963) speaks of the taboo of death by which adult silence on the subject in-

---

4. S. Freud's observations of children's ideas about death are only anecdotal. One wonders, for example, whether the young child who said he loved his mother so much he would keep her stuffed after she died was trying to integrate explanations given to him during his preceding visit to the natural science museum (1900, p. 254). Sometimes, I believe erroneously, Freud is thought to have held the definite opinion that children do not understand death. It is rarely noted that he introduced with the phrase "I was astonished to hear" (p. 254) his frequently quoted example of a ten-year-old who, after his father's sudden death, expected the father to come to supper. Later Freud added another observation of a four-year-old who fully grasped the finality of death (p. 255).

hibits children's comments. Anthony (1972) finds that communication between child and adult often confuses rather than clarifies the child's concept. Isaacs (1930) points to the obstacles owing to contradictory attitudes to death in our society—killing animals we consider distasteful or a nuisance; killing for sport, collecting purposes, or experiments. These obtain even when the adults' answers are not deceitful or evasive.

Several studies specifically investigate latency children's concept of death (Schilder and Wechsler 1934; Anthony 1940; Nagy 1948). Schilder and Wechsler's and Anthony's work may be contrasted to show different authors' approach and evaluation. In his sensitive paper on children's ideas about death, Moellenhoff questions Schilder and Wechsler's choice of subjects: seventy-six patients on the pediatric ward of the Bellevue Psychiatric Hospital. Several had lost their parents through death or had lived in successive homes without stable relationships. "But another factor influencing the results may be found in the method of procedure. To stimulate reactions Schilder showed the children pictures, the selection of which seems to me to have been rather unfortunate. The pictures portrayed hanged or stabbed persons, brutal scenes and ghosts . . . Is this a way to obtain data concerning a child's general speculations on life and death?" (1939, pp. 149–50). The interpretation of the results is equally questionable. Schilder and Wechsler's conclusion that the children think of death as a deprivation that can be revoked and remedied like any other deprivation bears no clear relation to the listed responses. Under the subheading, "Children do not believe in their own death," the following conversations are recorded "(Do you think you will die?) 'No, I don't know' . . . (Can a child die?) 'No, boys don't die unless they get run over.' 'If they go to a hospital I think they come out living.' 'I never die when I am sick—I stay.' 'I shall not die—when you are old you die. I shall never die. When they get old they die.' But afterward he says that he will also get old and die" (1934, p. 421).

Anthony studied 128 children of primary school age, the majority living in London, some in a rural area. They were seen at school, at home, and some 20 percent in a child-guidance clinic. Her methods included records by parents, definition of the word "dead" inserted into an intelligence test, and a story-completion test. A small number of younger children was studied through home records only. Evaluation of the data showed that most five- to twelve-year-olds were at the stage of being preoccupied with personal and cultural concomitants of the death process. The younger children had discovered the fact of death and, in a limited way, what it implies. Anthony is well aware of the limitations of her results. She relates her findings to fantasy, emotional development, and individual life experiences. Her sensitivity is illustrated by her not using the story-completion test with the few children who had experienced death in their own families. The stories contained no reference to death or violence but stressed painful feelings. Regrettably, Schilder and Wechsler's conclusions are quoted frequently—Anthony's are almost forgotten.

Children's Reactions to the Death of a Love Object Other Than a Parent

Our analytic experience shows that children's as well as adults' mourning depends, among other factors, on who died, what kind of relationship was maintained with the deceased, and how the loss affects the life situation of the bereaved. The death of a parent in childhood is, in many respects, so different from any other loss that we decided against including clinical material and theoretical discussion of other bereavements or to compare them with parental death. It appears that there are no analytic reports that specifically focus on understanding children's reactions to the death of love objects other than the parents. Most of the available clinical studies are based on data gained from observation, psychotherapy, interviews, or statistical records.

Reactions to the death of a sibling are discussed most frequently. Wolf (1958), Chaloner (1962), Cain, Fast, and Erickson (1964), Rogers (1966), and Kliman et al. (1969) discuss their clinical experiences with sibling loss most sensitively but without drawing general conclusions.

Several studies of the adult psychiatric population suggest that the experience of a sibling's death in childhood may have serious effects on personality development and later mental illness. Rosenzweig (1943) and Rosenzweig and Bray (1943) note the incidence of early sibling loss in adult psychotics. Pollock (1962) discusses its significance in relation to later neurotic disturbances.

Our group's analytic experience with children whose sibling died suggests that this kind of bereavement is governed by its individual circumstances, and the responses are determined by a large number of variables. This makes it even more difficult to generalize about reactions to sibling loss than is the case with the death of a parent.

A grandparent's death is, clinically, the most frequent bereavement in childhood. As such it is often mentioned in guidance articles for parents and professionals but there are no detailed analytic reports. Mahler (1950), Wolf (1958) and R. A. Furman (1970) discuss the topic briefly. Barnes (1964) includes a description of four-year-old Wendy's and two-and-a-half-year old Winnie's reactions to their grandfather's death in her report on the children's mourning of their mother. The tragic, close sequence of the two deaths affected the children's responses but there were also notable contrasts. Wendy, especially, could utilize her concept of death in coping with the loss of the grandfather. Nagera (1970) observes four-year-old Peter's reactions to his grandfather's death. This report has the usual advantages and disadvantages of such records. The parents' feelingful and conscientious observation of the child's behavior and of their interaction with him is paralleled by the inevitable omissions that stem from their involvement. For example, there is no record of Peter's behavior on the morning following the grandfather's death during the night. Although the boy had known that grandfather was very ill when he went to bed, Peter was taken to nursery school as usual and not told of the death till his return later that day. Did he know or sense what was going on that morning? Did he make his usual special visit to the grandparents' room or did he know to keep away? Did this relate to his unexplained avoidance of these morning visits subsequently?

Our understanding of mourning in childhood would be considerably enhanced by analytic data on children's reactions to the death of such love objects as grandparents, other relatives, friends, and also of pets. As R. A. Furman (1970) points out, in some such instances the child has maintained an important relationship with the deceased. It differs from the death of a parent in that it does not significantly affect the child's fulfillment of bodily and emotional needs. The death itself may be more timely and its form may not arouse as much anxiety as the premature deaths of young parents and children. This helps us to evaluate the significance of other factors and to compare these losses with parental bereavement. There are a few articles on children's reactions to the death of a pet (Tolsma 1964; Levinson 1967) but no analytic investigations. Several authors report on children's reactions to the death of a peer's mother (McDonald 1963, 1964; R. A. Furman 1969) and to the death of a peer (Wolf 1958). All these papers illustrate the children's capacities for understanding and feelingful response.

The death of President Kennedy prompted much research into children's reactions to this event (Wolfenstein and Kliman 1965). Most of the studies show that, since Kennedy was not a love object in his own right, his death sparked very different reactions in each child, depending on his own experiences, developmental concerns, family attitudes, and varying exposure to knowledge of the entire brutal sequence of events. Some of the detailed descriptions of individual children's reactions in the context of their personal background are most interesting (Alpert, Kliman, Krug and Dember, Zilbach; all 1965). Even these reports, however, contain so many unexplored variables that it is difficult to utilize them for an understanding of mourning reactions. Such studies nevertheless throw light on children's attitudes, thoughts, and feelings about news of death in their environment. Do they react similarly to the daily media reports of "ordinary" murders at certain stages? Have the children identified with the inconsistent attitudes of our social milieu which allow us to grieve loudly for a president but shrug off the deaths of thousands?

Reports on Psychotherapy with Children Whose Parent Had Died

Winnicott comments, "The difference between psychoanalysis and child psychiatry is chiefly that in the former one tries to get the chance to do as much as possible, . . . whereas in the latter one asks: How little need one do?" (1965, p. 213). This view is not shared by all but it highlights one of the differences between analysis and analytic psychotherapy. Some further aspects may be stressed. Since psychotherapeutic contacts do not allow us to make full use of analytic tools, we can gain only partial understanding of the patient's mental life. However, insofar as the difficulties are explored, the work focuses, as in analysis, on the patient's material, the therapist's clarification and interpretation, and the patient's responses to them. The study of this interaction furnishes the basis of our meta-psychological understanding. The extent to which this aim can be realized depends on many factors in each therapy, especially on the patient's disturbance.

When a therapeutic contact is primarily based on another approach, the patient may benefit, but the work does not add to our under-standing of his mental life. This applies to therapies with the main aims of instituting environmental changes, giving advice, and provid-ing a supportive relationship or corrective experience.

For the purpose of discussing clinical therapy data on bereavement reactions, I have selected only full case reports, omitting the many vignettes contained in some papers. The published reports of thera-pies vary greatly in the degree to which they enable us to understand metapsychologically the individual bereaved children.

Bonnard (1961) cites the cases of two boys, both aged thirteen, who suffered recent parental bereavement. Thomas was seen over a period of several years, but the report does not include material about the father's death or its relation to the boy's difficulties. John was seen only six times over a period of ten weeks, with some follow-up, but it was possible to understand some aspects of his reaction to the mother's long illness with cancer and subsequent death.

John was referred for truancy from school and stealing the weekly household money. There was no indication of maladjustment prior to the mother's death nine months earlier. The boy's conscious material and affects mainly concerned his misunderstanding of the mother's illness and partial loss of the relationship with the father. Bonnard gave the boy a realistic account of the course of the mother's illness and interpreted his past partial denial of the seriousness of the mother's condition, a denial that had been shared by the rest of the family and supported by the physician. John was able to integrate the new knowledge and correct his estimate of his own and the father's guilt over mother's death. John's symptoms subsided; he regained his previous good adjustment.

Winnicott (1965) describes a bereaved eleven-year-old boy. There were ten interviews with Patrick and four with his mother over a period of one year. Follow-up contact extended over the next four years. The father drowned while sailing with Patrick on the boy's eleventh birthday. His mother referred him for somatic complaints and withdrawal from schoolwork eight months after the tragedy. The interview material, given in great detail, shows how Patrick allowed himself first to recall the events, then affectively reach "very close to the actual agony of the drowning situation" (p. 234) and, later, to understand some genetic aspects of his difficulty with feelings and with parental relationships. The account of the therapy affords some understanding of how this child's defense structure and underlying conflicts were activated by the tragic experience of parental death and how his adult love objects contributed to the pathological reaction and also helped him find a healthier solution.

Barnes (1964) reports on her treatment-via-the parent of Wendy and Winnie, aged four and two and a half, when their mother died suddenly from an acute episode of a dormant multiple sclerosis. Barnes describes in detail Wendy's gradual comprehension of the finality of death, her fear of death for herself and others at times of illness, her many poignant memories of the mother, anger expressed in the context of her continuing oedipal phase, and deep and often verbalized sadness. Wendy was helped to mourn by her developmental closeness to her father and his capacity to mourn.

Barnes links Winnie's initial denial, and its sudden cessation, to the girl's closeness with the mother figures and her resulting identification with the mother's and grandmother's strong use of denial. Winnie began to express her thoughts and feelings openly when her grandmother went into a delayed mourning. By the end of the first year both children had completed the major stages of mourning, but incidents of separation, illness, and death continued to cause them anxiety. Among the reports of therapy with bereaved children, Barnes provides the most comprehensive view of the many factors that facilitated or interfered with the mourning process.

Kliman et al. (1969) include three cases of a parent's death, two treated in weekly psychotherapy, one in their Cornerstone Project nursery. Richard, aged eight at the time of referral, was seen for sixteen months. He had a learning difficulty and a memory disturbance, and appeared immature and restless. The report focuses on tracing the current problems to the child's difficulty in integrating many earlier overwhelming impressions and feelings—especially the father's lung surgery and death during Richard's fifth year. He mastered this task, with the help of therapy, and recovered emotional health.

Norma, ten and a half years old, was referred by her father and stepmother because of an episode of hysterical physical symptoms. She underachieved at school, spoke slowly and sparsely, and wanted to become a nun. When Norma was five, her then pregnant mother died of carcinoma of the pancreas one month after the diagnosis was made. The next years were marked by further losses—withdrawals, separations, and deaths of relatives. The therapy helped Norma to recover memories, feelings, and misconceptions about the mother's illness and death and related them to Norma's oedipal conflicts at the time of the death. Norma thought that her mother had died because she was having a baby. This work facilitated better integration and allowed Norma to accept her own wish to become a mother.

Quentin, aged five and a half, attended the Cornerstone nursery where the therapist visits daily and talks with the children about their concerns when their conversation or behavior provides an appropriate opportunity. Quentin's father had died six months earlier of a heart attack while he and the boy were alone in the car. The reported material focuses on Quentin's piecemeal accounts of the details of his tragic experience and his acknowledgment of sadness and anger. Quentin is reported to have benefited from this work.

All of Kliman's reports show the therapist's role in empathizing with the child's feelings and helping him to tolerate them. The relationship with and attitude of the surviving parent are omitted. With a child as young as Quentin one wonders particularly about this omission. It seems unlikely that he could profit from the therapist's help without his mother's cooperation and support.

The reports of weekly psychotherapy by Shambaugh (1961), Scharl (1961), Wallach (1961), and Wolfenstein (1966, 1969) are very difficult to discuss because the authors largely exclude the very aspect that affords the best insight into the children's mental lives, that is, the therapist's interpretations of the material and the patient's responses. The descriptions of the children's behavior and verbalizations also tend to be isolated from other factors that would enable us to consider them in specific contexts. These include the child's personality before his bereavement, the genetic origin of his reactions, the role of the surviving parent, the circumstances of the lost parent's illness and death, and the child's current daily life. The authors' conclusions are therefore difficult to follow.

The therapy of Shambaugh's seven-and-a-half-year-old patient began during the time of his mother's terminal hospitalization for cancer. Henry showed no problems and therapy was discontinued because the mother opposed it. It was resumed seven months after the mother's death. Shambaugh describes Henry's reversal of affect, alternating demandingness and attempts to be independent, jealousy of the younger sister, and later use of her as a vicarious object. Henry adopted the father's irresponsible attitudes, sought to be close to him, and hated the various housekeepers. He welcomed the stepmother and blamed himself, though not always consciously, for her rejection and withdrawal into illness. A turning point came when Henry felt a chest pain in the session and remembered his mother's chest operation. He became sad and resolved to stop playing and talking in therapy and to pursue his schoolwork instead. This was the first sign of his identification with the injunctions of his dead mother. Later, when the stepmother insisted on obliterating all traces of the dead mother, Henry could apparently dissociate himself from his parents' defenses and sadly kept a set of glass animals which served to contain his memories of his mother.

Shambaugh attributes Henry's initial behavior solely to regression caused by immaturity. His report suggests, however, that the model of, and relationship with, his father played a significant part. One wonders also about the effect on the therapy of the deceased mother's opposition to it.

Scharl reports on five-year-old Nancy and eight-year-old Linda who witnessed their father's decapitation in a car accident. Linda is said to have become a perfect child since the father's death, in contrast to her previous sulkiness. She was referred because she did not talk about her father and fought with her sister. The report describes Linda's initial drawing of a decapitated man and relates, later, primarily her interactions with various animals, colored by sadistic fantasies and marked feelings of guilt and inadequacy. Within a few months Linda's uncle and grandfather died and she was found to have a heart murmur. She became accident prone but warded off her fear of death. Scharl attributes the material to Linda's aggression toward the dead father and her attempts to find symbolic replacements. She relates Linda's improvement after the death to the strengthened identifications, less critical super ego, and more neutral relationships of latency. The impact of the traumatic events and the mother's attitudes are not considered (see the comment on p. 247 of this chapter).

Nancy is reported as having been perfect before father's death. She was his favorite; he spoiled and infantilized her. "She was extremely upset about her father's death and said, 'If Daddy is dead, life isn't worth living' " (Scharl 1961, p. 475). Later Nancy tried to charm everyone, showed elation and hyperactivity and periods of being a sad, dirty girl who disliked herself. Termination of treatment with both sisters occurred after a few months, timed by the mother's

remarriage and move. Scharl concludes that Nancy initially easily restored her lost object but that the further loss of uncle and grandfather
deprived her of the narcissistic supplies from men and she therefore
regressed and expressed her rage in the form of feeling dirty and
worthless. The material suggests several other factors: the regressions
coincided with Nancy's warding off recall of the traumatic death and
fear of dying; the elation and hyperactivity occurred during separations from the mother.

Wallach (1961) saw Billy for twenty months. He was referred by
his father and stepmother at age six because he stole and wore her un-
derwear, showed hostility to his little half-brother, and was found in
voyeuristic sexual play with a little girl. Billy's mother fell ill when
he was nine months old and died after thirteen months of hospitalization. His grandmother cared for him till age four when father
remarried. During the following two years Billy had two operations
and experienced the death of one brother and the births of two.
Wallach sees Billy's main difficulty as a feminine identification,
which serves to ward off feelings of loss of his mother. His material
in the sessions, however, contains many references to hospitals, operations, masturbation, castration fear, confusion about death,
and sexuality. It appears to relate to his experiences during the
phallic–oedipal phase rather than to the early death of the mother or
later separation from the grandmother and therapist.

Wolfenstein describes Ruth and Walter. R. A. Furman (1968) discussed these cases in detail. I quote excerpts from his paper. "We
could really understand Ruth [whose mother died during adoles-
cence] only through analysis of her pathological defenses and the neurotic conflicts and anxieties they warded off, provided there was any
reasonable semblance of the fulfillment of her reality needs. We are
left with the impression that Ruth's inability to mourn produced these
defensive responses. It would seem to me quite the contrary: that it
was her pathological defenses that made her unable to mourn" (p.
58).

Walter was ten years old when he lost his mother: "Walter's
grandmother's ability to fulfill his needs, facilitated by the reality situation of her gradual assumption of this role, and her active acceptance of his feelings created the circumstances in which one would
expect him to be able to mourn. Wolfenstein felt that 'a major decathexis of the lost parent was accomplished' . . . Despite her feel-

ing the significant decathexis occurred and despite the evidence that
he achieved the results we associate with successful completion of the
mourning task, she feels this was an adaptive reaction and not mourning. Her reasons are that there was 'no protracted sadness or withdrawal into painful preoccupation with memories of the lost object.' I
would add, visible to any observer of his manifest behavior. But as
analysts we can draw no conclusion from the description of his manifest behavior that he was never sad or painfully preoccupied'' (p.
61).

In 1969 Wolfenstein brings further case material, but it contains
the same omissions and therefore does not further an analytic understanding of bereavement reactions. The descriptions of the patients' aggressive manifestations and reactions to disappointments in
relationships may represent many different underlying mental processes.
They do not, as such, justify her claim that they invariably ensue
from the child's rage at the narcissistic deprivation caused by the loss
and by his inability to accept the parent's death. Mary was fourteen at
the time of her father's death after a heart attack. She came for help
at nineteen because she was depressed, had feelings of derealization,
felt unmotivated to continue in college, and was leading a promiscu-
ous life. Mary was seen twice and later three times weekly for three
years when she angrily discontinued after yet another disappointment
in a long series of neurotic relationships with men.

Wolfenstein views Mary's promiscuity as a protest against the father's death, which deprived the girl of his promised supervision of
her dating. Mary's disinterest in her schoolwork is seen as typically
due to ''the absence of external superego support and [with] the loss
of narcissistic supplies provided by parental praise and pride''
(p.446). Mary's penis envy and at times boyish behavior and interests
are related to the premature loss of the father: ''In her uncompleted
development at the time of her father's death, this girl had been left
still longing for a penis'' (p. 439). A normal fourteen-year-old's
pleasure in working and achieving no longer depends so closely on
the father; dating behavior would not be controlled solely by parental
supervision, and the wish for a penis from the father would not constitute a phase-appropriate major conflict. If Wolfenstein's assessment of Mary's conflicts is correct, the girl's difficulties are caused
by pathology which precedes the death of the father. In reading the
report one is tempted to speculate on the relation between Mary's dif-

ficulties and her struggles toward adolescent object removal, including a new identification with her mother. Mary had earlier viewed the mother as inferior but currently seemed to come to resemble her increasingly in behavior and attitudes.

Frank was four when his father committed suicide. Six months later he started therapy for enuresis and temper tantrums. His therapist left after the first year and Frank was transferred to another man. The report tells us only that Frank was attached to, and preoccupied with, a little red car which represented both the lost therapist and father who had committed suicide in a car.

Karl was nine when his school referred him for stabbing a child with scissors. After some improvement, Karl's difficulties with aggression worsened when he learned that his father refused to care for him and that he was to be sent to a residential institution. Karl's angry outbursts are viewed as rage at his mother's death and deprivation of his father.

Edward was eleven when his mother initiated his therapy during her terminal illness. She died during the year of therapy. He had always shown difficulties with aggression and had some facial tics. Both parents had been hospitalized repeatedly. The report discusses Edward's anger at the therapist as a displacement of his rage at their sickness and then the death of his mother. At another point in the paper Edward's fine scholastic achievements are discussed in terms of a successful identification with his mother's ambitions for him.

Diane started treatment at fifteen, one month before her mother's death. She had attempted suicide when her mother was hospitalized with terminal cancer. The report describes the homosexual nature of her relationships and her deep disappointment at rejection by a girl friend. This repeated her shock at the mother's death as well as the mother's withdrawal after the birth of a sister when Diane was in her third year. Diane's repeated suicidal attempts and increasing drug addiction "could be construed as demonstrating what happens to a motherless girl and attempting to coerce the return of her mother to take care of her. There was also the motive of wanting to rejoin her mother in death" (p. 451). Diane's attempts to cope with the mother's death by means of primitive introjections suggest that her pathology has very early genetic roots.

Reports on Analyses of Children Whose Parent Died

With analyses we assume that the method of treatment is basically uniform and provides access to a metapsychological understanding of the patient's mental life. With published accounts of analyses, however, we encounter several limitations. So much material and insight have to be condensed in a report that, inevitably, a great deal is omitted. The author's aim in presenting the case, the need for confidentiality, and practical considerations are among the factors that determine which facets are included. I became aware again of some of these limitations when I compared our group's detailed knowledge and discussion of each case with the written version included in this book. A further difficulty arises in utilizing analytic data for an understanding of normal processes. Patients usually come for treatment when there is considerable pathology. We cannot equate pathological and normal reactions. We use analytic data only to further our insight into the nature and interplay of the many factors that influence psychic and behavioral phenomena.

In the literature I found reports of eleven analyses of parentally bereaved children. They show a great diversity of individual responses and, manifestly, similar reactions are differently determined. Each case reveals such a complexity and multitude of variables that it is difficult to gauge the significance of specific factors. The developmental factor is particularly difficult to single out. Since some of the younger patients show a capacity for the mental processes associated with mourning, the children's difficulties cannot be caused by a developmental incapacity to mourn. Rather, the material seems to confirm Laufer's conclusion: "While itself not pathogenic, object loss can become the nucleus around which earlier conflicts and the latent pathogenic elements are organized" (1966, p. 290). Our experience confirms this, but we have also worked with children whose disturbances did not attach itself to or interfere with their mourning (see analyst's report on Ken, p. 27).

Laufer's (1966) analysis of Michael continued for almost four years. It started in his fifteenth year because of shyness, lack of friends, and poor schoolwork. Laufer saw him as a very disturbed boy whose passivity warded off object-related aggression since his pre-oedipal phase. Michael's mother became sick and died during the first year of his analysis. He was unable to integrate the reality of the mother's death and to allow himself appropriate expression of sadness and anger. Michael's identification with the mother as house-keeper helped him to take care of himself but it contained also pre-oedipal and oedipal pathology and endangered his masculinity and adolescent object removal. Difficulties with the task of mourning and adolescent development reinforced one another. The analysis of Michael's masturbation conflict provided an avenue to understanding the oedipal pathology and enabled Michael to express affects and to progress in his adolescent growth.

Laufer describes how Michael's current experiences and rela-tionships affected his responses but, it seems to me, he underes-timates the interference caused by the family situation. Instead of having the example and support of responsible mourning adults, Mi-chael had to care for his overwhelmed and immature stepfather and grandmother.

Root's (1957) report of a neurotic nineteen-year-old girl focuses primarily on elucidating her adolescent development. There is little information about the death and how the family dealt with it. Her hysterical symptoms were triggered by her marriage at age seventeen and expressed an unconscious wish for, and fear of, pregnancy. The analysis revealed genetic factors of pre-oedipal and oedipal guilt and aggression, as well as difficulty with object removal. This was closely tied to her incomplete mourning for her mother who had died in a car accident when the patient was ten and a half years old. External and internal circumstances appear to have combined to effect an in-cestuous oedipal identification with the mother and to deny the emo-tional significance of her death. The analysis enabled her to get in touch with her grief. She accomplished an object removal, together with a decathexis of the mother and acceptance of herself as a sexual adult.

Novick's (Nagera 1970) patient was sixteen years old when he began his analysis. A.'s mother died from cancer when he was ten. He cried and missed her for a brief period. "The lack of real mourn-ing in the family and the lack of support during his own mourning combined with other factors to produce in A. a pathogenic reaction to the loss" (p. 397). These other factors were pre-oedipal and oedipal difficulties, revived by the loss of the mother, by the onset of pu-berty, and by two hydrocele operations. A. copied mainly with the loss by identifying with the mother's pathological character. This also reinforced a negative oedipal position and anal regression.

Gauthier's (1965) patient was ten and a half when his father died suddenly. He had been in analysis for eighteen months for symptoms of enuresis, anxiety, and difficulty in mixing with peers. Gauthier's report excludes all references to current relationships, events, and behavior outside the sessions, as well as links between the material and its genetic determinants. He notes especially the boy's longing for his father, expressed initially in a barely warded off wish to die and later in fantasies. Aggressive feelings appear to emerge in displacements to the analyst and in thoughts about the father's sins and afterlife. In the latter part of the eight months described, John becomes interested in continuing the generations and shows advanced forms of identification with the father. Gauthier describes the outcome of John's mourning as normal but notes that John has not expressed painful feelings. The reader is impressed with the sadness inherent in John's material at many points. Also, one wonders whether affective discharge occurred outside the analysis.

Kearney (Nagera 1970) started B.'s analysis when he was five and a half. A year later his mother had a mastectomy and died from metastases when B. was close to eight. At the time of referral B. showed "massive oral fixations, disturbances of mood and social-emotional responsiveness" (p. 390). Fears of death, separation, and punishment long predated the mother's illness. B.'s alternate denial and awareness of his mother's physical state appears to correlate with her handling of it with the child. Kearney describes the boy's different attempts to deal with the impending disaster. During the two months after the mother's death B. is described as a traumatized child, overwhelmed by shock and helplessness. Periods of sadness, crying, and longing alternated rapidly with defensive reversal of affect and attempts to distract and protect himself. Guilt and anger, stemming from his earlier relationship with the mother, contributed to initial primitive identifications.

Kearney contrasts these reactions with adult sustained sadness. B.'s feelings, however, appear strikingly similar to adults' affects during the acute phase of mourning (Lindemann 1944; Pollock 1961). The particular form of the boy's responses suggests early determinants in line with the given pre-analytic symptomatology. These and the role of the surviving parents are not mentioned.

R. A. Furman (1964a, 1967, 1968) reports on Billy's reactions to his mother's illness and death and the first year of mourning. Billy was referred for enuresis, teasing of his two older brothers, and feminine interests and gestures at age six, two weeks before an unexpected recurrence of his mother's previously operated breast cancer. She died four months later. Helped by the father's care, emotional support, and realistic information, Billy did not deny the mother's illness or death. Initially he expressed much anger at it and then, for many months, sustained deep sadness and longing which led to considerable decathexis. A temporary interference with mourning was understood to relate to Billy's concern over the mastectomy. He had seen the mother's operative site but received no explanation. Episodic mourning and identifications marked the later stages of mourning. The nonadaptive aspects of these identifications—excited teasing—could be traced to the earlier pathological relationship with the mother. The outcome of mourning was normal. Phase-appropriate maturation continued.

Chethik's (1970) Mark was five years old when his analysis began. Severe castration anxieties pointed to phallic concerns, but Mark functioned like a very disturbed toddler. On his sixth birthday the mother was hospitalized for a mastectomy. She then deteriorated and died within ten months. During that time the grandmother also developed cancer and died before the mother. For one and a half years several housekeepers cared for the children until the father remarried. His attitudes are not mentioned but it does not appear that he lent much emotional support. Mark could be helped to cope with the mother's illness and achieved ego growth and positive oedipal feelings. The terminal hospitalization and death, however, caused a setback. Mark largely denied facts and feelings, endowed the analyst with the maternal role, and comforted himself with infantile autoerotic behavior. In time Mark could be helped to be more in touch with his feelings and to regain acceptable functioning. His difficulties with the housekeepers and new mother were understood to relate to his feelings of disloyalty and fear of driving away yet another love object.

Chethik relates Mark's difficulty with mourning to several factors: insufficient structuralization of the personality resulting in threat to the integrity of the self, primitive level of aggression with attendant guilt and fear of retribution, long-standing difficulty in distinguishing inner and outer reality, and severe castration anxiety heightened by the mother's amputation and bodily disintegration.

Bergen's (1958) four-year-old Ellen started analysis because of anxiety around dirt and broken objects and a hand-washing ritual. Quite recently Ellen had seen her dying mother escape from her father, who had stabbed her and attempted to kill himself. Ellen and two of her younger sisters were cared for by an aunt who could not discuss the tragic realities and respond to Ellen's many questions. Initially, fear of repeated abandonment was paramount. Following her visit to the mother's grave, however, Ellen brought into the analysis her concept of death, sad affect, and reliving of the tragedy. This led to clarification, decathexis, and adaptive identifications by the time she was six. It took longer to effect realistic understanding and emotional detachment in regard to the father, whom Ellen visited occasionally in prison. Eventually she could cathect her aunt and uncle as oedipal objects and continue her development.

Meiss (1952) reports on Peter who had experienced many separations, emotional withdrawals, and illnesses before his father died suddenly when Peter was three years old. Initially Peter had talked a great deal about his father, had dreamt about him repeatedly, and played with a doll he called Daddy, but when his mother moved house and went to work, he became willful and ate poorly, the latter a lifelong reaction to stress. A period of work with the mother helped to improve her feelings for the boy and Peter responded by resuming his oedipal development. The analysis began when Peter was five. He had recently begun to suffer from insomnia, from fears of mother dying, and from thoughts that told him that daddy was angry at him. There are no data on whether or how mother and analyst explained the father's death. His confused ideas about heaven and resurrection derived from a maid. The analysis showed that Peter's fear of father's anger represented a premature superego identification with the angry avenging father, reinforced by earlier castration threats and oedipal ambivalence. Peter was helped to achieve an identification with a kindly and just father, the one he so fondly remembered and still longed for. Meiss attributes Peter's precocious superego development and his intense transference to the loss of the father.

First (1970) reports on the first year of analysis of five-year-old Robert. His father died from a blood disease after one year of illness when Robert was nineteen months old. Robert's serious disturbance, especially pronounced in the area of object relationship, appeared to stem from his mother's difficulty in relating to him and from many changes in nursemaids. There are no data on how Robert reacted to the death of the father, who had been warm and loving with him, or what had been explained to Robert, as the mother herself was quite unclear and ambivalent about the father's illness. The aspect reported in regard to the father is Robert's conflict over identifying with him as a damaged, helpless person and, later, as a powerful dead monster. Neither of these attitudes appears to be rooted in memories of the father but represents other conflicts.

Gyomroi (1963) analyzed Elizabeth, who lost both parents early in her second year when she and her one-year-older sister were sent to Auschwitz. Elizabeth arrived in England at age four and was a member of Miss Goldberger's home from then on. After a manifestly adequate though precarious adjustment during the latency years, Elizabeth could not function independently in adolescence. Gyomroi poignantly relates her efforts to help Elizabeth, in late adolescence, to become a person in her own right and to "remodel her ego, which was distorted by a normal attempt at adaptation to an abnormal environment and thwarted by the severe blocking of her libidinal development" (pp. 509–10). Elizabeth's primitive pathology stems from a multitude of traumatic factors in her pre-oedipal period. The significance of the loss of the mother, without a substitute, is no doubt central and accounts for the arrest in the development of object relationships and self-representation.

Effect of Childhood Bereavement on Adult Functioning

Among studies of adults who had suffered death of a parent in their childhood, only Jacobson, and Fleming and Altschul, provide full-length analytic reports. Jacobson (1965) describes Robert, a married man and father in his thirties, who complained of recurrent depressions and feelings of depersonalization. His difficulties were traced to his reaction to the death of his mother, toward the end of his oedipal phase. She died in childbirth and the newborn child also died on the same day. Robert spent a helpless, lonely childhood in the care of a "gloomy," strict grandmother. He comforted himself with fantasies of his mother's return. In this way he also warded off his idea that father had killed mother and baby in sexual intercourse and his unconscious identification with his "sinful" parents. Jacobson comments that Robert's denial of the mother's death was prompted by the evasiveness of the surviving love objects and the murderous primal scene fantasies derived from his knowledge that during childbirth something terrible had happened to mother and infant.

Fleming and Altschul's (1963) patient, a twenty-nine-year-old woman, entered analysis because of anxiety and depression. At fifteen her parents had sent her to England to escape the holocaust of Nazi Germany which killed them when she was about eighteen. The analysis of her difficulty in the transference showed that she warded off her unconscious attachment to her parents and feelings about their loss. Her relationships and self-image were arrested at the beginning of adolescent object removal and colored by the difficulties she had at the time of separation from her parents. The analysis activated the mourning and enabled the patient to mature. The authors note that developmental immaturity and prior defense structure interfered with mourning. I would add other factors: no factual evidence of death, anxiety about its sadistic nature, survivor guilt, stress of adapting to a new country and language, and lack of opportunity to share grief.

Lewin's and Deutsch's data are not detailed. Lewin (1937) analyzed a group of patients suffering from a "neurotic hypomanic reaction." They had lost a parent through death in early latency and made a superficially good adjustment by taking on the dead parent's role. This complicated their adolescent development, at which time the hypomanic mechanisms were instituted to ward off incestuous impulses. Deutsch (1937) states that her two patients, bereaved at age five, showed unmotivated depression in one case and, in the other, lack of interest in object relationships, combined with a general affect block. She stresses the lack of affective reaction at the time of the loss as crucial for the pathological outcome.

Dorpat (1970) considers the effects of parental suicide. He treated seventeen such children as adults for a variety of disturbances. He finds that the ego strain associated with the parent's suicide was greatly heightened by lack of emotional support and lack of opportunity to express grief at the time of the tragedy.

Barry studied the significance of maternal bereavement in large numbers of psychiatric patients. In 1949 he considered bereavement before the age of eight particularly crucial. His later collaborative work as well as that of others (Barry and Lindemann 1960; Barry Jr., Barry III, and Lindemann 1965) shows that the death of the mother in

children under five is most significant for the incidence of adult psychoneuroses and dependency. Archibald et al. (1962) investigated a
large group of clients at a mental hygiene outpatient clinic and compared their data with other studies. They find among these patients an
appreciably greater frequency of bereavement in childhood, but consider the early parental death a nonspecific trauma whose effects
depend upon complex interaction of many variables. Pollock (1962)
similarly records the marked incidence of early parental and sibling
loss among his neurotic patients and stresses the multitude of individual factors.

Hilgard and Newman (1959) find that the onset of psychoses in
adults is often connected with the anniversary of the parent's death in
childhood, particularly when the patient reaches the age at which the
parent died or when his child becomes as old as the patient was when
he was orphaned. Brown's (1961) and Beck, Sethi, and Tuthil's
(1963) studies show that parental bereavement below fifteen years of
age has a significantly higher incidence among adults with depressive
illness.

In our work with parents we frequently found that a parent whose
own parent died in childhood encountered difficulty as a parent but
showed no disturbance in other areas of functioning. Sometimes this
difficulty interfered with the entire ability to function as a parent; at
other times it involved only certain periods. For example, some
parents lost empathy with their children when the latter reached the
age at which the parents had suffered bereavement; others experienced an interference during that critical period but could later resume parenting; still others showed different styles of parenting before and after the period of their own parent's death, apparently based
on different models for identification. In the literature there seems to
be only one report of such an aftermath of early parental bereavement. Pfeffer (1973) describes the psychotherapy of an older man
who experienced mild depressions and anxiety at the time of his son's
belated object removal. This related to the patient's own father's
death in latency.

Altschul points out that some children may "adapt successfully to
loss, but in our experience they are not likely to come under psychoanalytic investigation" (1968, p. 303). Some studies investigate normally functioning adults who suffered parental bereavement in childhood. The work of Hilgard, Newman, and Fisk (1960) is particularly

interesting because the authors detail the factors they find significant in having facilitated normal development after the father's death in childhood. The home was kept intact by the mother, who served the dual role of homemaker and breadwinner. A network of support existed outside the home, which the mother appropriately utilized. Relationships before the death were stable, well defined, compatible, and generally healthy. The children had developed an emotional tolerance for separation before the loss occurred. Grief and mourning occurred immediately after the death.

Assistance with Mourning

In discussing their analyses of adults who lost a parent in childhood, the authors leave the impression, or specifically indicate, that these patients could be helped to complete their mourning and resolve successfully the related difficulties (Deutsch 1937; Lewin 1937; Pollock 1961; Fleming and Altschul 1963; Jacobson 1965; Remus-Araico 1965; Altschul 1968). Whereas Remus-Araico advocates the introduction of occasional "timeless interviews" to facilitate the mourning process in early bereaved patients, most analysts used the customary daily sessions. Fleming and Altschul, and Altschul, explicitly state that analysis invariably activates the mourning and thereby facilitates further maturation. Jacobson notes: "In the analysis of orphaned adults we can regularly observe the development of a delayed mourning process during treatment after their defenses have broken down" (1967, p. 434). The reports on completed analyses of bereaved children similarly suggest very good treatment results as far as facilitating their mourning is concerned. R. A. Furman (1964a) finds that analysis is not contraindicated during a child's mourning but may, on the contrary, assist the patient in his task without interfering with the analytic process. Many papers on analytic psychotherapy also report a favorable outcome with the help of therapeutic intervention (Bonnard 1961; Winnicott 1965; Kliman et al. 1969). Barnes (1964) describes the helpful effect of treatment-via-the parent for bereaved youngsters under five. Similar positive reports come from other forms of treatment. Kliman et al. (1969) discuss the benefits of parent guidance, stressing the parent's need to appreciate the different rhythms of his and his child's mourning and to curb the tendency to transfer to the child aspects of the relationship with the deceased spouse. Ottenstein, Wiley, and Rosenblum (1962) studied families in which the father had died. Since the mothers' difficulty with mourning had immobilized their dealing effectively with the children, the authors extended casework help to the mothers. Paul (1969) used family therapy to help bereaved children with the expression of grief in instances where the surviving parent had fostered unhealthy defensive measures. Kliman et al (1969) report on helping young orphans in the setting of the Cornerstone Project nursery. Moller (1967) assisted bereaved pupils as a school psychologist by offering them a sympathetic relationship and an opportunity to talk about the loss.

The twenty-three cases treated by analysis and treatment-via-the parent in our study also benefited, as did many other patients with whom we worked in other forms of treatment. We recognized, however, many important variables and limitations. The extent to which a bereaved patient can be helped and the preferred form of treatment depend on the pathology of his personality before the loss and on the nature of his life circumstances at the time and after his bereavement. These may interfere with the patient's ability to cope with the death and to continue his development, and they may also augment earlier pathology. Among these circumstances are the form of death, the availability of realistic information, the consistency of physical-need fulfillment and emotional support for mourning, coincident stresses, and opportunity to form a relationship with a new parent figure at the appropriate time. The previous pathology and the effects of attendant and subsequent circumstances both determine the nature of the patient's difficulties and their accessbility to therapeutic intervention. A. Freud (1952, 1960) suggests that very early bereavements followed by very unfavorable life circumstances tend to produce disturbances which may not be treatable. Gyomroi's (1963) and some of our cases come close to this. Although these patients benefited greatly from their analyses, the task was extraordinarily difficult and could not have been approached by other forms of therapy. In this connection it is pertinent to mention another of our findings, that is, that assistance is most effective when it occurs at the time of bereavement or shortly thereafter. One does not think here of individual therapy as an initial form of help but of assistance to the surviving parent in the form of counseling. Through such work the attendant and subsequent circumstances of the death may be ameliorated so that the child has an optimum chance of utilizing his capacities for mourning.

This does not prevent all difficulties but forestalls some. Kliman et al. (1969) concur here in stressing the need for providing help to bereaved families early as a prophylactic measure.

The community apparently makes a strong demand for professional help with all situations involving death and dying, including bereavement in childhood. During recent years, many newspapers and family magazines have published articles on this subject. In some papers, several contradictory views appeared in succession, which must make it quite difficult for the lay reader. In going over a number of educational articles written primarily for parents, it seems to me that one area is most controversial. It concerns the handling of death with prelatency children. Many authors thoughtfully suggest being realistic about the cause of death, supporting the expression of feelings, providing continued love and care, and recognizing the difficulties that children and adults have with mourning. They neglect, however, the need to teach a concrete concept of death in early life. They underestimate the young child's interest and capacity for understanding as well as the importance of factual knowledge of death for coping with a bereavement.

The following articles, though not a complete list and varied in format and scope, have impressed me as particularly helpful. Chronologically, the earliest article is by Mahler (1950). It stresses the need to explain death and its causes realistically to children of all ages and to keep in mind their individual and age-appropriate ability to integrate facts and feelings. Wolf's (1958) booklet is perhaps the most detailed and comprehensive. It deals sensitively, concretely, and consistently well with many situations in which the child confronts death and faces his parent and teacher with his questions and reactions. Spock's (1960) contribution emphasizes how important it is that the parent's attitude and feeling coincide with the content of his words in discussing all aspects of death. Chaloner's (1952) article utilizes the experience of a death in the family most thoughtfully. McDonald (1963) describes the reactions of nursery school children to a peer's mother's death and the teachers' efforts to help them. She uses this experience to discuss how parents and teachers can assist children in developing a concept of death and why this is so important. Grollman (1967) talks forthrightly and with feeling on how to explain the death of a loved one to children of different ages and how to include them in the family's rites and mourning. R. A. Furman's (1970) paper is intended for pediatricians but can be equally helpful to parents and other professionals. He addresses himself first to the task of helping young children to learn about death and to develop tolerance for feelings associated with loss. Then he discusses how children react to different types of bereavement and how adults can help them in mourning. Ramos (1972) presents briefly Kliman's views on helping children both before and after bereavement. Similar points are emphasized.

When a child's parent dies, each surviving member of the family faces so complex and difficult a situation that no form of assistance may seem adequate to the task. Yet, many children and parents are fortunate enough both in the makeup of their personalities and in the circumstances of their lives that they can master the stress and profit even from very limited help.

Bibliography

Abraham, Karl. 1911. "Notes on the Psychoanalytical Investigation and Treatment of Manic-Depressive Insanity and Allied Conditions," in *Selected Papers.* London: Hogarth (1927), pp. 137–57.

———. 1924. "A Short Study of the Development of the Libido, Viewed in the Light of Mental Disorders," in *Selected Papers.* London: Hogarth (1927), pp. 393–407.

Alpert, Augusta. 1965. "Choice of Defenses Used by Prelatency Children in Reaction to the Assassination," in *Children and the Death of a President,* ed. M. Wolfenstein and G. Kliman. Garden City, N.Y.: Doubleday, pp. 99–106.

Altschul, Sol. 1968. "Denial and Ego Arrest," *Journal of the American Psychoanalytic Association* 16, no. 2 : 301–18.

Anderson, Charles. 1949. "Aspects of Pathological Grief and Mourning," *International Journal of Psycho-analysis* 30 : 48–55.

Anthony, J., and Scott, P. 1960. "Manic-Depressive Psychosis in Childhood," *Journal of Child Psychology and Psychiatry* 1 : 53–72.

Anthony, Sylvia. 1940. *The Child's Discovery of Death.* London: Routledge and Kegan Paul.

———. 1972. *The Discovery of Death in Childhood and After.* New York: Basic Books.

Archibald, Herbert C., Bell, D., Miller, C., and Tuddenham, R. D. 1962. "Bereavement in Childhood and Adult Psychiatric Disturbance," *Psychosomatic Medicine* 24 : 343–51.

Archives of the Foundation of Thanatology. 1969–70. New York, vols. 1 and 2.

Arthur, B., and Kemme, M. L. 1964. "Bereavement in Childhood," *Journal of Child Psychology and Psychiatry* 5 : 37–49.

Barnes, Marion J. 1964. "Reactions to the Death of a Mother," *Psychoanalytic Study of the Child,* vol. 19. New York: International Universities Press, pp. 334–57.

Barry, H. 1949. "Significance of Maternal Bereavement before the Age of Eight in Psychiatric Patients," *Archives of Neurology and Psychiatry* 62 : 630–37.

Barry, H., Jr., and Lindemann, E. 1960. "Critical Incidence for Maternal Bereavement in Psychoneuroses," *Psychosomatic Medicine* 22 : 166–81.

Barry, H., Jr., Barry, H., III, and Lindemann, E. 1965. "Dependency in Adult Patients following Early Maternal Bereavement," *Journal of Nervous and Mental Disease* 140 : 196–206.

Beck, A., Sethi, B., and Tuthil, R. 1963. "Childhood Bereavement and Adult Depression," *Archives of General Psychiatry* 9 : 295–302.

Becker, Diane, and Margolin, Faith. 1967. "How Surviving Parents Handled Their Young Children's Adaptation to the Crisis of Loss," *American Journal of Orthopsychiatry* 37 : 753–57.

Benda, Clemens. 1962. "Bereavement and Grief Work," *Journal of Pastoral Care* 16 : 1–13.

Bender, Lauretta. 1954. *Dynamic Psychopathology of Childhood*. Springfield, Ill.: Thomas.

Benolie, Jeanne Quint. 1971. "Assessments of Loss and Grief," *Journal of Thanatology* 1, no. 3 : 182–93.

Beres, D. 1965. "Superego and Depression" (presented to the Cleveland Psychoanalytic Society, April 16).

Bergen, Mary E. 1958. "The Effect of Severe Trauma on a Four-year-old Child," *Psychoanalytic Study of the Child*, vol. 13. New York: International Universities Press, pp. 407–29.

Bibring, E. 1953. "The Mechanism of Depression," in *Affective Disorders*, ed. P. Greenacre. New York: International Universities Press, pp. 13–48.

Binswanger, Ludwig. 1957. *Sigmund Freud: Reminiscences of a Friendship*. New York: Grune and Stratton, p. 106.

Birtchnell, J. 1969. "The Possible Consequences of Early Parent Death," *British Journal of Medical Psychology* 42 : 1–12.

Blos, Peter. 1967. "The Second Individuation Process of Adolescence," *Psychoanalytic Study of the Child*, vol. 22. New York: International Universities Press, pp. 162–87.

Bonaparte, M. 1928. "L'Identification d'une fille à sa mère morte," *Revue française psychoanalytique* 2 : 541–65.

———. 1939. *Five Copy Books*. London: Imago (1950).

Bonnard, Augusta. 1961. "Truancy and Pilfering Associated with Bereavement," in *Adolescents*, ed. S. Lorand and H. Schneer. New York: Hoeber, pp. 152–79.

Bowlby, John. 1951. *Maternal Care and Mental Health*. Geneva: World Health Organization Monograph.

———. 1960. "Grief and Mourning in Infancy and Early Childhood," *Psychoanalytic Study of the Child*, vol. 15. New York: International Universities Press, pp. 9–52.

———. 1960a. "Separation Anxiety," *International Journal of Psycho-analysis* 41 : 89–113.

———. 1961. "Processes of Mourning," *International Journal of Psycho-analysis* 42 : 317–40.

———. 1963. "Pathological Mourning and Childhood Mourning," *Journal of the American Psychoanalytic Association* 11 : 500–41.

Brandon, S. G. F. 1962. *Man and His Destiny in the Great Religions*. Manchester, England: Manchester Univ. Press.

Brown, F. 1961. "Depression and Childhood Bereavement," *Journal of Mental Science* 107 (July) : 754–77.

Burlingham, Dorothy, and Freud, Anna. 1942. *Young Children in War-Time*. London: Allen and Unwin.

Cain, A., Fast, I., and Erickson, M. 1964. "Children's Disturbed Reactions to the Death of a Sibling," *American Journal of Orthopsychiatry* 34 : 741–52.

Chaloner, L. 1962. "How to Answer the Questions Children Ask about Death," *Parents' Magazine,* November, p. 48.

Chethik, Morton. 1970. "The Impact of Object Loss on a Six-year-old," *Journal of the American Academy of Child Psychiatry* 9, no. 4 : 624–43.

Clayton, Paul, Desmarais, Lynn, and Winokur, George. 1968. "A Study of Normal Bereavement," *American Journal of Psychiatry* 125 (Aug.) : 168–78.

Deutsch, Helene. 1937. "Absence of Grief," *Psychoanalytic Quarterly* 6 : 12–22.

Dorpat, T. L. 1970. "Psychological Effects of Parental Suicide on Surviving Children" (presented to the Scientific Meeting of the Seattle Psychoanalytic Society, Feb. 9).

———. 1971. "Psychological Effects of Parental Suicide on Surviving Children," (report) *Bulletin of the Philadelphia Association for Psychoanalysis* 21, no. 1 : 45–46.

Eissler, Kurt K. 1955. *The Psychiatrist and the Dying Patient.* New York: International Universities Press.

Eliot, Thomas D. 1930. "The Adjustive Behavior of Bereaved Families: A New Field for Research," *Social Forces* 8 : 543–49.

———. 1955. "Bereavement: Inevitable but Not Insurmountable," in *Family, Marriage and Parenthood,* ed. Howard Becker and Reuben Hill. Boston: Heath, pp. 641–68.

Engel, G. L. 1961. "Is Grief a Disease? A Challenge for Medical Research," *Psychosomatic Medicine* 23 : 18–22.

Federn, Paul. 1952. *Ego Psychology and the Psychoses.* New York: Basic Books, p. 375.

Fenichel, Otto. 1945. *The Psychoanalytic Theory of Neuroses.* New York: Norton.

First, Elsa. 1970. "The First Year of Analysis of A Fatherless Boy," *Journal of Child Psychotherapy 2,* no. 4, Dec. 1970, pp. 39–53.

Fleming, Joan, and Altschul, Sol. 1963. "Activation of Mourning and Growth by Psycho-Analysis," *International Journal of Psycho-Analysis* 44 : 419–31.

Flugel, J. C. 1940. "Introduction," in Sylvia Anthony *The Child's Discovery of Death.* London: Routledge and Kegan Paul.

Frankl, L., and Hellman, I. 1962. "The Ego's Participation in the Therapeutic Alliance," *International Journal of Psycho-Analysis* 43 : 333–37.

Freud, Anna. 1945. "Indications for Child-analysis," *Psychoanalytic Study of the Child,* vol. 1. New York: International Universities Press, pp. 127–49.

———. 1952. "The Mutual Influences in the Development of Ego and Id," *Psychoanalytic Study of the Child,* vol. 7. New York: International Universities Press, pp. 42–50.

———. 1958. "Adolescence," *Psychoanalytic Study of the Child,* vol. 13. New York: International Universities Press, pp. 255–78.

Freud, Anna. 1960. "Discussion of Dr. John Bowlby's Paper," *Psychoanalytic Study of the Child,* vol. 15. New York: International Universities Press, pp. 53–62.

———. 1962. "Assessment of Childhood Disturbances," *Psychoanalytic Study of the Child,* vol. 17. New York: International Universities Press, pp. 149–58.

———. Communication to Erna Furman, Dec. 26, 1963. "On Object Constancy."

———. 1965. *Normality and Pathology in Childhood.* New York: International Universities Press.

———. 1970. In Humberto Nagera, "Children's Reactions to the Death of Important Objects: A Developmental Approach," *Psychoanalytic Study of the Child,* vol. 25. New York: International Universities Press, p. 379.

Freud, Anna, and Burlingham, Dorothy. 1943. *War and Children.* New York: International Universities Press.

———, and ———. 1944. *Infants without Families.* New York: International Universities Press.

Freud, Sigmund. 1893. *Studies on Hysteria,* standard ed., vol. 2 : 1–305. London: Hogarth (1966).

———. 1897. *Draft N. Notes III,* standard ed., vol. 1 : 254–57. London: Hogarth (1966).

———. 1897. *Letter 66,* standard ed., vol. 1 : 257–58. London: Hogarth (1966).

———. 1900. *The Interpretation of Dreams,* standard ed., vol. 4 : 1–338. London: Hogarth (1953).

———. 1909. *Notes upon a Case of Obsessional Neurosis,* standard ed., vol. 10 : 153–318. London: Hogarth (1955).

———. 1911. *Formulations on the Two Principles of Mental Functioning,* standard ed., vol. 12 : 213–25. London: Hogarth (1958).

———. 1913. *Totem and Taboo,* standard ed., vol. 13 : 1–161. London: Hogarth (1955).

———. 1915. *Mourning and Melancholia,* standard ed., vol. 14 : 237–58. London: Hogarth (1957).

———. 1915a. *Thoughts for the Times on War and Death,* standard ed., vol. 14 : 273–302. London: Hogarth (1957).

———. 1915b. *On Transience,* standard ed., vol. 14 : 303–07. London: Hogarth (1957).

———. 1918. *From the History of an Infantile Neurosis,* standard ed., vol. 17 : 23–122. London: Hogarth (1955).

———. 1921. *Group Psychology and the Analysis of the Ego,* standard ed., vol. 18 : 67–143. London: Hogarth (1955).

———. 1923. *The Ego and the Id,* standard ed., vol. 19 : 3–68. London: Hogarth (1961).

———. 1926. *Inhibitions, Symptoms and Anxiety,* standard ed., vol. 20 : 77–178. London: Hogarth (1959).

———. 1927. *Fetishism,* standard ed., vol. 21 : 149–57. London: Hogarth (1961).

———. 1928. *Dostoevsky and Parricide,* standard ed., vol. 21 : 175–96. London: Hogarth (1961).

Fulton, Robert. 1967. "On the Dying of Death," in *Explaining Death to Children,* ed. E. A. Grollman. Boston: Beacon, pp. 31–47.

Furman, Erna. 1957. "Treatment of Under-Fives by Way of Parents," *Psychoanalytic Study of the Child,* vol. 12. New York: International Universities Press, pp. 250–62.

———. 1969. "Treatment via the Mother," in *The Therapeutic Nursery School,* ed. Robert A. Furman and Anny Katan. New York: International Universities Press, pp. 64–123.

———. 1970. "Research on Bereaved Children," *Archives of the Foundation of Thanatology,* vol. 2, no. 2. New York, pp. 75–77.

Furman, Robert A. 1964. "Death and the Young Child: Some Preliminary Considerations," *Psychoanalytic Study of the Child,* vol. 19. New York: International Universities Press, pp. 321–33.

———. 1964a. "Death of a Six-year-old's Mother during His Analysis," *Psychoanalytic Study of the Child,* vol. 19. New York: International Universities Press, pp. 377–97.

———. 1967. "A Technical Problem: The Child Who Has Difficulty in Controlling His Behavior in Analytic Sessions," in *The Child Analyst at Work,* ed. Elisabeth R. Geleerd. New York: International Universities Press, pp. 59–84.

———. 1968. "Additional Remarks on Mourning and the Young Child," *Bulletin of the Philadelphia Association of Psychoanalysis* 18, no. 2 : 51–64.

———. 1969. "Sally," in *The Therapeutic Nursery School,* ed. Robert A. Furman and Anny Katan. New York: International Universities Press, pp. 124–38.

———. 1970. "The Child's Reaction to Death in the Family," in *Loss and Grief: Psychological Management in Medical Practice,* ed. Bernard Schoenberg, Arthur C. Carr, David Peretz, and Austin H. Kutscher. New York and London: Columbia Univ. Press, pp. 70–86.

———. 1973. "A Child's Capacity for Mourning," in *The Child in His Family: The Impact of Disease and Death;* Yearbook of the International Association for Child Psychiatry and Allied Professions, vol. 2, ed. E. J. Anthony and C. Koupernik. New York: Wiley, pp. 225–31.

Gauthier, Y. 1965. "The Mourning Reaction of a Ten-and-a-half-year-old Boy," *Psychoanalytic Study of the Child,* vol. 20. New York: International Universities Press, pp. 481–94.

Geleerd, Elisabeth R. 1965. "Two Kinds of Denial: Neurotic Denial and Denial in the Service of the Need to Survive," in *Drives, Affects and Behavior,* vol. 2, ed. Max Schur. New York: International Universities Press, pp. 118–27.

Gesell, Arnold, and Ilg, Frances L. 1946. *The Child from Five to Ten.* New York and London: Harper, 1946.

Gibney, H. H. 1965. "What Death Means to Children," *Parents' Magazine,* March, p. 64.

Gorer, Geoffrey. 1965. *Death, Grief, and Mourning.* Garden City, N.Y.: Doubleday.

Greene, W. A. 1958. "Role of a Vicarious Object in the Adaptation to Object Loss," *Psychosomatic Medicine* 20 : 344–50.

Greenson, R. 1949. "The Psychology of Apathy," *Psychoanalytic Quarterly* 18 : 290–302.

Grinstein, A. 1956–72. *The Index of Psychoanalytic Writings,* 11 vols. to date. New York: International Universities Press.

Grollman, Earl A. 1967. "Prologue: Explaining Death to Children," in *Explaining Death to Children,* ed. E. A. Grollman. Boston: Beacon, pp. 3–27.

Gyomroi, E. L. 1963. "The Analysis of a Young Concentration Camp Victim," *Psychoanalytic Study of the Child,* vol. 18. New York: International Universities Press, pp. 484–510.

Harrison, Saul I., Davenport, Charles W., and McDermott, John F. 1967. "Children's Reactions to Bereavement," *Archives of General Psychiatry* 17 (March) : 593–97.

Hart, Henry Harper. 1972. *Conceptual Index to Psychoanalytic Technique and Training.* Croton-on-Hudson: North River Press.

Hartmann, Heinz. 1950. "Comments on the Psychoanalytic Theory of the Ego," *Psychoanalytic Study of the Child,* vol. 5. New York: International Universities Press, pp. 74–96.

Hilgard, J. R., and Newman, Martha F. 1959. "Anniversaries in Mental Illness," *Psychiatry* 22 : 113–21.

———, ———, and Fisk, F. 1960. "Strength of Adult Ego following Childhood Bereavement," *American Journal of Orthopsychiatry* 30 (Oct.) : 788–98.

Hug-Hellmuth, Hermine von. 1912. "The Child's Concept of Death," *Imago,* 1 : 286–98, trans. *Psychoanalytic Quarterly* 34 (1965) : 499–516.

Irion, P. E. 1954. *The Funeral and the Mourners.* New York: Abingdon.

Isaacs, Susan. 1930. *Intellectual Growth in Young Children.* London: Routledge (1945).

Jackson, Edgar N. 1967. "The Theological, Psychological, and Philosophical Dimensions of Death in Protestantism," in *Explaining Death to Children,* ed. E. A. Grollman. Boston: Beacon, pp. 171–95.

Jacobson, Edith. 1946. "The Effect of Disappointment on Ego and Superego Formation in Normal and Depressive Development," *Psychoanalytic Review* 33 : 129–47.

———. 1953. "Contribution to the Metapsychology of Cyclothymic Depression," in *Affective Disorders,* ed. P. Greenacre. New York: International Universities Press, pp. 49–84.

———. 1954. "The Self and the Object World: Vicissitudes of Their Infantile Cathexes and Their Influence on Ideational and Affective Development," *Psychoanalytic Study of the Child,* vol. 9. New York: International Universities Press, pp. 75–127.

———. 1957. "On Normal and Pathological Moods," *Psychoanalytic Study of the Child,* vol. 12. New York: International Universities Press, pp. 73–113.

———. 1964. *The Self and the Object World.* New York: International Universities Press.

————. 1965. "The Return of the Lost Parent," in *Drives, Affects and Behavior*, vol. 2, ed. Max Schur. New York: International Universities Press, pp. 193–211.

————. 1967. "Introjection in Mourning," *International Journal of Psychiatry* 3, no. 2 : 433–35.

Joffe, W. G., and Sandler, J. 1965. "Notes on Pain, Depression, and Individuation," *Psychoanalytic Study of the Child*, vol. 20. New York: International Universities Press, pp. 394–424.

Jones, Ernest. 1953–57. *The Life and Work of Sigmund Freud*, 3 vols. New York: Basic Books.

Joseph, Florence. 1962. "Transference and Countertransference in a Case of a Dying Patient," *Psychoanalytic Review* 49, no. 4 : 21–34.

Journal of Thanatology. 1971–72. 2 vols. to date. New York: Foundation of Thanatology, Health Sciences Publishing Co.

Kalish, Richard A. 1969. "Grief and Bereavement: A Selected Annotated Bibliography of Behavioral Science and Psychiatric Writings," in *Death and Bereavement*, ed. Austin H. Kutscher. Springfield, Ill.: Thomas, pp. 343–58.

Karpe, R. 1961. "Freud's Reaction to His Father's Death," *Bulletin of the Philadelphia Association for Psychoanalysis* 6 : 25–29.

Katan, Anny. 1937. "The Role of Displacement in Agoraphobia," *International Journal of Psycho-Analysis* 32 : 41–50 (1951).

————. 1961. "Some Thoughts about the Role of Verbalization in Early Childhood," *Psychoanalytic Study of the Child*, vol. 16. New York: International Universities Press, pp. 184–88.

Keller, W. R. 1954. "Children's Reactions to the Death of a Parent," in *Depression*, ed. Paul H. Hoch and Joseph Zubin. New York: Grune and Stratton, pp. 109–20.

Klein, Melanie. 1935. "A Contribution to the Psychogenesis of Manic-Depressive States," *International Journal of Psycho-Analysis* 16 : 145–74.

————. 1940. "Mourning and Its Relation to Manic-Depressive States," *International Journal of Psycho-analysis* 21 : 125–53.

Kliman, G. 1965. "Oedipal Themes in Children's Reactions to the Assassination," in *Children and the Death of a President*, ed. M. Wolfenstein and G. Kliman. Garden City, N.Y.: Doubleday, pp. 107–34.

————, Feinberg, Daniel; Buchsbaum, Betty; Kliman, Ann; Lubin, Harriet; Ronald, Doris; and Stein, Myron. 1969. "Facilitation of Mourning during Childhood" (presented to the American Orthopsychiatric Association, New York, April).

Kroeber, Theodora. 1964. *Ishi, Last of His Tribe*. Berkeley, Cal.: Parnassus.

Krug, Othilda, and Dember, Cynthia Fox. 1965. "Diagnostic and Therapeutic Utilization of Children's Reactions to the President's Death," in *Children and the Death of a President*, ed. M. Wolfenstein and G. Kliman. Garden City, N.Y.: Doubleday, pp. 80–98.

Krupp, George R. 1962. "The Bereavement Reaction: A Special Case of Separation Anxiety—Sociocultural Considerations," *Psychoanalytic Study of Society* 2 : 42–74.

Kubler-Ross, Elizabeth. 1969. *On Death and Dying*. New York: Macmillan.

Lampl-de Groot, J. 1960. "On Adolescence," *Psychoanalytic Study of the Child*, vol. 15. New York: International Universities Press, pp. 95–103.

Laufer, M. 1966. "Object Loss and Mourning during Adolescence," *Psychoanalytic Study of the Child*, vol. 21. New York: International Universities Press, pp. 269–93.

Lehrman, S. R. 1956. "Reactions to Untimely Death," *Psychiatric Quarterly* 30 : 564–78.

Levinson, B. M. 1967. "The Pet and the Child's Bereavement," *Mental Hygiene* 51 (April) : 197–200.

Lewin, Bertram D. 1937. "A Type of Neurotic Hypomanic Reaction," *Archives of Neurology and Psychiatry* 37 : 868–73.

Lindemann, Erich. 1944. "Symptomatology and Management of Acute Grief," *American Journal of Psychiatry* 101 : 141–48.

Lipson, Channing T. 1963. "Denial and Mourning," *International Journal of Psycho-Analysis* 44 : 104–07.

Loewald, H. W. 1962. "Internalization, Separation, Mourning, and the Super Ego," *Psychoanalytic Quarterly* 31 : 483–504.

Mahler, M. S. 1950. *Helping Children to Accept Death*. New York: Child Association of America, pp. 98–99, 119–20.

———. 1961. "On Sadness and Grief in Infancy and Childhood: Loss and Restoration of the Symbiotic Love Object," *Psychoanalytic Study of the Child*, vol. 16. New York: International Universities Press, pp. 332–51.

Marris, P. 1958. *Widows and Their Families*. London: Routledge and Kegan Paul.

McDonald, Marjorie. 1963. "Helping Children to Understand Death: An Experience with Death in a Nursery School," *Journal of Nursery Education* 19, no. 1 : 19–25.

———. 1964. "A Study of the Reactions of Nursery School Children to the Death of a Child's Mother," *Psychoanalytic Study of the Child*, vol. 19. New York: International Universities Press, pp. 358–76.

Mendelson, M. 1960. *Psychoanalytic Concepts of Depression*. Springfield, Ill.: Thomas.

Meiss, M. 1952. "The Oedipal Problem of a Fatherless Child," *Psychoanalytic Study of the Child*, vol. 7. New York: International Universities Press, pp. 216–29.

Miller, Jill Barbara Menes. 1971. "Reactions to the Death of a Parent: A Review of the Psychoanalytic Literature," *Journal of the American Psychoanalytic Association* 19, no. 4 : 697–719.

Mitford, Jessica. 1962. *The American Way of Death*. New York: Simon and Schuster.

Moellenhoff, Fritz. 1939. "Ideas of Children about Death," *Bulletin of the Menninger Clinic* 3 : 148–56.

Moller, Hella. 1967. "Death: Handling the Subject and Affected Students in the Schools," in *Explaining Death to Children*, ed. E. A. Grollman. Boston: Beacon, pp. 145–67.

Nagera, Humberto. 1970. "Children's Reactions to the Death of Important Objects: A Developmental Approach," *Psychoanalytic Study of the Child,* vol. 25. New York: International Universities Press, pp. 360–400.

Nagy, Maria. 1948. "The Child's Theories Concerning Death," *Journal of Genetics and Psychology* 73 : 3–4, 26–27.

Natanson, M. 1959. "Death and Situation," *American Imago* 16 : 447–57.

Ottenstein, Donald, Wiley, Kathryn, and Rosenblum, Gershen. 1962. "Some Observations on Major Loss in Families," *American Journal of Orthopsychiatry* 32 : 299–300.

Parkes, C. M. 1964. "Grief as an Illness," *New Society,* April 9, p. 11.

———. 1965. "Bereavement and Mental Illness," *British Journal of Medical Psychology* 38 : 1–26.

———. 1967. "The Nature of Grief," *International Journal of Psychiatry* 3 : 435–38.

Paul, Norman L. 1969. "Psychiatry: Its Role in the Resolution of Grief," in *Death and Bereavement,* ed. Austin Kutscher. Springfield, Ill.: Thomas, pp. 174–95.

Peniston, D. Hugh. 1962. "The Importance of 'Death Education' in Family Life," *Family Life Coordinator* 11 (Jan.) : 15–18.

Pfeffer, Arnold Z. 1973. "Towards a Psychoanalytic Understanding of Psychotherapy" (presented to the Scientific Meeting of the Cleveland Psychoanalytic Society, Jan. 19).

Pine, Fred, and Furer, Manuel. 1963. "Studies of the Separation-Individuation Phase: A Methodological Overview," *Psychoanalytic Study of the Child,* vol. 18. New York: International Universities Press, pp. 325–43.

Pollock, George H. 1961. "Mourning and Adaptation," *International Journal of Psycho-Analysis* 42 : 341–61.

———. 1962. "Childhood Parent and Sibling Loss in Adult Patients," *Archives of General Psychiatry* 7 : 295–305.

———. 1972. "Bertha Pappenheim's Pathological Mourning: Possible Effects of Childhood Sibling Loss," *Journal of the American Psychoanalytic Association* 20, no. 3 : 476–93.

Provence, Sally, and Lipton, Rose C. 1962. *Infants in Institutions. A Comparison of Their Development during the First Year of Life with Family-Reared Infants.* New York: International Universities Press.

Putnam, Marian C., Rank, Beata, and Kaplan, Samuel. 1951. "Notes on John I.: A Case of Primal Depression in an Infant," *Psychoanalytic Study of the Child,* vol. 6. New York: International Universities Press, pp. 38–60.

Rado, S. 1928. "The Problem of Melancholia," *International Journal of Psycho-Analysis* 9 : 420–38.

Ramos, Suzanne. 1972. "The Hardest Lesson of All," *New York Times Magazine,* Dec. 10, p. 94.

Remus-Araico, J. 1965. "Some Aspects of Early-Orphaned Adults' Analyses," *Psychoanalytic Quarterly* 34 (April) : 316–18.

Robertson, James and Joyce. 1971. "Young Children in Brief Separation: A Fresh Look." *Psychoanalytic Study of the Child,* vol. 26. New York: Quadrangle Books, pp. 264–315.

Rochlin, Gregory. 1953. "Loss and Restitution," *Psychoanalytic Study of the Child,* vol. 8. New York: International Universities Press, pp. 288–309.

———. 1959. "The Loss Complex: A Contribution to the Etiology of Depression," *Journal of the American Psychoanalytic Association* 7 : 299–316.

———. 1961. "The Dread of Abandonment: A Contribution to the Loss Complex and to Depression," *Psychoanalytic Study of the Child,* vol. 16. New York: International Universities Press, pp. 451–70.

———. 1967. "How Younger Children View Death and Themselves," in *Explaining Death to Children,* ed. E. A. Grollman. Boston: Beacon, pp. 51–85.

Rogers, R. 1966. "Children's Reactions to Sibling Death," Proceedings of the First International Congress of Psychosomatic Medicine, Spain. *Excerpta Medica (Amsterdam),* ser. 134, pp. 209–12.

Root, Nathan. 1957. "A Neurosis in Adolescence," *Psychoanalytic Study of the Child,* vol. 12. New York: International Universities Press, pp. 320–34.

Rosenzweig, S. 1943. "Sibling Death as a Psychological Experience with Special Reference to Schizophrenia," *Psychoanalytic Review* 30 : 177–86.

———, and Bray, D. 1943. "Sibling Deaths in the Anamnesis of Schizophrenic Patients," *Archives of Neurology and Psychiatry* 49 : 71–92.

Sachs, Hans. 1942. "Beauty, Life and Death," in *The Creative Unconscious,* ed. A. A. Roback. Cambridge, Mass.: Science Art Publishers, pp. 147–240.

Sandler, J., and Joffe, W. G. 1965. "Notes on Childhood Depression," *International Journal of Psycho-Analysis* 46 : 88–96.

Scharl, A. E. 1961. "Regression and Restitution in Object Loss: Clinical Observations," *Psychoanalytic Study of the Child,* vol. 16. New York: International Universities Press, pp. 471–80.

Schilder, Paul, and Wechsler, D. 1934. "The Attitude of Children Towards Death," *Journal of Genetics and Psychology* 45 (Dec.) : 406–51.

Schur, Max. 1972. *Freud Living and Dying.* New York: International Universities Press.

Shambaugh, B. 1961. "A Study of Loss Reaction in a Seven-year-old," *Psychoanalytic Study of the Child,* vol. 16. New York: International Universities Press, pp. 510–22.

Shoor, M., and Speed, M. 1963. "Delinquency as a Manifestation of the Mourning Process," *Psychiatric Quarterly* 37 : 540–58.

Siggins, Lorraine D. 1966. "Mourning: A Critical Survey of the Literature," *International Journal of Psycho-Analysis* 47, no. 1 : 14–25.

Smith, Joseph H. 1971. "Identificatory Styles in Depression and Grief," *International Journal of Psycho-Analysis* 52, no. 3 : 259–66.

Solnit, Albert J. 1970. "A Study of Object Loss in Infancy," *Psychoanalytic Study of the Child,* vol. 25. New York: International Universities Press, pp. 257–72.

Solnit, A. J., and Stark, M. H. 1961. "Mourning and the Birth of a Defective

Child," *Psychoanalytic Study of the Child,* vol. 16. New York: International Universities Press, pp. 523–37.

Spiegel, Leo A. 1966. "Affects in Relation to Self and Object," *Psychoanalytic Study of the Child,* vol. 21. New York: International Universities Press, pp. 69–92.

Spitz, R. A. 1945. "Hospitalism: An Inquiry into the Genesis of Psychiatric Conditions in Early Childhood," *Psychoanalytic Study of the Child,* vol. 1. New York: International Universities Press, pp. 53–74.

———. 1946. "Anaclitic Depression: An Inquiry into the Genesis of Psychiatric Conditions in Early Childhood II," *Psychoanalytic Study of the Child,* vol. 2. New York: International Universities Press, pp. 313–42.

Spock, B. M. 1960. "Telling Your Child about Death," *Ladies Home Journal,* January, p. 14.

Statistical Abstract of the United States. 1971. Table 472, 92nd annual ed. Washington: U.S. Dept. of Commerce, Bureau of the Census, p. 296.

Steiner, Jerome. 1970. "Group Function within the Mourning Process," *Archives of the Foundation of Thanatology* 2, no. 2 : 80–82.

Sterba, Richard. 1948. "On Hallowe'en," *American Imago* 5 : 213–24.

Stern, Karl, Williams, Gwendolyn M., and Prados, Miguel. 1951. "Grief Reactions in Later Life," *American Journal of Psychiatry* 108 : 289–94.

Stern, Max M. 1968. "Fear of Death and Trauma," *International Journal of Psycho-Analysis* 49, nos. 2–3 : 457–61.

———. 1968a. "Fear of Death and Neurosis," *Journal of the American Psychoanalytic Association* 16, no. 1 : 3–31.

Sugar, M. 1968. "Normal Adolescent Mourning," *American Journal of Psychotherapy* 22 : 258–69.

Tolsma, F. J. 1964. "Psychological Disturbances after a Pet Dog's Death," *Psychiatria, Neurologia, Neurochirurgia (Amsterdam)* 67 (Sept.–Oct.) : 394–405.

Toolan, J. M. 1962. "Depression in Children and Adolescents," *American Journal of Orthopsychiatry* 32 : 404–15.

Van Gennep, A. 1960. *The Rites of Passage,* trans. M. B. Vizedom and G. L. Caffee. Chicago: Univ. of Chicago Press.

Vernick, Joel J. 1972. *Selected Bibliography on Death and Dying.* Bethesda, Md.: National Institute of Child Health and Human Development.

Wahl, C. W. 1958. "The Fear of Death," *Bulletin of the Menninger Clinic* 22, no. 6 : 214–23.

Wallach, Helen D. 1961. "Termination of Treatment as a Loss," *Psychoanalytic Study of the Child,* vol. 16. New York: International Universities Press, pp. 538–48.

Wetmore, Robert J. 1963. "The Role of Grief in Psycho-analysis," *International Journal of Psycho-Analysis* 44 : 97–103.

Winnicott, D. W. 1949. *The Ordinary Devoted Mother and Her Baby.* London: Brock.

Winnicott, D. W. 1954. "The Depressive Position in Normal Emotional Development," in *Collected Papers*. London: Tavistock (1958), pp. 262–77.

———. 1960. "Ego Distortion in Terms of True and False Self," in *The Maturational Processes and the Facilitating Environment*. New York: International Universities Press (1965), pp. 140–52.

———. 1965. "A Child Psychiatry Case Illustrating Delayed Reaction to Loss," in *Drives, Affects and Behavior,* vol. 2, ed. Max Schur. New York: International Universities Press, pp. 212–42.

Wittels, Fritz. 1939. "Unconscious Phantoms in Neurotics," *Psychoanalytic Quarterly* 8 : 141–63.

Wolf, Anna W. M. 1958. *Helping Your Child to Understand Death*. New York: The Child Study Association of America.

Wolfenstein, Martha. 1965. "Death of a Parent and Death of a President: Children's Reactions to Two Kinds of Loss," in *Children and the Death of a President,* ed. M. Wolfenstein and G. Kliman. Garden City, N.Y.: Doubleday, pp. 62–79.

———. 1966. "How is Mourning Possible?" *Psychoanalytic Study of the Child,* Vol. 21. New York: International Universities Press, pp. 93–123.

———. 1969. "Loss, Rage and Repetition," *Psychoanalytic Study of the Child,* vol. 24. New York: International Universities Press, pp. 432–62.

Young, Michael, Benjamin, Bernard, and Wallis, Chris. 1963. "The Mortality of Widowers," *Lancet* 2 : 454–56.

Zetzel, E. R. 1960. "Symposium on 'Depressive Illness,' Introduction," *International Journal of Psycho-Analysis* 41 : 476–80.

Zilbach, Joan J. 1965. "The Impact of the Assassination of President Kennedy on Child Psychiatric Patients," in *Children and the Death of a President,* ed. M. Wolfenstein and G. Kliman. Garden City, N.Y.: Doubleday, pp. 135–56.

Zilboorg, G. 1937. "Considerations on Suicide with Particular Reference to That of the Young," *American Journal of Orthopsychiatry* 7 : 15–31.

———. 1943. "Fear of Death," *Psychoanalytic Quarterly* 12 : 465–75.

Index

A., case of (Novick), 286–87
Abraham: 188, 254, 255, 257; on depression, 184, 187, 265; on definition of mourning, 242, 250
Addie, case of, 47, 125; vignettes, 65, 100, 113, 167
Affective responses in mourning. *See* Grief
Aggression: effect on object representation, 54, 56, 122; discharge, in depression, 196; role in grief, 258–59. *See also* Grief
Alpert, 277
Altschul, 247, 248, 269, 292, 293
Ambivalence, 56, 65, 122, 248, 258–59; role in depression, 195–96. *See also* Grief
Anthony, S., 272, 274; on concept of death, 271, 274–75
Apathy: compared with depression, 189–90; illustrated, 191–94; this study on, 194–97; affecting motility, 196
—definition: clinical, 189; questions raised by, 189–90; by other authors, 190
—observation of: in infants, 189; in adults, 190
—underlying psychic conditions of: varied, 190, 194–95; defensive, 195–97
Archibald et al., 292
Archives of the Foundation of Thanatology, 233
Arnold, case of, vignette, 58
Arthur, case of, vignette, 98
Anderson, 242, 247, 264
Assistance with mourning, professional: therapy, forms of, 1, 6–7, 293–96; indications for, 26, 294–95; role of therapist, 44–45, 116, 170; assessment of results, 293–95; educational articles, 295–96

B., case of (Kearney), 287
Barnes, 2, 19, 36, 293; on case of Wendy, 99, 279; on duration of mourning, 260, 265; on outcome of mourning, 266, 267; on concept of death, 270, 272, 276; on case of Winnie, 279
Barry, 291
Barry and Lindemann, 291
Barry Jr., Barry III, and Lindemann, 291–92
Beck, Sethi, and Tuthil, 292

Becker and Margolin, 236, 246
Benda, 246
Bender, 273
Benolie, 234
Bereavement in childhood, other than parental, 275–77
Bereavement in childhood, parental: incidence of, 2–3; task for bereaved, 163–64. *See also* Loss of love object; Mourning, developmental capacities; Parent, death of; Parent, surviving
—compared with: bereavement in adulthood, 12, 127–28; other bereavements in childhood, 127, 275–77
—studies of: research value discussed, 6–7, 240, 261–62, 277–78, 285; other, 236, 291–94; psychotherapies, 278–84; analyses, 285–90; cases analyzed as adults, 290–91
—effects of: in infancy, 40–43, 122–23, 166, 173, 293; on ego functions and activities, 44–46, 122–23, 173–78; on mourning, 127–28; on personality, 163–72, 173; on later losses, 178–79, 182–83
—outcome: pathological, 163–72, 267–69; normal, 172, 267
—related to preceding losses: 178–82
Beres, 186
Bergen, 233, 247, 272; on case of Ellen, 289
Bess, case of, vignette, 24–25
Bibring, E., 186, 188, 190, 259; on depression, 184–85
Billy, case of (Furman, R. A.): vignettes, 64, 103, 182; case report, 288
Billy, case of (Wallach), 282
Birtchnell, 257, 268
Blos, 178
Bonaparte, 257
Bobby (3½), case of, vignette, 56–57
Bobby (2½), case of, vignette, 171
Bonnard, 293; case of, John, 278
Bowlby, 187, 243, 252, 263, 270; on parent loss in infancy, 166, 187, 265; on concept of mourning, 234, 252; on factors impeding recognition of death, 246, 248, 250, 270; on decathexis in toddlers, 253; on affects in mourning, 257, 258, 259, 260